Beyond the H
The History of the Rugby

CW00538003

RLC Lionhearts versus Featherstone Lions Challenge Cup 2001

By Julian Harrison

London League Publications Ltd

Beyond the Heartlands
The History of the Rugby League Conference

A CIP catalogue record for this book is available from the British Library.

First published in Great Britain in October 2004 by:
London League Publications Ltd, P.O. Box 10441, London E14 8WR

ISBN: 1-903659-17-5

Cover design by: Stephen McCarthy Graphic Design
                               46, Clarence Road, London N15 5BB

Layout: Peter Lush

Printed and bound by: Antony Rowe Ltd, Chippenham, Great Britain

The Rugby League Conference is sponsored by Totalrl.com

This book is dedicated to all my family, in particular my youngest son Elliot, in the hope that he will grow to love rugby league as I have done.

Foreword

At last it seems as though the visionaries are overpowering the traditionalists as rugby league spreads its wings throughout the British Isles through the Rugby League Conference. Even Martyn Sadler, the long time advocate of summer rugby league, must be amazed and delighted that the professional, and now the amateur game has embraced the summer concept, with the effect that there are now thousands more participants enjoying rugby league at all levels. It really is a rugby revolution.

Spreading the game to the non-traditional areas has always been a problem, but the switch of Super League to summer stimulated nationwide interest, the long held prejudices against summer rugby were severely questioned, and new opportunities suddenly appeared.

Up to 1996 only the Student Rugby League (SRL) had significantly spread beyond the traditional areas, but now the SRL was to provide the building blocks for a new competitive structure as many former students wished to continue their new found interest. Under the stewardship of Tom O'Donovan, the RFL national development executive, a group of individuals gathered at various times and in varying combinations to discuss potential initiatives. These included Hector McNeil, the London Skolars impresario, ultimate visionary Lionel Hurst, the author Julian and me.

Julian provides the details of what materialised, but the explosion from 10 embryo clubs in 1997 to today's 66 in the RLC is nothing less than sensational. The pyramid competitive structure we see today looks remarkably like the plan initially created by Hector McNeil. Lionel Hurst, as the inaugural chairman of the RLC, provided the inspiration and vision, and Julian performed wonders as the first full-time administrator. The RFL and Super League willingly provided financial and administrative support.

As a director of London Broncos in 1996, development and expansion were part of my role and the club supported the creation of West London Sharks - inaugural members of the RLC. I became chairman and bucket carrier in the early years and it is great to see that the club is still flourishing, achieving the ultimate goal this year of reaching the RLC Grand Final for the first time with one of the founder players - the legendary Alex Sanerive - at the helm.

The concept of the RLC as a development tool for non-traditional areas has now been expanded to include all areas as the summer game, by popular demand, is spreading rapidly through the heartlands, with some famous traditional clubs like Woolston and Dudley Hill now embracing all-year-round rugby league.

Julian did a magnificent job as RLC administrator and he is the ideal person to record the RLC story to date. It is surely just the start of a much longer tale.

Bev Risman
One of the founders of the Rugby League Conference

Introduction

I am indeed honoured to have been asked to write a few words of introduction to Julian Harrison's book on the Rugby League Conference. The very fact that, after a mere seven years of existence, the Conference has inspired the writing of a book speaks for itself.

What began with a few enthusiasts, exiled for various reasons from their rugby league heartlands homes, has now blossomed into a nationwide network of clubs. This is indeed an amazing success story for our game and the Rugby Football League itself is to be congratulated for its wisdom in supporting so wholeheartedly this concept.

I have been privileged to be involved since those very early pioneering days. That has been my good fortune and it gives me very great pleasure on behalf of our game to pay well-merited tribute to, and thank most sincerely, those missionaries, inspired by the vision and determination of people like Lionel Hurst, who combined to enjoy themselves by playing, administering or simply being involved in the sowing of the rugby league seed in the barren acres which have now proved to be so fruitful.

Harry Jepson OBE
President, Rugby League Conference

Harry Jepson with a Rotherham Giant – RLC Grand Final 2000. Julian Harrison is on the left.

Preface

The creation of the Rugby League Conference is one of the most important innovations since the sport's inception at the George Hotel in Huddersfield in 1895. When Rugby League embraced a summer season in 1996 I knew that the right time had arrived to introduce this great sport on a nationwide basis. By the time of my address to the gathering at the House of Commons in 1998 there was a clear aim that there should be a "team in every town". This indeed is the clarion call of summer development. The great success of this new concept is due to the many talented and dedicated men and women throughout the land. The backbone of the RLC is the new intelligentsia who are products of the university system. It is such graduates who are spearheading the new revolution.

Nonetheless the RLC cannot flourish in isolation. On joining the London Broncos in 2001 it was apparent that time was short and swift action was necessary. Firstly, along with Bev Risman and Graeme Thompson the National Pyramid Plan was devised. This was revealed to many sectors of the game at the headquarters of UK Sport in London. Some of our proposal has been adopted and put into effect. However there is still much of the plan that remains to be brought into being. Secondly, it was vital that the Super League Board was reformed. Our motion for directors to stand down if they also had club loyalties was carried unanimously. This has led to Rugby League's first independent board of directors. Furthermore in order to enter the nation's consciousness a national media profile is essential with a principal office in London and quality coverage on terrestrial television – especially international matches.

The RLC requires more grading with the implementation of a National Division 4 – North and South – and regional premier leagues. All of this to be underpinned by high standards off, as well as on, the field of play. Moreover the RLC champions should take part in a new Champions' League alongside the winners of the appropriate domestic leagues in the countries mentioned below. As the sport continues to develop in Scotland, Ireland, Wales and other nations in Europe then so must the Cheltenham Regency Cup be expanded to include France, Russia, Holland, Serbia and so on.

A special executive would be of great benefit to oversee all of the above. It should be comprised of people of wisdom and experience and varied skills with an understanding of the origins and aims of the RLC and beyond.

Finally, good luck and best wishes to all of you in the shires. You have my eternal affection and respect for all your hard work and courage.

Lionel Hurst
Chairman of the Rugby League Conference 1997 to 2000

Photo: Lionel Hurst speaking at London Broncos press launch in 2001

About the author

Julian Harrison was one of the founders of the Southern Conference League (the precursor to the Rugby League Conference) and acted as the competition's secretary during the pilot season of 1997. Following two years working in Student Rugby League, he then became the RLC's first full-time administrator, a post he held until April 2002. His path to rugby league was multi-faceted. With family roots in South Leeds, he became a Hunslet supporter, but his active involvement in the game began while undertaking a Post Graduate Certificate in Education at Leeds University in 1992-93. Here he met John Kear, then the RFL coaching executive, and became sufficiently enthused to join Leicester RLFC when he moved to the East Midlands to work at the University of Leicester.

With a wife and family all born in Leicester, he has done his best to promote the virtues of rugby league to his own personal audience, with some success. He even met his wife Lesley through Leicester Phoenix Rugby League Club. His participation in the game is now confined to spectatorship and he can often be found on touchlines at amateur rugby league venues all over the country.

Acknowledgements

I have done my best in this book to portray as accurately and truthfully as possible the complex processes that led to the emergence and development of the Rugby League Conference (RLC). However, as the foundation of the competition involved a multitude of developments and independent actions, it has been a very difficult task to undertake. There is a focus on my own personal involvement at club and organisational level, but I hope this has not been to the detriment of honesty and faithfulness to the truth. It has been my aim to show that the origins and evolution of the RLC were not down to any one individual or simple development line, but can be attributed to many interdependent processes and actions. I hope that in this I have been successful.

Inevitably I will have missed things and where there have been omissions and mistakes I trust the reader will forgive me.

There are far too many people who have contributed to the writing of this book to thank them all individually. I have received assistance from numerous clubs and individuals in written, verbal and pictorial form, but I must mention the following who have been particularly helpful and supportive: Chris Wilson, Ruth Sigley, Richard Lord, Dave Flaherty, Phil Gowing, Phil Jackson, Paul Walmsley, Ron Banks, Steve Harrison-Mirfield, John Haigh, Phil Caplan, Niel Wood, Lionel Hurst and Harry Jepson OBE. Peter Lush, Dave Farrar, Michael O'Hare and Steve McCarthy deserve special gratitude for their patience, attention to detail and hard work producing the book.

I'd also like to single out Bev Risman. Bev is, for me, the most significant influence on my career and involvement in rugby league. His input and achievements are the stuff of legend and if ever there should be a specific national award given for contribution to the development of rugby league outside of the heartland areas, Bev would be the most worthy of recipients.

Lastly, and above all, my thanks go to Lesley, Leomi, Luke, Joel and Elliot for their support and encouragement and for putting up with the many long hours spent away from them in the cause of rugby league over the years!

Julian Harrison

Contents

1. Early days   1
2. Moving forward   9
3. The beginning – establishment   13
4. 1997: The pilot season   27
5. 1998: Awakening   41
6. 1999: Six new teams   53
7. 2000: Strengthening   63
8. 2001: The North East   87
9. 2002: Looking ahead   105
10. 2003: Further expansion   127
11. 2004: Into the heartlands   143
12. Into the future   159

Appendix 1: Matches, memories and people   162
Appendix 2: Club profiles   174
Appendix 3: Club performances   179
Appendix 4: Grand Finals   181
Sources and references   182

Julian Harrison was heavily involved in many of the events covered by this book. Except in chapter 12, he refers to himself in the third person.

This book is not an 'official' history of the Rugby League Conference, but a personal account by Julian Harrison. It does not claim to represent the views of the Rugby League Conference, the Rugby Football League or any other individuals involved.

South London Storm versus Australian Legends 2003:
Former London Broncos captain Jason Hetherington about to receive the ball

Rugby Raiders versus Wolverhampton Wizards at Rugby School in May 2004.
This was Rugby's home debut.

Derby City's Lee Marsden about to pass the ball despite the close attention
of two Rotherham Giants in June 2004 (Photo: John Finch)

1. Early days

The mid-1990s was a momentous time for rugby league in Great Britain. Exactly 100 years on from the code's foundation, 1995 witnessed another sensational development – the advent of Super League and summer professional rugby league. The impact of this was felt immediately both in the wrangling over proposed club mergers, later rescinded; but also that the sport's most important event, the World Cup held in October, was played amid turmoil in the Australian game, resulting in only players aligned to the Australian Rugby League (ARL) representing the world champions, with those from the rival Super League camp excluded.

Super League produced a fast-flowing sport played in summer on harder pitches with family-orientated side-shows and on-pitch entertainment. Rugby league was reaching out to a new, more national, audience. Three Super League clubs (Sheffield Eagles, Paris St Germain and London Broncos) came from non-traditional rugby league areas, which also added to the sense of a new dawn. And in August, rugby union went open, which had important implications for rugby league and the relationship between the two codes.

In 1996 another development also ensured that the perception of rugby league was changing. Wigan - the sport's most successful club and then holders of the BBC Television Sport 'Team of the Year' title - entertained rugby union's Bath in a 'cross-code challenge' with one game played under league rules at Maine Road, Manchester, and a return under union rules at Twickenham. Not surprisingly each side won the match played in its respective code and Wigan's aggregate victory of 101-50 was less significant than the fact that the games had taken place at all. Barriers between the codes were coming down. Wigan also competed in, and won, the Middlesex Sevens union competition, also at Twickenham, and this further emphasised that rugby league and rugby union could share each other's skills and events.

This sense of rugby partnership was not new to many rugby league enthusiasts involved in the game in areas of the country outside the game's traditional heartlands. At the same time as Wigan and Bath were locking horns, for example, the respective rugby clubs at Leicester University were also doing battle. While two-way player movement between the sports had been hampered by rugby union's nominal amateur status, rugby league clubs in the sport's development areas existed side-by-side with their union counterparts – often as tenants of union clubs – and arguably there was more appreciation of the mutual benefits of playing and sharing both codes than there was in the rugby league heartlands.

A combination of rugby détente and a new image, playing season and expanded basis for professional rugby league, ensured that a movement that in time may indeed eclipse all others as far as securing a vibrant future for rugby league is concerned, found fertile roots from which to develop. That movement was initially called the Southern Conference League (SCL) in the 1997 pilot season, but is now known as the Rugby League Conference (RLC).

Rugby league has made many attempts to develop nationally, with failures and short-term impacts combined with notable successes and lasting initiatives. Towns in which current and potentially future RLC clubs now exist had been part of this past legacy. Coventry, for example, played in the Northern Union, later the Rugby Football League in the years immediately prior to the First World War, and in 1912 there was a flurry of potential rugby league activity in Devon – with allegations of 'broken time' payments leading to suspensions from rugby union, although a proposed Northern Union Western League never started. Though this only lasted a year, it did bring the name of James Peters into the spotlight. Peters (the first black player to win an England rugby union cap) moved from Plymouth to play league with Barrow and St Helens. His links with the borough of Greenwich, led to the current Greenwich Admirals RLFC naming a trophy after him.

Cheltenham staged the final test match in the inaugural tour of A.H. Baskerville's New Zealand 'All Golds' in 1908, the crowd of 4,000 witnessing a test match and the first sending off in an international fixture: the New Zealand prop, T.W. Cross. Cheltenham became home to the Cheltenham (later Gloucestershire) Warriors club and staged two RLC Grand Finals.

Development in Wales, Scotland and London has been well documented. Both the first and last have had leagues and indeed professional clubs in the past - and, in London's case, the present. All three currently host domestic amateur competitions linked directly and indirectly to the RLC. The cross-league and cross-national use of personnel in these areas with the RLC competition, showed the strong links between rugby league enthusiasts, players and development personnel. The experiences of a vast array of people in previous rugby league contexts and development initiatives were a particular strength for the launch of the SCL in 1997.

Scotland has players and coaches who have appeared for Scottish representative sides, including at full international level, and also – though not always concurrently – RLC and other clubs in development areas of England. Former Scottish development officer and current player performance manager at the Rugby Football League (RFL), Graeme Thompson has had significant involvement with the RLC, in youth development and the Amateur Four Nations tournament and with RLC trailblazers Crawley Jets. Finally, one of the initial founders of the competition, London Skolars chairman Hector McNeil has, as part of an extensive rugby league career, considerable experience of Scottish rugby league, both in playing and organisational terms and was the initial treasurer of the Scottish Rugby League Development Association.

Games between development Scottish and English sides also took place prior to the advent of the RLC and in the early years of the competition. The first Scottish amateur club, the Forth and Clyde Nomads, played in the North East League in the 1995-96 season. A Scottish Development XIII played Birmingham Bulldogs in 1997 and Scarborough Schools played Glasgow Schools at under-11 level as a curtain-raiser to the 2000 Challenge Cup Final at Murrayfield.

London is a more vivid illustration of a past legacy of development links. The London Amateur Rugby League has a rich history back to 1965. The amateur game has carried on in the capital and in its environs - the London League encompassed teams from as far away as Cambridge, Huntingdon, Swindon and even (as the Southern ARL) Aberavon - through thick and thin ever since. Links with London's professional side have also been evident. Players and coaches such as Frank Feighan, Colin Fenn, Dave Gillan and Bill Goodwin have all had direct involvement in the amateur game.

These connections did not stop once the RLC came into being, but got stronger. Two individuals illustrate this. Paul Johnstone coached the Fulham 'A' team, but also coached at various RLC clubs, including Oxford Cavaliers, South London Storm and St Albans Centurions. Paul is a man of many rugby league talents. He is not only a leading coach in the southern half of the country, but also compiled the official RLC fixtures for a number of seasons. Secondly, no history of London rugby league (both professional and amateur) would be complete without mentioning dual-code international, Great Britain captain and ex-Leeds star Bev Risman. He was not only the most capable of development officers and administrators, but also influenced so many others participating in rugby league. As team manager at Fulham, he used London amateur players in his squad. As the director of development at London Broncos, Bev played a leading role in bringing the Southern Conference League and Rugby League Conference to fruition, ensuring that talented players from the Broncos and other sources, had outlets in the amateur game. This was evident in clubs where Bev had a strong involvement – for example London Skolars and West London Sharks.

In other parts of the country, too, there had been considerable rugby league activity at amateur level prior to the advent of the SCL and RLC, with development leagues that covered relatively virgin rugby league territory. The Midlands and South West Amateur Rugby League Association (MASWARLA), for example, was formed in the mid-1980s and at its height had 14 teams, including clubs that re-emerged much later in the RLC, such as Wolverhampton and Cheltenham. Another link with the later development was the involvement of Cheltenham-based lawyer Lionel Hurst, the initial founder of the Cheltenham club and one of the main driving forces behind the SCL and RLC. Leicester also played in the MASWARLA competition and were also leading members of another development league, the East Midlands Amateur Rugby League Association (EMARLA). Again, there were common factors in both 1980s and 1990s developments. Leicester, Birmingham, Cambridge and Derby were all EMARLA members, as were Telford All Blacks, Garibaldi and Shirebrook (the last two clubs based in North Nottinghamshire mining communities) who, though not strictly speaking the same clubs, influenced the development of RLC clubs in the Shropshire town and in Mansfield and Worksop.

There were, therefore, some fairly long-standing club operations in existence when the idea of the Southern Conference League began to materialise. For example, Leicester were founded in 1986, Birmingham in 1989 and Ipswich Rhinos in 1992. Notwithstanding these, there were clubs with longer histories in London. Also, Hemel Hempstead Stags (though not an initial member either of the SCL or RLC) had been formed in 1981 by Australian Bob Brown who is still involved at the club.

There were other pockets of interest that provided a boost to the existence of the game in the amateur leagues in non-traditional regions.

Student Rugby League (SRL) begun in the 1960s (initially at Leeds and Liverpool) and by the mid-1990s had a national presence. Clubs were particularly prominent in areas in which the SCL would initially focus – London and the Midlands. The pinnacle of the student game, the National League, at various times over the late 1990s and early 2000s, comprised Loughborough, Leicester, Coventry and Birmingham Universities. SRL clubs were similar in make-up to their amateur counterparts and were also a precursor to the embryonic SCL and RLC clubs that formed post-1997. Students from rugby league areas moving to locations outside the heartlands wanted to play the game they knew. In joining or forming student clubs, they enticed others from virgin rugby league areas to take up the sport. Student rugby union club players were also attracted to the game. The same applied to players from other sports, American football being a good example. As always with students, methods of persuasion were rife – a vibrant social club with sporting endeavours were popular.

All these factors were true in the amateur context. Of course, amateur clubs benefited considerably from recruiting local student players and liaison between student and amateur clubs benefited both. Amateur clubs provided an additional playing outlet for students. Coaching initiatives, promotional opportunities and even direct competition between the two strengthened the connections. Some clubs went further. London Skolars – an ever-present SCL and RLC club – were formed as an outlet for graduates to continue playing the game. Former Nottingham Trent University students provided the impetus for the formation of Nottingham Outlaws, and, more recently, the Leeds Akademiks followed a similar route to the London Skolars and became an official graduates club. All three clubs did not restrict their composition to students or former students, but the bonds between them and the student sector continue to the present day.

In East Anglia and parts of the South (as well as Scotland), the Armed Forces were also be a tremendous ally, fulfilling the same purpose and role as the student sector. Over the years, many clubs experienced the benefits of forces' players and coaches. A similar case could be made for the police. Dave Doran who became one of the key coaches in the early years of the Rugby League Conference, making his mark at Oxford Cavaliers, and also the RLC Lionhearts representative side, was one of the initial band of club contacts that registered interest in the SCL. His club at the time wasn't Oxford, but the Metropolitan Police.

What was life like for the average amateur rugby league club in a development area before 1997? This is important in assessing the conditions that led to the radical re-structuring of the game in non-traditional areas in that momentous year. There are bound to be differences as well as similarities in club circumstances. That was as true in the 2004 season with an RLC competition of 66 clubs as it was in the pre-SCL era. Those differences may relate to differing competitions, league structures, geography, player strength, administrative and organisational capacity and media profile.

However, there were many similarities. There was a reliance on rugby union – players, grounds and facilities – and on ex-patriot northerners and current and former students or servicemen. When the clubs played in winter

4

on Sundays, they were uncertain of their teams as the rugby union contingent played the previous day. Fixture lists would change considerably, often weekly, and fixtures were postponed or cancelled at short notice due to clubs not having enough players. There was little youth development.

Another problem was an absence of qualified - or indeed - any coaches with rugby league experience. Where such coaches existed, they probably doubled-up as players, managers, physios and kit-washers. There were too few administrators. The most common situation was a one or two-person administrative team, and few, if any, sponsors.

There was minimal assistance from rugby league governing bodies or professional rugby league personnel. Governing body involvement simply constituted the very basics – insurance and registration organisation and a degree of fixture co-ordination. The clubs had a low profile locally. Rugby league had to compete directly with rugby union because both games were played in winter. The national exposure to rugby league as a professional sport was hampered by the game – in terms of consensus – not being considered to be a national pastime. The pending move to summer, through the advent of Super League, was going to exacerbate this sense of profile alienation in development areas if games in these areas were going to continue in the winter, the Super League off-season.

Despite all these difficult circumstances, rugby league clubs and the people involved in them remained passionate and dedicated as well as innovative in their attempts to develop both club and sport.

Take Leicester RLFC as an example. Julian Harrison joined Leicester Rugby League club in 1995. He well recalls his introduction to the club: "I turned up for training at a local rugby union club not knowing what to expect. I was greeted by darkness, not a soul about. I walked around the corner to the stadium that I knew was the venue for the club's home matches, thinking that my information must have been wrong and that training had moved. On entering the stadium car park, my hopes were raised by the sight of a minibus full of young blokes in sports kit just leaving. I thought they were being taken to rugby league training. However, they went in the wrong direction, so I went back to the training venue, to see if anyone had turned up and, if not, go home. This time, there was a light on in the clubhouse and moving towards it, I was aware of about 10 lads throwing a rugby ball about in darkness on the pitch. I was greeted in the clubhouse by Paul Walmsley, the Leicester coach, who explained – in graphic language – that the lights weren't working, that training had been cancelled, but the players who had turned up, some from quite a distance, just wanted to have a quick game of touch-and-pass. Paul went out to join them and I – because I had a long-term injury – went out to watch. I realised afterwards that I wanted to do something to help develop this club, if only to ensure that they could train in the light next time."

In many ways, Leicester RLFC was the typical amateur rugby league club in a development area. The club played in EMARLA with Birmingham, Derby, Nottingham, Bulwell, Clowne, Shirebrook, Garibaldi, Peterborough and others. However, fixtures were sporadic and the club tried to arrange extra fixtures elsewhere. Entrance into nines tournaments and holding their own (won in

1995 by Leicester and in 1996 by Birmingham) was mixed with participation in BARLA's Southern Counties Cup. The club, desperate for playing opportunities to keep their enthusiastic but small band of players interested, even explored the possibility of entering BARLA's Yorkshire Cup.

In the same vein, 1995 saw Leicester entering negotiations with Peterborough and Northampton Knights to produce a merged, East Midlands super-club to compete in BARLA's flagship National Conference League. Northampton were already a member but the club was struggling to compete on the pitch. The thinking was that all clubs would benefit from such an arrangement – greater playing numbers, pooled resources, a bigger, regional profile and a fantastic competition in which to play. However, the writing was soon on the wall. Peterborough pulled out before a ball was kicked. The surviving dual-club operation fared little better and, after a fixture against a Hull trialist XIII on 5 August, the clubs went their separate ways – Northampton continuing in the National Conference and Leicester, the East Midlands League. The major consolation was that the players had had the opportunity of appearing at one of rugby league's famous venues, because the Hull game was at the Boulevard.

It was obvious to everyone at Leicester RLFC that things had to change if there was to be a future for the game in the city. Moving back to East Midlands rugby league after the hopes and experience of the merger was detrimental to club morale. The club lost players and ceased operations for a while. Paul Walmsley and Julian Harrison decided to invest energy into junior rugby league. With the assistance of sports development people at Leicester City Council, they formed a junior club, the Aylestone Terriers – named after the local area - following a coaching course also involving people from Sheffield Eagles. Harrison was in regular contact with Gary Hetherington in this period, figuring that if anyone in professional rugby league could appreciate the problems of developing initiatives away from the game's heartlands, it would be the man who had been so successful in leading the Eagles into Super League. This twinning experience would be repeated when similar arrangements were conceived in the early years of the SCL and RLC.

The Terriers venture was – despite its brief existence – a positive move. The club, encouraged by then Sheffield development officer, Ralph Rimmer, joined the South West Yorkshire junior league, organised their own gala event and appeared at a rally at Sheffield-Hillsborough Hawks as well as being part of the curtain-raising warm up to the Eagles Super League fixture against Halifax Blue Sox in 1996. Even though the club is now defunct, Aylestone Terriers left a legacy in professional rugby, unfortunately in the other code. Two young Leicestershire rugby stars played league for the Terriers. They were Ollie Smith and Luke Myring, who having gone through rugby union player development went on to play for Leicester Tigers. Smith is an up-and-coming England full international. A third ex-Terrier, Ben Spokes, is with the Northampton Saints union club.

Sheffield Eagles also benefited from their links with Leicester. Lawrence Taylor and Curtis Thomas were stalwarts of Leicester rugby league, and both had trials at the Eagles, eventually securing contracts. Although only Taylor played Super League, the fact that both players had impressed and had received a good grounding in rugby league in the lower ranks of the East Midlands League showed the potential for the professional game.

Off the field, the Leicester club was also creating a profile for itself and the game. They attempted to involve local rugby union clubs to develop mutually-beneficial relationships. The club joined forces with a local cable television company to produce an introductory programme on the game. Taking advantage of the 1995 World Cup, club spokesman Julian Harrison appeared regularly on BBC Radio Leicester and the commercial station, Leicester Sound. BBC East Midlands also did a feature on the club's 1995 Nines Tournament. Having nearly folded, and then risen again, the club became 'Leicester Phoenix'.

However, it was abundantly clear that more fundamental and radical changes were necessary for the game to survive in places such as Leicester. Such changes would be beyond the control of one individual or club. A revolution was needed, one in keeping with the upheavals in professional rugby league in 1995.

One other factor is significant. The importance of rugby union has to be fully recognised. In most cases, if it wasn't for the support of rugby union, rugby league would not have survived and grown into the national presence at amateur level it has today. Players are the obvious example of this relationship between the two codes. However, rugby league clubs had to play somewhere and in the absence of council facilities, where else could they play other than at rugby union clubs? For this to happen, there had to be co-operation and collaboration beyond the players. Relationships between the administrators of the two sports at club level were not always harmonious and many rugby league clubs had a nomadic existence, moving to new union venues in the search for a cross-code relationship of lasting mutual benefit. However, the two sports at national level appeared to those at local level as being continually embroiled in conflict and suspicion, the same, by-and-large, could not be said in rugby league development areas. Relationships take time to work, and those rugby league clubs who have found their ideal partner in union have found a relationship that works and thrives. Some rugby league people do not recognise the attributes of rugby union and remain averse to anything about it. However, such people might pause to reflect that league and union in many areas prosper together, and rugby league's advance as a genuinely national sport owes much to the input of people from the other code.

There was a legacy of rugby league participation over a surprisingly long period of time throughout the length of the country. Nevertheless a combination of factors – among them, as we have seen, the enthusiasm of those involved, the realism that something had to be done to fuel that enthusiasm, Super League and a summer professional game – resulted in the autumn of 1996 being a watershed for the game in development areas. If ever there was a time for action, it appeared to be then.

Blackpool Sea Eagles 2004 squad for the North West Divisional Plate Final against Crewe Wolves (Photo: Paul Clarke)

Cardiff Demons versus Valley Cougars at the picturesque Taff Wells RFC, July 2004

8

2. Moving Forward

As well as the factors outlined in the previous chapter, there was also a combination of circumstances involving a number of individuals and organisations during the latter half of 1996 that were instrumental in the formation of the Southern Conference League. As fate would have it, the people concerned all recognised – in many cases, independently of each other – that, in words used in the new Sky Television coverage of the sport, it was time to 'seize the day'. These people did not come to the realisation through one particular route, or even had a uniform vision of the future. However, the common factor was the concept of a development league played in summer for clubs outside the game's heartlands. Like a domino effect, once news reached someone else that other people were thinking along similar lines, so the realisation that there was substance to the idea and that it could happen became more concrete.

Various views surfaced as to how to make it happen. Some thought that a high-profile Super League game, played as an on-the-road fixture for promotional reasons as well as competition points, would provide a stimulus to grassroots development and assist in the profile of particular clubs. This was certainly the train of thought in Leicester where club chairman Julian Harrison had actively pursued the idea, first with Neil Tunnicliffe and Maurice Lindsay of the Rugby Football League and then, prompted by their interest, with Peter Wheeler of the Leicester Tigers rugby union club and Tom Smeaton, chairman of Leicester City FC. Indeed, though the venture was unsuccessful at that time (as we shall see, there was success in the concept a number of years later), it did pave the way for an opening of relations between sporting partners in the city.

Harrison concentrated on the involvement of Sheffield Eagles and, though ultimately fruitless, this persisted well into the New Year. Similar things happened in Oxford, focusing on the London Broncos. Oxford Cavaliers had been recently founded, playing their first fixture – and winning – against Bath on 14 July 1996. As part of the plan to promote the game in the Oxford area, and the Cavaliers as well, club representatives and others had been investigating the possibility of a Super League fixture at Oxford United's planned new stadium (a stadium that would take a few years to come to fruition). Bristol City's Ashton Gate was also considered as a potential host for a London Broncos fixture, possibly against Australian opposition.

Among those investigating this initiative were two figures who became initial members of the first Southern Conference League executive committee – John Nugent (a solicitor then based in Northampton) and Lionel Hurst. Hurst, following his sterling efforts with MASWARLA, had carried his missionary zeal into this period and was involved not only in the formation of the new Oxford Cavaliers club, but also attended the inaugural meeting in May 1996 of another club who have featured throughout the competition to date, Worcester Royals (now Worcestershire Saints). Hurst clearly had ambitions for rugby league in these areas and understood the current national climate in the sport. Incidentally it was around this time that he launched the

1895 club that has now turned into a high-profile promotional and fund-raising support body for international rugby league. At the dinner that launched the 1895 club, he spoke about the idea of a national amateur summer competition for the development areas. Guests at the dinner included Peter Deakin, Tom O'Donovan and Martyn Sadler, all of whom later were involved in the RLC in different ways. Hurst's speech followed up an article he had written for *League Express* in the spring, where he had also aired the idea of a summer competition.

As part of discussions about the possibility of a league for the likes of Oxford and Worcester, Hurst talked to Niel Wood, then director of Student Rugby League. Recognition of the close ties between the student and amateur games was a core factor in these two men coming together.

Hurst was an instrumental figure in the formation of the Southern Conference League. However, the central figures who made it happen initially were elsewhere: Bev Risman and Julian Harrison.

Arguably, one of Risman's most important feats was his pivotal role in the establishment of the development league that became the Southern Conference League. Risman had the advantage of his background in the sport, and his then position as director of development at London Broncos. In this role, he oversaw the growth of young players from the London area with the Broncos, and had a wider brief that ran from his previous employment as Niel Wood's predecessor at the Student Rugby League, to the various amateur clubs in and around the capital.

The development league idea had also been raised in the rugby league press. An article in *League Express* had appeared in November 1996, mentioning the possibility of a national third division, below Super League and the professional leagues. Risman had read this and had decided that action was required. London Skolars had just had their application to join BARLA's National Conference League rejected. That Conference was national in name only – Skolars would have been the only southern presence. A national concept to join with the existing structures was needed. However, he could not act alone.

While meeting with Neil Tunnicliffe to discuss the prospective Super League game, Leicester RLFC chairman Julian Harrison had also mentioned the possibility of the RFL employing a project officer for the Midlands and Southern areas of England, first to investigate the potential of a development league and then to take action to bring it about. Harrison, who was working part-time at Leicester University, was determined not only to ensure the survival of his own rugby league involvement at Leicester, but also to gain a personal role in rugby league development in the southern half of the country. His view was quite simple. Rugby league needed to be in the hands of those who knew it best in these areas, people who were 'doers' as well as 'talkers', people who had a passion to make it succeed. Harrison considered he fitted these categories. He also had the time on his hands. It was a calculated risk. He needed employment on the one hand, but he needed the time to make things happen in this particular sphere of rugby league on the other. His ultimate hope was that the two would coincide.

Circumstances would dictate that Risman and Harrison got together. Harrison wrote to Risman and they met on 20 November 1996. That meeting launched a series of actions. Risman utilised his experience, contacts and position to approach the RFL and others in positions of influence. Harrison became the operational driver, talking to grassroots contacts, developing interest among potential league clubs, and formulating on paper the vision and the plan to make it happen. While Risman ensured that the London end of professional operations was supportive and prepared for action, Harrison focused on informing and continually gaining advice from Gary Hetherington (now at Leeds Rhinos) and also Ralph Rimmer at Sheffield Eagles.

The remainder of November 1996 set the trend for the future. More and more people came on board. One of the early tasks was to bring together those who were willing and able to work on the project and had the same vision, so that a collective of individuals could work together. This meant Lionel Hurst, whose name was one of the first mentioned to Harrison by Risman at their inaugural meeting. It meant Neil Tunnicliffe at the RFL. It also meant the Student Rugby League Alumni, the graduate arm of the Student Rugby League, which had Niel Wood and Bev Risman among their directors. The third director was Hector McNeil of the London Skolars and the manager, Abe Kerr, a graduate of Manchester Metropolitan University. McNeil and Kerr would be key figures, their experience of grassroots rugby league, both in the student sector and in and around London, proving invaluable.

Harrison went about the task of formulating a plan of operations and, in effect, a development league version of the RFL's *Framing the Future* document. Lionel Hurst confirmed the support of the Oxford Cavaliers club and also raised the importance of financial support through commercial sponsorship. Paul Walmsley, Leicester's coach, contacted fellow EMARLA club, Birmingham. Conversations were ongoing between Risman, Harrison and the RFL, primarily through Neil Tunnicliffe.

A combination of independent and interdependent developments and thoughts had catalysed through a coherent and uniform group into a clear vision for the future. The first hurdle had been cleared. More would follow.

Ipswich Rhinos 2004 semi-final squad (Photo: Kevin Cook)

Middlesex Lions versus Cambridge Eagles July 2004

3. The beginning - establishment

In Julian Harrison's opinion, the most important period in the history of the competition to date is indisputable: "The time when the Southern Conference League was established and then realised has to be the most significant. Impressing on the powers-that-be that this development was not only desirable but essential, and then putting the many months of planning into action during the pilot season was not only immensely satisfying, but also vital for the national development of our sport. Quite simply, if we hadn't been successful during this period, the Rugby League Conference wouldn't have existed, there wouldn't be such a national dimension to the game, a national presence in the National Leagues would be virtually non-existent and hundreds if not thousands of new enthusiasts for rugby league throughout the country would never have materialised."

In December 1996, there was an idea and a vision. On 17 May 1997 when the competition commenced, there were 10 teams making that a reality. Those five months had action, excitement and passion coupled with uncertainty, worry and considerable nerves.

In addition to the key elements identified in the previous chapter: the volunteers, the RFL, the Student Rugby League and both the London Broncos and Sheffield Eagles; BARLA also had some input. Harrison's links with the South West Yorkshire junior section, instigated by Ralph Rimmer, ensured that there was an opportunity to broadcast to a more experienced rugby league community the realities of the new situation and life at more remote rugby league outposts, such as Leicester. On 2 December, he spoke at a meeting in Hoyland about life at Leicester Rugby League. Mike Morrissey, who would become BARLA chair in June 1997, was present and it was apparent that a national development league was also in the minds of some at the amateur governing body. This was also borne out by features in the rugby league press. Despite feeling that there was still a sense of aversion to rugby league development in the southern half of the country from some people in the north, Harrison also felt more optimistic that the Southern Conference League concept could become a reality because of the joining-up of rugby league forces and organisations, and provide a vehicle for closer relationships between those organisations. Everyone would benefit.

In the meantime, Harrison continued work on a plan of action document, effectively a schedule, and a larger piece of work entitled *The Way Forward* that was a first attempt at providing both a constitutional and organisational framework for the new competition. On 5 December the former was completed and circulated to the following the next day: Bev Risman, Neil Tunnicliffe, Abe Kerr, Ralph Rimmer, Lionel Hurst, and two club representatives – Jamie Walsh of Birmingham and Bob Brown of Hemel Hempstead. This was the initial guiding document of the Southern Conference League, circulated to clubs as they expressed interest, for information and to involve them in framing the league in which they would participate.

Risman, Tunnicliffe, Kerr and RFL development executive, Tom O'Donovan met shortly after the circulation of the plan of action. O'Donovan's brief was the national development of the sport. He was a key figure in the competition's early years and instrumental in the initial establishment of the league as it was under his direct remit. He had previously been BARLA's national development officer and had considerable experience. His relative absence from involvement in the process of establishing the competition so far was raised by O'Donovan at the meeting. However, he was appeased and there was generally a positive outcome to this gathering, including recognition of the need for a quick follow-up meeting involving both Lionel Hurst and Julian Harrison.

Planning for that meeting, scheduled initially for Thursday 19 December in Oxford, was not entirely smooth, and it did not actually take place until 22 January 1997. A combination of factors provided a temporary halt in what had been up until that time a period of good progress and fortune.

Nevertheless, Bev Risman felt that a meeting on 19 December was still necessary. So on that Thursday prior to Christmas, possibly the first action-oriented meeting devoted entirely to the embryonic league was held. Julian Harrison joined Risman, Abe Kerr, Hector McNeil and London development officer Dave Evans (another man with Student Rugby League history) at Crystal Palace to discuss happenings to date and things to do prior to the eventual *tête-à-tête* with the Rugby Football League officials. Harrison's document received positive feedback, and discussion also focused on likely candidates for the new league. Harrison had discussed this with Lionel Hurst, and between them a number of names had come to the fore in addition to those already earmarked as the most likely starters: London teams, Leicester, Birmingham and Oxford. Among those names were Bath, Basingstoke, Telford, Derby and Hemel Hempstead. Other possibilities were outlined at the meeting – Abe Kerr, for example, mentioning Bedford Swifts, an existing rugby union club considering forming a rugby league section. A number of responsibilities were delegated at the meeting. Harrison was to update the plan as a result of the meeting, introducing consideration of how – and where – to enlist new teams. He was also to keep the RFL informed and to advertise in the press - union and league - for prospective clubs.

McNeil and Kerr were to talk to London clubs about the Southern Conference idea and nurture possible involvement. Bev Risman was to continue to liaise on financial and administrative matters with the RFL, the London Broncos and Super League.

Bearing in mind Tom O'Donovan's concerns at the previous meeting, it was important to keep him informed. However, it was also felt important to be as organised as possible prior to increased RFL involvement, so as to convey a sense of professionalism and to act in such a manner. Time was of the essence. Much needed to be done before the meeting with the RFL.

The turn of the year saw further press interest in the potential development league. *League Express*, which had raised the possibility of such a competition two months previously, contacted Julian Harrison at the beginning of January for further information on developments. Harrison – unused to the attention of national publications in his rugby league career to date – saw an opportunity to grab the attention of the game and push forward the agenda that had been created. Despite seeking Risman's advice on what should be said, Harrison – naively – gave full vent to his feelings.

The finished product, while espousing the unity of purpose within the SCL fraternity, came across as being critical of BARLA and the perceived neglect of amateur rugby league in the East Midlands.

"The opportunity was there to speak and I took it," Harrison reflected, "but I should have been more professional in the way the message was delivered and I should have thought more about the current efforts of people within BARLA to move things along. I was a little frustrated that things hadn't happened previously and conscious of the legacy of past attempts and that realistically, if it (a national amateur game) was going to happen, it had to happen now". Tony Hannan, the *League Express* reporter in question, duly reported the positive overtones emanating from the RFL and notified Harrison of the fact that BARLA were considering pushing forward an eight-team winter initiative in the London area that could dovetail nicely into any new summer set-up. The article did at least provoke thought and informed the readership of what was happening. It also included possibly the first ever picture of a Leicester rugby league team in a rugby league publication.

Club interest was beginning to gather pace. Early contact was made with Mike Cunningham from Oxford Cavaliers. He was positive about summer rugby and the need for a bigger profile for the game in the south of England. While expressing concerns over the extent of potential rugby union influence in the competition, he realised that financial input was important and that there needed to be a significant element of control at grassroots level. He also considered it more likely that a league would begin in 1998, with the summer of 1997 devoted to friendly matches and promotion. With this in mind, Oxford had begun to organise games against suitable opposition.

When it comes to acknowledging the long-standing contribution of volunteers in development areas, Dave Flaherty of Ipswich Rhinos was one of the leaders. His involvement was not just at club level – he had been a key figure in the Civil Service game in the South East region – but his drive meant that Ipswich were prominent in the pilot season. Julian Harrison first spoke to him on the eve of the 22 January meeting and immediately recognised a key ally. Ipswich participated in the London ARL and had a history of enterprising fixture arrangement. They played annually against Cambridge University and had made international contact with Scotland and Kazakhstan. In addition, they made inroads into schools and produced a high quality match programme. The club were exactly the sort of operation that the SCL and RLC wanted to produce.

Contact was also made with some other clubs, and networks began to develop. Barry Butterfield at Cambridge Eagles, Sam Cook at Reading and Worcester Royals' Andrew Cave joined the growing band of SCL supporters. Both Cambridge and Reading also played in the London ARL, with Cambridge, established in 1990, finalists in the 1993-94 Southern Counties Cup. Their opposition in that final, Fulham, were also informed of developments in relation to the SCL, via the ever-enthusiastic Flaherty. In addition to these rugby league clubs, Bev Risman was also approaching prospective union set-ups in the London and Home Counties area, among them Henley RFC.

Following on from the Crystal Palace gathering, the next SCL meeting took place on 22 January in Oxford. Present that day were Tom O'Donovan and Neil Tunnicliffe from the RFL, Bev Risman, Julian Harrison, Lionel Hurst and Mike Cunningham of the Oxford club. On and off-field developments were discussed in greater detail than on any previous occasion and it was clear that there was a more tangible note to proceedings when compared to the potential and, on occasions, hypothetical conversations of the past. For a start, eight rugby league clubs were identified as the most likely starters. These were the SRL Old Boys from London (the present London Skolars club), Oxford Cavaliers, Leicester Phoenix, Birmingham, Ipswich Rhinos, Reading, Cambridge Eagles and Kingston - five clubs from the London ARL, two clubs from EMARLA and one club, Oxford, without a current league. These clubs would come under a uniform basic development scheme, thus avoiding the necessity - and financial repercussions - of providing eight separate development officers.

One club missing from the list was Hemel Hempstead. Despite involving Bob Brown from the Hertfordshire club in the circulation list of information and in informal discussions, Hemel had their competition needs well catered for. Having only recently left BARLA's National Conference League, the club were about to join the Rugby League Alliance First Division. Another possibility not included in the eight was Portsmouth, for, while not actually existing as a club, it was felt that the Royal Navy presence would make any club operation on the south coast viable. Bev Risman reported that at every club that had been approached there had been great interest. He also listed a number of rugby union clubs worthy of consideration – Henley, High Wycombe, Camberley, Guildford and Esher. Following the meeting in Oxford, Risman held discussions that afternoon with representatives of Wasps.

The SCL and RLC have always maintained a commitment to standards. There was a need to act professionally and responsibly, with recognition that previous attempts to sustain development leagues had perhaps foundered because of an imbalance between on-pitch and off-field focus. A sound administrative structure was required for the new league, with practical measures needed for a pilot project in the summer of 1997 and a full competition to commence the following year. The pilot season would combine actual competition and a joint marketing and development initiative. Various strategies and events were suggested – the Super League 'on-the-road' notion that had been mooted and worked on in Leicester, Oxford and Bristol; a possible rugby league festival and nines tournament in Oxford; the annual Varsity Match and initiatives in areas throughout the south. Minimum standards were vital, both in assessing club suitability and ensuring a successful organisation and competition. Such standards needed to be demanding, appropriate and realistic – to encourage development, but not to discourage participation. Costings were also required in order to assess the financial viability of running the pilot competition in 1997 and in full in 1998. Lionel Hurst proposed that the RFL underwrite the costs of a pilot competition.

To move things forward, Julian Harrison was asked to produce a document by Monday 10 February, the date when RFL chief executive Maurice Lindsay was due to return from Australia. The document would include information contained in both the plan of action and *The Way Forward*, but with actual costings and a one-page précis. While Harrison felt that he could produce something based on what he perceived was needed and desirable, he realised that he had to produce something realistic and therefore consultation with Risman was essential. Accordingly, six days following the Oxford meeting, Harrison visited Risman at his Crystal Palace office. Discussion focused on the content and format of the 'Lindsay document', tactics to be used and the plans to be formalised. Risman's experience and knowledge proved vital to producing an appropriate document, and he took responsibility for providing a costed appraisal of what it would mean financially for the RFL. A link with Gerrard Grundy (who had taken over from Abe Kerr as the SRL Alumni's development manager) was mentioned, with the aim being an administrative 'double-act' – Harrison as secretary of the SCL, with Grundy being general administrator. While the latter's position could be subsumed within his current work, there would be administration costs involved and these would need to include a position of secretary as Harrison wasn't currently employed within the sport.

February opened with yet another meeting at Crystal Palace, though this time not one devoted entirely to the SCL. The London Rugby League Steering Group covered all rugby league activity in and around the London area, involving various partners for the common good. The Sports Council were directly represented through Andy Sacha, and the RFL by Tom O'Donovan. On 5 February 1997, the group was joined by a figure synonymous with the Rugby League Conference, whose name would eventually be given to the winners' trophy, Harry Jepson OBE. Jepson, a past Leeds RLFC chairman and rooted in grassroots development in the Hunslet area of that city, was on the RFL board of directors. His presence elevated the significance of the gathering. This was Harrison's first attendance at this group, and he joined more seasoned campaigners in Risman, Dave Evans (London Broncos development officer) Henry Miles (London ARL secretary), and Gerrard Grundy. The meeting was productive with Jepson agreeing to the need to pursue the formation of a development league. More importantly he also made it clear that he agreed with the request for RFL funding. As to how much, Risman had a clear notion. He proposed an amount sufficient to cover the positions of SCL co-ordinator and development officer. Risman and Harrison had, by this time, completed the 'Lindsay document' and O'Donovan took it away to consult with Neil Tunnicliffe, before forwarding a version to Maurice Lindsay.

At this stage in the process, things appeared – on the surface – to be progressing seamlessly. There was a conformity and uniformity of feeling and purpose. The SCL was the right initiative. It would help to bring about a wider national game. It would enthuse, promote and develop rugby league. It would involve the various necessary components – the professional governing body, amateur organisers and volunteers, the student sector, and, albeit indirectly, sport's primary organisation, the Sports Council. Henry Miles confirmed that a Southern Conference League could complement nicely the existing amateur league in London. Miles was quick to offer his advice to

Harrison, who had become potentially his secretarial colleague. Following the 5 February London Steering Group meeting, there also appeared to be a consensus on the provision of funding from the RFL. It seemed only a matter of time before things fell into place.

A report in *The Independent* on 25 February stated that the RFL were to appoint a development officer for South Wales, to maintain interest in the game there. To Harrison, that provided further justification for supporting the SCL initiative: "To my mind, it seemed inconceivable that we could be unsuccessful in our request for financial support. If the RFL could support Wales where current activity was not on a par with that coming under a prospective SCL umbrella, how could it not support us? I felt that if our request for funding went unanswered, questions would be asked, and answers would need to be given."

Concern, however, existed among those working on the SCL project, including Harrison. This was based on past feelings and experiences, but also focused on the present and on the need for things to happen quickly while the impetus and interest was high. Harrison discovered another measure of that interest. On buying the latest copy of *Open Rugby*, the predecessor to *Rugby League World*, Harrison was delighted to read information on the SCL. The rugby league press was helping maintain interest.

It should be noted that this period in the fortunes of rugby league development was also characterised by financial movements at both Super League clubs featured in the SCL project, Sheffield Eagles and London Broncos. The latter development received considerable attention as it concerned Richard Branson. The timing of his involvement at the Broncos was advantageous for the SCL. A higher profile for the professional club and a desire to help spread the game in London was positive boosts for the prospects of a successful development league.

While work continued on *The Way Forward*, the 'Lindsay document' was now with Tom O'Donovan. However, this situation was soon to be reversed as on the same day, 19 February, that the first draft of the former was completed, Harrison received feedback from Neil Tunnicliffe to say that amendments were needed to the latter. The amendments required were a more detailed breakdown of costs and of minimum standards criteria. Further discussions between Risman, Harrison and Tunnicliffe produced a final version for the RFL hierarchy. It was sent to Maurice Lindsay on 1 March for consideration by the RFL board of directors, with Risman adding the required costings. Nothing could now be done at this level until a decision was taken on the document.

This waiting game was not repeated when it came to club and organisational level though. Things progressed with more people and clubs coming on board. As mentioned previously, the Birmingham club were well established members of the East Midlands League and were similar in make-up to Leicester Phoenix. The driving forces behind the club were founder John Simkin, chairman Jim Eccles and secretary Jamie Walsh, though Birmingham could also boast a certain Ellery Hanley as club president. Eccles and Walsh were former professional players, with Wigan and Castleford respectively, and Walsh provided the contact with the SCL initiative.

While Bev Risman continued to keep in touch with the Royal Navy in Portsmouth, interest also emanated from the Metropolitan Police. The Met were an established club in the London ARL and were coached by Cumbrian Dave Doran. His contact with Harrison had been prompted by the *Open Rugby* feature. Abe Kerr at the December meeting at Crystal Palace had indicated the potential of a rugby league arm to the Bedford Swifts rugby union club. That was being nurtured by a former Doncaster player, Darryl Cook, with the blessing and co-operation of club president Mike Smith. Cook was contacted by Julian Harrison on 27 February. While overwhelmingly supportive of the SCL concept and progress, the Bedford man did express concern at the prospect of SCL players being directly targeted by more prestigious league outfits in the south with club development at SCL level therefore being hindered by player movement and recruitment to higher levels. This was not the first time that this issue had been mentioned and it would not be the last. There is an argument that this is a natural - though not necessarily desirable to all parties - process in sport at all levels. However, the impact on embryonic rugby league clubs of players moving to more established set-ups could not be ignored. Nevertheless, Cook's enthusiasm was immediately apparent. Twenty-four hours later, he spoke to Harrison again, reporting on the first training session, and was delighted at the response from the players. There had been 20 present and the prospect of more to come.

Harrison was also contacted by someone not connected with a club, but who was still keen to add his weight and skills to the project. Andy Stevens was known to Bev Risman for his expertise in promotion and marketing. After receiving some basic information from Harrison, Stevens produced some initial ideas that could help clubs' abilities to market and promote themselves and rugby league in their areas. These ideas included the use of open-age players for development purposes, sending letters to colleges doing Sports Science courses seeking joint initiatives in coaching or administration and innovative local sponsorship programmes linked to rugby league development.

Clearly, the Southern Conference League was recruiting some quality people. While this was encouraging and illustrated perfectly the validity of the concept, for Risman and Harrison in particular it was rapidly turning into an administrative headache. It was difficult having to deal with evermore contacts, a demanding timetable of producing documents, a constant flow of information and ideas and then sharing these with more and more people and the game's press. This all happened at the same time as everyday work and life, which meant that there weren't enough hours in the day and resources to cater for everything.

There was a remedy – in the short term at least. A meeting of interested clubs and others would allow all the ideas and information to be shared and developed in one place at one time, with an opportunity for questions to be put to those in some position to answer.

The location of the meeting had to be central and its timing was also crucial, bearing in mind people's work and other commitments. Of course, finding a day when everybody could be available was – and is – never easy, but the meeting was scheduled for Hemel Hempstead RLFC at 7.00pm on

Tuesday 18 March. Hemel offered a rugby league venue and central location close to the motorway network. However, there were also concerns. Hemel had not been identified as an initial SCL club, and Harrison also sensed that as it was a bona-fide rugby league operation without any rugby union input, this might open up elements of criticism of the dual-code relationships that were present at most prospective SCL clubs and very much part of the organisational framework for the new competition. Nevertheless, Hemel were willing hosts and keen to assist.

Lots of issues were being discussed. Andrew Cave at Worcester Royals had made tremendous progress in getting the club off the ground. He was concerned about playing standards. Harrison assured him that all the clubs would be experiencing transformations of one kind or another and that a focus on promotion and getting games played was as important at this stage as the quality and equality of on-pitch play. Ipswich's Dave Flaherty advised that progress would not be all plain-sailing and that there would be problems. Harrison was well aware of this, but little did he know that another significant problem was about to strike.

With hopes for a viable competition rising, the beginning of March saw consideration of possible fixture formats. Even at the end of January (prior to knowing the extent of club interest), Dave Flaherty had raised the idea of a five-team tournament for the early summer period based on the rugby union 'five nations' model. This would involve a representative side from various regions, though the absence of an obvious candidate from the South West proved a minor flaw in the plan. However, things had moved on by March and at this stage Reading's Sam Cook proposed a more traditional structure based on a league format. One of the burning questions was how structured a pilot competition should be? Should it be a home and away based fixture format, a merit table or simply organised friendlies? Of course, finance would be a big determinant in this, but without knowing what – if any – figure was in the offing from the RFL, other factors needed to be considered. Key was the ability of individual clubs to field sides in a competitive league on a regular, week-by-week basis. For some this would be no problem, for others it might prove more difficult. This was an early example of the perennial issue of catering for a wide variety of clubs at different stages of development in a unified competition. Cook clearly imagined a more regulated structure. However, Harrison was keeping options open.

Mike Cunningham of Oxford rang him on 4 March, concerned about the fixture situation. Oxford had already arranged a number of games and Cunningham wondered whether he should cancel these to make way for SCL fixtures. Not knowing how things would pan out, Harrison advised him to keep things as scheduled because he thought at the time that clubs would be left to make their own arrangements for matches with SCL opposition and therefore not have to commit to regular rugby. Thus SCL fixtures could be fitted around existing club schedules. In a few weeks the situation became clearer and this laissez-faire approach to fixture formatting was dropped.

The growth of potential clubs that would ensure a regular fixture list continued during March. West London was the next focus of attention. George McCoombe of Brent-Ealing RLFC contacted Harrison to propose the formation of merged super-club to compete in the SCL formed from his own, plus London Colonials and London Warriors, though Bev Risman was also keen for them to include Twickenham. Clearly, bearing in mind the strength of these teams, Colonials in particular, this amalgamation would be a force to be reckoned with on the pitch. Contact was also made with another London ARL club, Basingstoke Beasts, and also EMARLA's Derby City, though both of these did not actually take to the field in the pilot season.

Publicity, too, was also on the increase with new opportunities arising. The SRL Alumni, as mentioned, were key figures in the SCL project, and their newsletter *League Leader* provided a means to promote the SCL and clubs to Alumni members. And on 3 March, Harrison received a letter from BBC commentator and dual-code international, Ray French, expressing his support for the SCL concept and his willingness to assist in whatever way he could.

Everyone still awaited some kind of feedback or decision from the RFL. On 6 March, Bev Risman phoned Julian Harrison to say that he had heard from Neil Tunnicliffe that the RFL would support the summer's pilot season, on condition that control of the funds would remain within the hands of development executive, Tom O'Donovan and his departmental budget. The go-ahead had effectively been given, and Harrison began to contact people with the news and with planning arrangements for the Hemel meeting on 18 March, which he hoped Neil Tunnicliffe would attend on behalf of the RFL.

That meeting would not take place, at least on the scheduled date. On 11 March, Harrison took a phone call from the RFL informing him that Tom O'Donovan had called a meeting regarding the SCL. Not long afterwards, he got another phone call from rugby league headquarters, but this time with a different tone. There had been no indication beforehand of annoyance and Harrison had certainly felt that things were progressing well but also, despite understandable concerns and worries, that everyone was content with how things had been done. That second call temporarily shattered that illusion, as a heated exchange took place between Harrison and O'Donovan over the arrangement and context of the planned clubs meeting in Hemel. O'Donovan's view was that it was inappropriate to call such a meeting without his involvement and prior to any information on the league being confirmed. Harrison said that the meeting was to be informal and that in his view it was well known that a meeting was due to take place because the need for one had been mentioned at the London Steering Group meeting, and that arrangements had been made prior to the announcement of the RFL decision on funding the previous week.

Harrison was furious, feeling that a movement that had been successful so far based on mutual respect, co-operation and the collaboration of clubs was in danger if demands were going to be imposed centrally without the input of others. He felt that there was a danger of development by coercion by the RFL, not by consensus, and that unnecessary obstacles were being thrown up. What was so wrong with club representatives meeting to have an informal group discussion over a drink in a clubhouse? On reflection, more effective communication would have been beneficial, as would a greater appreciation of the pressures faced by O'Donovan in keeping a hold on what was happening to a budget for which he had control and was accountable. This was something that Harrison himself would realise a few years later.

Nevertheless, the situation needed rectifying. Bev Risman acted as peacemaker. Harrison spoke to him; Risman contacted O'Donovan, and a compromise was reached. The RFL meeting dealing with specifics and facts (the focus of the first phone call of the day) would be brought forward from early April to 20 March, with clubs' involvement in a meeting taking place later on. Tensions were eased - Harrison was asked by O'Donovan, via Risman, to 'calm down' - and perhaps a better understanding was achieved.

All relevant parties were informed of the new meeting arrangements and Harrison and Bev Risman decided to meet three days before meeting the RFL on 20 March, to discuss the agenda, and their strategy for the meeting. Various matters were discussed, including a view of an eight-team mainstream competition in the pilot season, with a subsidiary league for additional teams coming under the umbrella of the SCL, but without funding support from the RFL budget. An organisational framework was also conceived, and thought was given to the starting date, length of the season and the impact of organised festivals.

Clearly both men had views on who would be included in the mainstream competition and those in any subsidiary league, but much depended on applications from clubs, some of whom were in the early stages of formation and had been awaiting positive signals from the RFL before proceeding. While not wishing to make the application process particularly lengthy and arduous, there was a need for specific information from clubs on areas such as player strength, facilities, finance and administration etc, to complement what was already known about them on and off the pitch.

In advance of the key meeting with the RFL, Risman had contacted Harry Jepson and the idea of the new league being run by a small committee had received a seal of approval from the RFL director. Other conversations had also taken place, including one that dealt with the subject of the position of RLC chairman.

Thursday 20 March 1997 dawned – a pivotal moment had arrived. The meeting was to begin at 2.30pm at the Red Hall headquarters of the Rugby Football League in Leeds. Bev Risman and Julian Harrison met two RFL employees, Tom O'Donovan and Neil Tunnicliffe. The latter was taking up a project co-ordinating role on behalf of the RFL. There was, of course, a notable absentee. Lionel Hurst had sent his apologies; work commitments had prevented his attendance. However, Hurst's input into how the process had materialised into the current situation was very evident. He had made a considerable impression on those with whom he had come into contact – this was one of Hurst's lasting legacies, not only with regard to the SCL and RLC – and it was clearly O'Donovan's view that Hurst would make an ideal inaugural chairman of the league.

From the outset, therefore, Hurst carried the mantle of chairman and was also perceived to be the sole holder of that position. However, technically at least, that was not the case, because the position of RLC chairman was to be shared with the RFL contingent, O'Donovan and Tunnicliffe. The rationale was not only shared responsibility and a reflection of the RFL stake-holding, but also practical reasons, in case Hurst could not always attend meetings. The rest of the executive committee comprised solicitor John Nugent, Risman and Harrison. They were later to be joined by Stuart Sheard (now football manager/player performance manager at Super League club Huddersfield Giants), after discussions among the committee revealed the need for a representative from BARLA. For administration, Harrison was to act as SCL secretary with general administration being the responsibility of the SRL Alumni's Gerrard Grundy.

Ten clubs were identified as short-listed candidates to be invited to submit an application to join the new league. Alphabetically, these were Bedford Swifts, Birmingham, Ipswich Rhinos, Kingston, Leicester Phoenix, North London (SRL Old Boys), Oxford Cavaliers, Reading Raiders, West London and Worcester Royals. There was no mention of the inclusion of further rugby union clubs (only Bedford were union-based), and a number of rugby league clubs that had expressed an interest were also not included within the chosen 10.

While other organisational matters were discussed at the meeting, it was the selection of clubs that was the main focus. It seemed some were not in a position to participate. However, this was certainly not the case with Cambridge Eagles. Barry Butterfield is one of the most enthusiastic and colourful characters in the RLC story. He is passionate about the game and his club. As a result, the Eagles are still flying the flag for the game in the Cambridge area 14 years after formation. Much of that is due to Butterfield's perseverance. The day after the meeting at Red Hall, Harrison spoke to Butterfield on the phone and told him the bad news. "I had to inform him that Cambridge had not been short-listed, and he wasn't happy," reflected Harrison. "All I could do was inform him of what had been discussed at the meeting. I really felt for him." In contrast to this phone call, Harrison had the pleasant task of informing the 10 selected club representatives. And for Cambridge, there would also be a happy ending.

Aside from registering interest in the potential Southern Conference League, what were clubs actually doing during the early months of 1997? The top-level developments had a galvanising effect on club operations, and strengthening in some cases occurred simultaneously with playing matches. For others, focus was solely on being in a position to play in any prospective summer league.

Leicester Phoenix fell into the second category. From the end of December 1996, the club had made a conscious decision to 'go for it'. That meant establishing a plan of action and a division of labour among club personnel. While Julian Harrison would focus on publicity (in addition to his broader SCL remit), secretary Howard Ludbrook concentrated on organisation and coach Paul Walmsley on the recruitment of more players. The club's work on junior development, it was hoped, would continue. It was a busy time at the East Midlands club. Negotiations – unfortunately, with no end result – were still ongoing with Sheffield Eagles over their Super League fixture in the city, and Harrison turned to Australia (via an academic contact) for ideas regarding general development. Slowly, but surely, Leicester succeeded in their core aims – an expanded committee, more players and a bigger profile. The potential of playing in a flagship RFL-supported competition had great appeal. Of course, local factors would ensure that there would be differences between clubs in their preparation, but deep down a realisation that this was a window of opportunity not to be missed, provided the spur for action. The SCL was achieving some of its aims without actually existing.

April 1997 was the month of final preparations before the big kick-off. At the start of the month, the final line-up of clubs was still unknown. That was soon rectified. Thursday 10 April saw the first meeting of club representatives and the new SCL executive committee, who met separately prior to the main meeting. Lionel Hurst opened proceedings in a fashion that was to become almost legendary in the years to come. He has a gift for speaking and instilling pride and enthusiasm in his audience, and he made clear the importance of the gathering on that April day in Oxford. Not all club representatives could be present, and Julian Harrison and Gerrard Grundy represented Leicester and North London Skolars respectively; but those that were there witnessed the birth of the Southern Conference League. Ten clubs would be involved in 1997, split into two regional divisions:

Central Division: Birmingham, Leicester Phoenix, Oxford Cavaliers, Reading Raiders and Worcester Royals.

Eastern Division: Bedford Swifts, Ipswich Rhinos, Kingston, North London Skolars and West London.

This was announced by the Rugby Football League and all seemed finalised. However, there was late drama. Following the Oxford meeting, Sam Cook from Reading contacted Tom O'Donovan to withdraw his club's application. They felt they weren't ready and, admirably, didn't want to let down their compatriots and the integrity of the new competition. A replacement was needed. Though regrettable and disappointing to all concerned, Reading's withdrawal provided a new opportunity for Cambridge Eagles. Harrison contacted Barry Butterfield with the news and both men were delighted – Butterfield for obvious reasons, and Harrison because he felt that the Eagles had been harsh victims of the earlier short-listing process. Cambridge's inclusion - and geographical position - necessitated an adjustment to the divisional make-up. They would play in the Eastern Division, with Bedford Swifts switching to the Central Division.

With the executive committee and administration up-and-running, Tom O'Donovan was keen to liaise with Lionel Hurst and Julian Harrison. With such a tight schedule prior to the start of the season, effective communication was paramount. Other preparations needed to be made and initiatives started. For example, information was needed on various club details – playing kit and equipment, public relations, a coaching audit, insurance and facilities. It was important to check both arrangements and costs. Match officials were also required. To this end, Gerrard Grundy was given responsibility for with liaising with Student Rugby League director Niel Wood who would arrange for the provision of referees for each game.

Lionel Hurst and John Nugent were to investigate possibilities of grant aid, and, of course, the fixtures needed to be drafted. Two divisions of five meant that two clubs (one in each division) would be absent from the divisional fixtures each week. The remedy was simply to match them up. Thus began the cross-conference fixture, a feature both of this pilot season, and the RLC proper. For 1997, with costs clearly in mind, club pairings needed to take geography into account and it was on the basis of equitable travel that the cross-conference pairings were made. Bedford were paired with West London, Birmingham with Cambridge, Leicester with Ipswich, Oxford with Kingston and Worcester with North London. The job of producing the first list of fixtures went to a surprising, and surprised, person. Julian Harrison recalls: "It was my responsibility to do the fixtures, and one weekend afternoon I sat down and tried to do just that. After an hour or so of getting absolutely nowhere, I gave up. I had a mental block and simply couldn't work out how to do it. In desperation I asked my partner, now my wife, Lesley, if she would have a go. It took her about five minutes."

Earlier on, it was mentioned how Leicester's relationship with Sheffield Eagles was used as a basis for twinning arrangements in the SCL. O'Donovan was particularly keen to develop this further, and asked Harrison for suggestions, with the RFL then attempting to put them into practice. The idea was for Super League clubs to engage in coaching and promotional support, in return for any assistance that could be given in development regions towards establishing a new supporter or player base for the Super League clubs. Some of the arrangements did last, at least for a season. Some didn't even get off the ground. Some changed, with new combinations attempted. Clearly, much depended on the circumstances and enthusiasms of the clubs involved and more practically, what specifically could be offered.

A further meeting of the executive committee and then of the committee and the clubs was held in Oxford at the end of April. The clock was ticking. Anticipation and excitement increased. So too did nerves. Fixtures were released. Referees were appointed. Pitches and players were prepared. Interviews were conducted. Like a dress rehearsal before a first performance, attention was given to detail within an aura of the unknown. The Southern Conference League was about to begin.

West London Sharks versus Greenwich Admirals July 2004

South Wakefield versus Bradford Dudley Hill 'A' July 2004

London Skolars' first try in professional rugby league scored by Kirk Wotherspoon

4. 1997: The pilot season

Saturday 10 May 1997 witnessed the annual rugby league pilgrimage to Wembley for the Challenge Cup Final, this year between St Helens and Bradford Bulls. A crowd of 78,022 saw St Helens triumph 32-22. The match programme included a page-long feature on an amateur competition that was to start one week later, which featured towns that most would not have known hosted rugby league sides. That article was the perfect advertisement for the start of the Southern Conference League on Saturday 17 May.

Some who had been at Wembley for the Cup Final were also present on the opening day of the SCL at the competition's inaugural fixture - Leicester Phoenix versus Birmingham at the Saffron Lane Stadium. These included BBC commentator and *Rugby Leaguer* journalist, Ray French. French was joined by photographer Gerald Webster and *League Express's* Martyn Sadler, who would have a more direct involvement in the competition in the future. The referee for the game was director of Student Rugby League, Niel Wood. He had also been present, as a player for St Helens club Pilkington Recs, in the first round of BARLA's National Conference League in 1986. He would also have a more significant role to play in the RLC some years later.

The fact that one fixture has been highlighted as the inaugural game deserves explanation. On the morning of Saturday 17 May, there were two games scheduled. However, when Ray French and Gerald Webster arrived in Leicester that Saturday lunchtime they also brought with them the news that the other game – North London versus Kingston – had been cancelled, due to the latter's inability to raise a side. Unfortunately, this would not be an isolated occurrence for this club in 1997.

Three games had also been scheduled to take place 24 hours later – Worcester Royals versus Oxford Cavaliers, Ipswich Rhinos versus Cambridge Eagles and Bedford Swifts versus West London. Attention on that first day, therefore, focused entirely on Leicester, a situation unique in the annals of the club's history and reflected in the vast coverage given to a match that had previously been lucky to grab the small print in the local newspapers when part of the EMARLA fixture list.

With Julian Harrison concerned not only with his own club's performance on the opening day, but the operation of the competition as a whole, the last thing he needed was further bad news in addition to the cancelled fixture at North London. However, when match referee Niel Wood walked into the foyer at the Saffron Lane Stadium an hour or so before the two Midlands clubs were due to kick off, he explained to Harrison the difficulties that he had experienced getting match officials for that weekend's games. Indeed at that moment the East Anglian derby between Ipswich and Cambridge was without an appointed referee. Wood was slightly appeased when Harrison introduced him to Phil Jackson, a stalwart of rugby league in Leicester and the East Midlands generally and a qualified match official. Though Jackson could not take up the pending Ipswich appointment, he offered his services in the future and became a regular official in the SCL and RLC and in Student Rugby League. The relative dearth of qualified referees in areas covered by the fledgling competition was a concern and, despite significant development and improvement, still remained so in certain areas seven years on.

Despite problems elsewhere, at 2.30 that afternoon, Leicester and Birmingham kicked off, the former in their traditional colours of red, white and blue, the latter – equally traditionally – in maroon and gold, with Niel Wood refereeing. A legacy was born. The teams were:

Leicester Phoenix: Mike French, Phil Inman, Andy Clancy, Ben Harbottle, Dominic Senior, Paul Walmsley, Ben Pearson, Richard Zmijewsky, Andy Clay, Duncan Carter, Pete Whitehead, Julian French, Mick Bryant.
Subs: Dave Walker, Simon Moore, Shaun Murray, Hitesh Patel.
Birmingham: Tony Williams, Tom Reading, Dave Wilson, James Brabin, Henry McLeod, Dean Burbidge, Duncan Green, Cliff Kirlew, Alex Thomas, Steve Harrison-Mirfield, James Scott, John Townend, James Topham.
Subs: Darren Parkin, Andy Swann, Graham Kettlewell, Jason Cattell.

Those present were treated to a game befitting the occasion and reflecting the great rivalry between the two teams. Birmingham full back Tony Williams registered the first score in the competition, though he did so in unusual fashion with an early drop-goal. His team-mate James Brabin then became the competition's first try-scorer with an eighth minute touchdown as Birmingham took control of the game in the first quarter. Their decision to continue playing over the winter period, in contrast to their opponents, looked to be vindicated as Dean Burbidge added to the score to give the visitors an 11-0 lead. Leicester came back into the game with tries from Pete Whitehead and Mick Bryant, Dave Wilson restored Birmingham's advantage before half-time capitalising on an error from the home side's winger, Dominic Senior, and the teams took their half-time oranges with the score 19-14 to the visitors.

If the first half thrilled those present with its passion and quality, the second half was even better; the teams were equally matched and locked in a titanic struggle. That it was ultimately to be Leicester's day was due more than anything to the key moment when centre Ben Harbottle received the ball and raced 90 metres to put Leicester ahead 24-23. It was a lead that they never relinquished and late tries from man-of the-match and former Great Britain student international Mike French and prop Duncan Carter, gave Leicester a deserved but perhaps flattering 36-23 victory. Niel Wood's refereeing summary on the official team sheet confirmed the spectacle: "A good, clean, fast game played in excellent spirit".

Praise was also forthcoming from both rugby league newspapers, and not only for the on-pitch activity. In a separate feature from the match coverage, Ray French was glowing in his praise not only of the performances on the field, but also the Southern Conference League itself, and the vision of the two competing clubs. In interviewing Julian Harrison and Birmingham winger Henry McLeod, French illustrated the enthusiasm behind the scenes, the talents on display and the significance of Student Rugby League input.

Other comments were also complementary. Martyn Sadler in *League Express* wrote: "At one time we used to think that southerners were too soft to play Rugby League. That's why they played rugby union, or so many League diehards thought. But to judge by Saturday's match the Southern

Conference will be contested just as fiercely as any competition you could find in the game's heartland."

Rather prophetically, Sadler also commented: "The competition has been established under the auspices of the Rugby Football League, with BARLA giving its blessing, in a fine example of co-operation between the governing bodies. Could this be the prototype for further agreements in the near future? That, of course, remains to be seen, but the Conference is designed to put League firmly on the sporting map in a swathe of cities where the game has had a limited profile until now."

After quoting Julian Harrison who said: "Next season we could have a much bigger Conference. But we have to ensure that the quality of our competition is as high as possible", Sadler responded: "On that note perhaps the Southern Conference can teach the rest of the game a thing or two."

Phil Hodgson in the *Rugby Leaguer* ended his report by acknowledging the occasion's significance: "A superb day for rugby league and, on this evidence, a new dawn for amateur rugby league in the south".

Twenty-four hours after the game in Leicester, the three remaining fixtures in the round took place. In the clash of the new sides at Worcester rugby union club's superb Sixways facility, the Royals from Worcester defeated the Cavaliers from Oxford 56-24, easing secretary Andrew Cave's fears over playing standards and delighting his brother, Dean, the club's team manager. At Bedford Athletic Stadium, Bedford Swifts put up a spirited display against more experienced opposition from West London and were even leading at one point, before that experience eventually told and the visitors ran out comfortable 52-28 winners. The most intense atmosphere was reserved for Humber Doucy Lane in Ipswich. East Anglian derby games are an established feature of the SCL and RLC fixture list. In 1997, the sole derby competitors were Ipswich Rhinos and Cambridge Eagles and they met in the opening round of the competition. Unfortunately, despite the strenuous attempts of Niel Wood, a qualified referee could not be found for the game, an embarrassing problem that was exacerbated by the presence of television cameras from Anglia Television. Paul Girdler, the Ipswich chairman, stepped into the match official's shoes and gave a very good account of himself. The game lived up to expectations of a tight, no-holds-barred encounter and after 40 minutes the score was deadlocked at 16-all. Ipswich then took the lead, but that inspired the visitors who registered four further tries, including a second for both Jason Walker and Lee Brodie; the final result was the Eagles winning 42-28.

The early weeks of the season were ones of great promise as the clubs gradually felt their way and grew in confidence. At the top of the two divisions, Leicester and North London set the pace. Leicester brought Worcester down to earth following their opening weekend success with a 32-10 victory at Sixways on 31 May. North London increased early concerns for the Ipswich Rhinos with a 48-26 victory on the same weekend and elsewhere, it was encouraging to see sides come back from opening weekend defeats to register their first points of the season – Birmingham went to Cambridge and won 33-14 and Oxford Cavaliers, with a hat-trick try-scoring hero in Craig Aven, beat the unlucky Bedford Swifts 38-22.

It appeared that there was something positive for everyone to take from the first encounters in the new competition. Regrettably, however, this was not the case, for behind the scenes there were significant problems at the Kingston club. The first day no-show at North London proved not to be an isolated occurrence. Despite intervention from both Bev Risman and Gerrard Grundy, the assistance of London development officer, Dave Evans, and the recruitment - after a little persuasion - of two new administrators in Dan Wilkinson and Mark Henderson, the experiment of open-age football in the Southern Conference League for the Surrey outfit was too much too soon. On 7 June, despite being short of the requisite 17 players, Kingston took to the field at Oxford's Marston Ferry Road ground and played admirably, losing 40-30. It was to be their first and last performance in the 1997 competition, though the name of Kingston was not to be lost forever to the RLC.

'Predictably unpredictable' seemed to be a phrase well-suited to both Worcester Royals and Birmingham after the sides met in their first derby on the same day that Oxford entertained Kingston. Both sides had started the season with a victory and a defeat. Birmingham had a positive result the preceding weekend and combined with their greater experience and home advantage, the odds were definitely on them putting the Leicester loss behind them and inflicting a second successive defeat on their neighbours. An early Dave Wilson try and two Tony Williams penalties further seemed to justify that scenario. Worcester fought back and by half-time were ahead 10-8. Tries from Adeshino Obileye and Chris Nelson had put the visitors in the ascendancy and following the half-time interval, the crucial score came from Worcester with a try from Tony Wright. However, with Birmingham ferociously attacking the Worcester line, a kick to the corner hoped to catch the visiting defence unawares. Instead, Obileye caught the ball and went the full length of the field to register his second try and put Worcester into an unassailable position. A further score from Jon O'Connell inspired a fighting comeback from Birmingham, but tries from Brabin and a second from Wilson were only consolations as Worcester won 30-16. The Royals were back.

'Predictably victorious' could best describe North London and Leicester Phoenix. Both had a 100 per cent win record from the early fixtures, the latter putting 58 points past luckless Bedford with the former beating that score by four as they inflicted a 62-34 home defeat on Cambridge Eagles in week three of the competition. They had both become the sides to beat. North London owed much to their strong links with the student game, their ranks including former, present and future SRL international players such as Charlie Oyebade, Hakeem Ashorbi, Mike Scott, James How and Hector McNeil. The club could also call upon the services of antipodean players and were particularly blessed in the stand-off position with New Zealander Anton Verryt providing the craft alongside the guile and strength of McNeil.

Leicester too had a preponderance of players with experience of student rugby league, and had managed to recruit a significant number from Nottingham after the opening round of fixtures. These players were to have a significant impact on Leicester's season, but a greater, and more enduring, impact on the RLC when they formalised their social club of Nottingham Trent

University graduates into the Nottingham Outlaws club, making their debut in 1999.

An increasing interest from the media, both local and national, helped by coverage in the rugby league press, also characterised the first month of the competition, providing a baseline of press coverage that would significantly increase throughout the next seven years. It was now common for local newspapers to feature games, and for clubs to attract local radio and television coverage. Both *League Express* and the *Rugby Leaguer* brought the scores, match reports and club development progress to a national audience of rugby league enthusiasts. Every Saturday afternoon, Julian Harrison rang the scores through to the Press Association so that they could be in the national newspapers and on BBC Ceefax. It was unprecedented interest in a league that had witnessed less than 20 games.

Progress was also being made on the twinning front. Leicester, with an existing relationship with Sheffield Eagles to build upon, had continuing talks with their Super League counterparts who were keen to offer coaching sessions as well as inviting the club to their World Club Challenge fixtures. Oxford Cavaliers had an immediate benefit from their new link with Hull Sharks, with the provision of a full playing kit. This did cause some confusion to new spectators at Oxford games who were greeted with the site of an Oxford side resplendent in a white-and-black kit with Hull emblazoned on the back. Before the season was out, Worcester and Birmingham would also receive new playing kits, courtesy of St Helens and Bradford Bulls respectively, and the Worcester-St Helens relationship went even further. The Super League Saints hosted the SCL Royals at their August bank holiday fixture against Leeds, with the players spending the morning training under the supervision of Saints' academy coach, Nick Halafihi and then being introduced to the crowd prior to kick-off in the main fixture. Saints, as Challenge Cup holders, then paraded the trophy, courtesy of chief executive David Howes, at Worcester's Annual Dinner in November, probably the first time the Cup had made an appearance in the county.

It was, therefore, a content SCL executive committee that met on 6 June to review the competition's early stages. The meeting agenda pinpointed the prevailing concentration on both off-field and on-field matters and reflected the content of executive meetings under both the SCL and RLC banner in the years to come. The early season problems concerning refereeing appointments and Kingston as a club were both top of the agenda. Nothing much more could be done about the latter, but the former was now much more under control with the intervention of referees controller at the RFL, Greg McCallum, a greater list of available match officials and a realisation of the need to set up courses to ensure a steady supply in the future.

This also applied to qualified coaches and the suggestion was made to consider somebody from within the club set-ups to become a coaching co-ordinator or even an unpaid director of coaching. The embryonic SCL constitution was discussed, and this area benefited considerably from the involvement of John Nugent who also raised the idea of the SCL becoming a limited company. Despite the enormous progress made on creating a profile for the competition and thereby raising the profile of its constituent clubs, there was a sense that opportunities were still being missed, and various remedies were suggested. The involvement of RFL media guru Dave Callaghan, who would become a director of the RLC in subsequent years, was considered essential, as was feeding on the enthusiasm of Andy Stevens and taking advantage of sympathetic and powerful ears at both the All-Party Parliamentary Rugby League Group, through David Hinchliffe MP, and the league's obvious expansionist Super League ally, the London Broncos. The notion of devoting a page in each Super League programme to the competition was fine in theory, but in practice depended on the individual club's inclination, available space and whether there was any degree of enforcement by the RFL. As a result, coverage from this source was variable, as were the benefits from the other suggestions made, despite being enthusiastically undertaken and through no fault of the individuals concerned.

Of course, the nitty-gritty of every sporting competition - registration, insurance, health and safety, finance, equipment, disciplinary measures and procedures - had to be covered, but those present at the meeting also spent some time focusing on the future, both the immediate, the Championship Final, and the more long-term - prospective clubs. The dilemma of whether to hold a final as a curtain-raiser to a bigger game, thus ensuring a larger crowd and media attention, or as a stand-alone event, thereby guaranteeing sole focus, is one familiar to many people at the grassroots level of rugby league. There are persuasive arguments for both. The topic was discussed for the first time at SCL level at the 6 June meeting. Lionel Hurst was at the time a very keen proponent of the curtain-raiser scenario and had a London Broncos Super League fixture in mind. However, despite the validity of this argument, the decision was made to pursue the possibility of an event in its own right without any other distraction. Both Worcester and Bedford were possible venues, not only because of their general quality, but also because they were enclosed and could charge an entrance fee.

As far as extending the competition in 1998 was concerned, the names of South Norfolk Saints and their contact, John Evans, were mentioned. Evans had written to Julian Harrison and had outlined how far he had got with his potential club. The reality at the time was that there were players awaiting a go-ahead, but only Evans involved in any administrative, coaching or off-field capacity. There was initial scepticism and early feedback to John Evans was not positive. Such pessimism was unfounded, because the club from Thetford in rural East Anglia not only got off the ground but had a storming baptism in the RLC.

Evans had already contacted his home-town club, St Helens, for assistance. This related directly to the issue of twinning. It was considered generally that if such relationships were to have any degree of success, then some central control needed to be exerted. That task was given to Neil Tunnicliffe under the umbrella of both the SCL and the professional governing body. With the benefit of hindsight, it proved to be difficult to regulate club activities in this respect and the practice of clubs making tentative approaches of their own, while not always actively encouraged, was given an informal go-ahead. Clearly, if there were opportunities that came along for individual SCL and RLC clubs to establish any sort of relationship with a Super League equivalent, it would be folly to resist and a laissez-faire practice was established. It would be some years before another attempt was made to regulate such links, though this time on a regional basis, and again a similar outcome ensued.

With the talking over for the time being it was back to the action in the Southern Conference League. By the end of July, the competition had intensified in each division and there were now at least two other sides challenging the previous supremacy of North London and Leicester. This was particularly the case in the Central Division, where Birmingham were on a roll. Their early defeats by Leicester and Worcester had been put behind them, and the club now embarked on an undefeated run that saw them not only avenge those defeats, but also challenge the side from Saffron Lane for the divisional title. They were scoring points for fun – 50 points at Bedford on 21 June and 56 against Oxford the following week.

There was much talk before the competition had kicked off about the real significance and importance lying simply in the staging of these games. However, being rugby league, there was no less desire to win and compete in the SCL than there would be in any other area of the game. A good indication of this was experienced by Julian Harrison's partner, Lesley, following that Bedford versus Birmingham game. The couple had just witnessed another Leicester victory at Oxford and on leaving the ground, Harrison's mobile was busy receiving results and reports from the other games. As he was driving, Lesley took the calls, including one from Darryl Cook at Bedford reporting on a 50-20 defeat. Not knowing the personnel involved, Lesley confused the sides and expressed amusement at the size of the defeat, thinking that she was speaking to someone from Birmingham. She was put right by Cook in no uncertain terms. "Lesley now knew how much the competition meant to everyone," reflected Harrison.

On 5 July, Birmingham met Leicester at their Moor Lane ground. Unfortunately, another match official appointment disaster threatened to spoil the most crucial match of the season to date. With the appointed referee unable to officiate, frantic phone calls by Gerrard Grundy resulted in only one candidate stepping forward. While he was a qualified match official, he was also a Birmingham player! Steve Harrison-Mirfield, who had propped for Birmingham in the corresponding earlier fixture, was now earmarked for another role. In order to get the game on, both sides – with no alternative – agreed to him taking up the whistle. In an afternoon of great drama and feeling, Birmingham came out on top 39-28. The competitiveness of that encounter was matched by the emphatic nature of the next episode in the Birmingham campaign of retribution, for they destroyed Worcester Royals 66-4 to avenge their earlier defeat. The battle for top spot in the Central Division stretched to the final weekend of the regular fixtures.

In the Eastern Division, the challenge to North London's dominance came from West London. Despite suffering a 54-24 defeat when the two sides clashed on 28 June, the West Londoners slowly, but surely, kept the pressure on the Skolars by some convincing displays against Bedford and Ipswich respectively. North London, though, looked comfortable. In June they found out that their bid to gain entrance to BARLA's flagship competition, the

National Conference League – denied the previous year – had been accepted, thus ensuring that the club would operate both winter and summer seasons. The club were also grateful recipients of a grant from the National Lottery and had ambitions to launch their own internal club lottery and to begin development initiatives in local schools. Their more humble current circumstances, however, were still in evidence as prior to home matches against both Ipswich and Worcester, the club had to resort to marking out their pitch in flour, leading to the headline "Homepride of London" in *League Express's* report of the Worcester game on 21 June.

Notwithstanding these temporary problems, the North London side laid down the gauntlet on the pitch. Against a depleted but gritty Worcester side, who included manager Dean Cave as their only substitute, they turned on the style in the last quarter, with winger Alvin da Silva scoring a hat-trick of tries in five minutes near the end, in only his third game of rugby league.

The Royals, though disadvantaged on that particular day, were making significant strides off the pitch. Their chairman, Alan Curless, was particularly astute in using contacts made through his other chairmanship - of the local Chamber of Commerce - to initiate the business development of the club. They weren't doing too badly on it either. When they clashed again with North London one month later, the tables were turned. This time, it was the Londoners who fielded a side with fewer than the normal XIII and four substitutes, and the home side won 36-10 for the Skolars' first SCL defeat.

It was clear that the SCL had sparked a wave of enthusiasm and interest in rugby league in areas covered by the competition. It also focused the minds of people within the sport in northern England. Great Britain and Bradford Bulls hooker, James Lowes wrote a regular column in the *Rugby Leaguer*. He gave the embryonic league a welcome boost by recognising developments twice in successive weeks.

As an interesting aside, June 1997 was also the month when the equivalent league in Scotland began. Though there was little direct relationship between the two events, the exception being RFL involvement, that another initiative following similar lines was now up and running north of the border added extra weight to the convictions of the SCL pioneers. There might have been minimal interaction between England and Scotland but, as we have seen, that wasn't the case with regard to the practical relationship between the SCL and the Student Rugby League. On 22 June, various key individuals met at the offices of the SRL Alumni in London. Among these were Julian Harrison, Gerrard Grundy, Hector McNeil and Gary Tetlow, who – along with Australian Ken Edwards – had recently established a club in St Albans. Although the focus of the meeting was on the development of the Alumni itself, expanding and strengthening the graduate arm of the SRL, among other topics discussed was linking with the SCL, including taking advantage not only of player involvement, as this was already happening, but also through marketing ideas such as club lotteries.

There was much to feel positive about. In deepest East Anglia, Ipswich Rhinos had pulled off a massive coup by attracting ex-Great Britain, Hull and Featherstone player Steve Evans to the club as head coach. They were further boosted by the involvement of BARLA's director of coaching, Brian Chambers, who ran a coaching seminar in two schools, one a special school, in the Ipswich area, attended by local government representatives keen to see rugby league coaching and curriculum possibilities at first hand.

In Leicester, always a rugby hotbed, though, of course of the other code, the advent of the SCL and the success of the home side in particular, gave rise to comparisons between league and union. Coverage in the local newspaper, the *Leicester Mercury*, had been phenomenal, with match previews, reports and colour photographs. This upsurge in media interest had not escaped the attention of columnist Gaynor Nash. She wrote a weekly piece on women's sport in the paper, and, while pleased at the success experienced by the Phoenix rugby league side, bemoaned the fact that this was happening while more popular women's sports, in terms of playing numbers, were receiving negligible coverage. She got a response from Leicester Phoenix and was invited by PR officer, Susan Dalgliesh, to attend the home fixture with Oxford Cavaliers.

It just so happened that Nash's visit also coincided with another rugby event later that same afternoon at Leicester Tigers' Welford Road ground. The occasion was Rory Underwood's farewell match and presentation, and the reporter was taking in the league game before moving to the other code. Nash, despite her relative unfamiliarity with the sport, drew comparisons very favourable to the rugby league encounter. The headline captured this superbly: "Pace and power – and then there was Rory's farewell affair at Welford Road!"

The season was reaching its climax. Despite the efforts of their close rivals, West London, North London had already booked their place in the semi-finals prior to the last fixtures of the regular season as champions of the Eastern Division. Compensation for West London came with a semi-final place, but, as runners-up, they would have to travel for their play-off game.

It was definitely not as clear-cut in the Central Division. Both Leicester and Birmingham had qualified for the semis, but in what position was still questionable as they faced their respective opponents on the weekend of 2 and 3 August. Birmingham brushed past Oxford Cavaliers in their final game to leave them ahead of their East Midlands rivals who still had a game to play. However, Leicester had a difficult task ahead of them, for they had to travel to Ipswich, where few sides come away with the points. That game was one of the best of the season. On a memorable day, the two clubs first fielded junior sides that provided an inspirational appetiser to the main feast. Jim Gilmartin, a leading figure within the student game, journeyed down from West Yorkshire to East Anglia to referee a game that would live long in the memory of those who both witnessed and played in it.

Ipswich Rhinos raced into a 16-4 lead. Leicester came back to tie the game at the interval and the second half proved to be agonising for those willing the Leicester team on from the sidelines. No sooner would Phoenix go ahead and seem destined to win, then the Rhinos would storm back to leave the outcome in doubt again. In the end, Phil Inman, the Leicester winger who worked for the local newspaper, managed to create the headlines. He scored a hat-trick of tries, including one of the most bizarre and luckiest scores of the season. From a Leicester kick-off, scrum-half Ben Pearson sliced his kick. The ball, unintentionally, found its way into Inman's hands as the Ipswich defence hesitated, and the winger proceeded to finish with a flourish, rounding the Ipswich cover and scoring behind the posts. The Leicester victory, 42-34, ensured that they would be at home to West London in the semi-finals the following week. Birmingham would travel to face the side many perceived as the favourites: North London.

The final divisional tables were as follows:

SCL 1997 Central Division League Table

		Pl	W	D	L	Pts
1	Leicester Phoenix	10	9	0	1	18
2	Birmingham	10	8	0	2	16
3	Worcester Royals	10	5	0	5	10
4	Oxford Cavaliers	10	5	0	5	10
5	Bedford Swifts	10	0	0	10	0

SCL 1997 Eastern Division League Table

		Pl	W	D	L	Pts
1	North London Skolars	10	9	0	1	18
2	West London	10	7	0	3	14
3	Ipswich Rhinos	10	4	0	6	8
4	Cambridge Eagles	10	3	0	7	6
5	Kingston*	10	0	0	10	0

* Played only one fixture

If ever there was a day of contrasts, the semi-final day in the inaugural year of the Southern Conference League was one of them. The four best sides lined up in a monumental clash of regions – London versus the Midlands – with many people awaiting the outcomes and with destiny and history awaiting the winners. Semi-finals often do not produce classics, but instead occasions fraught with nerves, of which the compelling attraction is not necessarily the quality on show, but the drama.

That North London and Birmingham managed to produce a contest fit to grace any sporting arena was testimony to their great strength and abundance of talent. The only pity was that there had to be a loser and the 'privilege' of playing an equal part in such a stupendous match but losing went to Birmingham.

It nearly wasn't the case, as the men from Moor Lane roared back at the Skolars after the Londoners had taken an 18 point advantage. The final whistle went with North London ahead by only two points, 18-16, and with elation mixed with relief.

However, disappointment came to all at Saffron Lane, Leicester – including the home side who would go through to the Final. On the morning of the match, SCL secretary, and Leicester chairman, Julian Harrison received a phone call from West London to say that the club would not be travelling up the M1 because they hadn't sufficient available players. Officially injuries and illness were given as the reasons. Much would be said about games called off due to player shortage in the seasons to come, but Harrison realised on that particular occasion that every effort had been made by the West London club to fulfil the fixture. Harrison felt a sense of compelled resignation and circumstances dictated that a result was needed. There was no opportunity to re-schedule with the final taking place the following weekend, and amidst the tremendous disappointment was felt a high degree of trepidation at the possible consequences, bearing in mind the pilot season nature of the SCL in 1997 and the need for a positive image. The fact that his own side had reached the final was, of course, pleasing for Harrison, but it was an afternoon of mixed emotions for him and many others.

Nevertheless, it was fitting that the two most consistent sides and divisional winners contested the final which took place on Sunday 17 August at Staines Rugby Club in south west London. Staines RFC provided a training base for the London Broncos and Harlequins rugby union club as well as a future venue for the West London RLC side. In addition to the quality of the match facilities, the club house had been completely rebuilt in 1989.

There was to be drama and tragedy prior to the big day. The match official appointments had been secured, with Matt Walker and Phil Knaggs acting as touch judges and Julia Lee from Leeds as the referee. Tragically, Lee's mother passed away in the week preceding the final. Understandably, she did not feel in a position to commit to refereeing and a hasty replacement was needed. Gerrard Grundy, charged with the responsibility of finding a substitute referee was unable to do so in the time he had. He promoted Phil Knaggs to referee, conveying this news to Knaggs as he drove into the ground while Grundy himself took over the touch judge role.

Both clubs named a 20-man squad for the final:
Leicester Phoenix: Mike French, Ian Rafferty, Matt Isherwood, Ben Harbottle, Phil Inman, Paul Walmsley, Ben Pearson, Gus Dinn, Craig Carter, Duncan Carter, Julian French, Pete Whitehead, Mick Bryant, 'Tubbs' Reffell, Dave Walker, Russ Mooney, Hitesh Patel, Andy Clancy, Shaun Murray, Gavin Baker.
North London: Mike Adeyami, Charlie Oyebade, Hakeem Ashorbi, Bobby Brown, Alvin da Silva, Anton Verryt, Hector McNeil, Ian Lovitt, Graham Oliphant, Martin Smith, Lee Jones, Mike Scott, Jason Samuel, Marc Simon, Tim Williams, Paul West, James How, Oliver Hockey, 'Nam the Man', Martin Snell.

The teams lined up, observed a minute's silence in memory of Julia Lee's mother and then the very first summer Conference Final was underway. North London's early dominance brought back memories of their semi-final against Birmingham and a 16-4 lead seemed to be conclusive, at least in terms of who the winners would be. A repetition of the Londoners letting their opposition back into the game two weeks running was expected to be fanciful thinking.

Leicester, however, seemed to be inspired by the legacy of Birmingham's determination, and did indeed come back with two tries from captain and coach, Paul Walmsley, though he rather spoilt his own performance by being sent off towards the end of the game. But it wasn't enough, and the greater class of opposition destined for National Conference League rugby that winter told in the end.

North London won 32-16 to become the first summer Conference champions and the only ever winners of the Southern Conference League.

Eagle-eyed spectators witnessing Hector McNeil holding aloft the cup would have spotted a more familiar trophy, for McNeil was actually presented with the European Nations' Cup recently been won by Wales by SCL chairman Lionel Hurst and RFL development executive Tom O'Donovan. Such was the pilot nature of

that season that the RFL hadn't yet invested in a permanent trophy.

So the 1997 Southern Conference League finished. Despite some teething problems and events beyond its control, the general consensus, and significantly also the viewpoint of at least one RFL director, was that it had been a resounding success. Julian Harrison realised that the battle he had witnessed at Staines on 17 August, could indeed be replicated in the office and in correspondence should the game's governing authority at Red Hall in Leeds be anything other than like-minded.

If the SCL was not to be a 'one-season wonder', those competing in the league were going to have to have longer-term visions and in the case of some set-ups, develop from a 'team' into a 'club'. A period of self-reflection for clubs was important. Where are we at present? What do we have in place? Where do we want to be? How do we get there? For more concrete answers to these – and other – questions, there needed to be a development plan at league structure level as well and a guarantee of at least a second season. A chicken and egg situation was in evidence – new and existing clubs would develop if the league continued - though with the power to influence and affect action vested in one body and one place – the Rugby Football League in Leeds.

The demand was there. The season had proved that, and other clubs were showing an interest in joining the fray. In addition to South Norfolk Saints, Gary Tetlow's St Albans Centurions and new clubs in Chester and Cheltenham, the latter under the auspices of Ruth Sigley and Stephen Rigby, wanted to participate in 1998. Harrison had also had a season-long correspondence with Mark Richardson in Sussex, who, after meeting by chance former Widnes player Steve O'Reilly and then Rod Chinn of the local rugby union club, had established rugby league in Crawley. Their intentions were very evident, especially as, witnessed by Bev Risman, they had overcome a London Broncos team containing some Super League stars in a friendly fixture.

Would there be another season and a follow-up competition? If so, which clubs would play? Was there to be some form of security and financial assistance? Was the present administrative and managerial organisation sufficient? These questions, and others, would soon be addressed and answered. As Julian Harrison and Bev Risman reflected on the extent of what had happened since they had first met nine months before, both expected to have continued their involvement, should there be affirmative responses from the RFL. Neither would have envisaged that in a short period of time their roles would be changed dramatically.

Cheltenham Warriors' Ronnie Haines presenting Andy Farrell with a commemorative sword
prior to the game with Oxford Cavaliers on 25 July 1998. (Photo: Nigel Wachs)

Dom Swan with the ball for Bristol Sonics against Oxford Cavaliers in 2003
(Photo: Rob Walsh)

St Albans Centurions versus South London Storm. National League 3 in 2003

5. 1998: Awakening

Fortunately, the impact of a successful pilot season had not been lost on funders, supporters, organisers and clubs. The Rugby Football League was keen to build on the initial wave of enthusiasm generated by the competition. Clubs too were voicing their desire to continue, pointing not only to increased numbers of players and media interest, but also to the fact that a structured league provided the foundation and security to enable that increase in activity to prosper. Birmingham club secretary Jamie Walsh epitomised the feelings when asked if his club would like to be considered for the 1998 season. His response was unequivocal, that the Birmingham players had asked for "more of the same" following their close 1997 semi-final defeat by the North London Skolars.

In the months following the Staines Grand Final, the indications were that the pilot season would be succeeded by a season proper, but there were also no hints of any fundamental changes to the way the competition was to be run. Julian Harrison and Lionel Hurst met up in Stratford-upon-Avon to reflect upon what had been achieved so far and to speculate on and consider options for the way forward.

Shortly afterwards, the SCL executive committee met up at Richmond in Surrey. The meeting focused on a range of important issues, some of a legal nature, and also agreed a name change for the competition. While the 'Southern' prefix covered most clubs in 1997, Leicester and Birmingham were not in that category, and with encouraging noises being made from Chester, a name change seemed appropriate.

Additionally, it was felt that geography had played a part in the marginalisation of rugby league through 'northern only' connotations, and the new league shouldn't fall into the same trap. The decision was made to keep the 'Conference' moniker, but to have a broader name, and what could be better than simply referring to the name of the sport itself? Hence, the Southern Conference League (SCL) became – in one meeting – the Rugby League Conference (RLC).

This was not the only change. Gerrard Grundy and Julian Harrison had been the initial administrative team. However, in the final months of 1997, both men's futures turned away from the competition. Grundy resigned from his position as development manager of the Student Rugby League (SRL) Alumni, and, knowing of Harrison's desire to work full-time in the sport, Alumni director Bev Risman offered him the opportunity of being Grundy's replacement. In discussing where this left Harrison, still the SCL secretary, both men believed there would be no conflict of interest or insurmountable problems in timetabling work commitments. The opportunity to formalise a link between two successful development initiatives seemed appropriate. This view was also shared by another SRL Alumni director Hector McNeil, who supported a proposal whereby remuneration would be paid to the SRL Alumni for the time Harrison spent on RLC duties. At an end of season executive and clubs meeting held at Leicester Phoenix's ground at Saffron Lane Stadium, Risman put this proposal to the rest of the RLC committee.

Although there would be no decision made then, it wouldn't be long in coming, and it proved to be disappointing for those in the SRL Alumni camp. For Harrison, it was devastating. By the proposal being turned down, he had to withdraw as secretary and thus indirectly from the RLC executive as well. This was not something he wished to do, but his hands were tied. He recalls: "Having been there from the very beginning, seen a dream realised and played a central part, to suddenly have to leave was a major disappointment. What made it worse was that I had no choice in the matter. I was also surprised and disappointed that an opportunity to formalise further links between the Conference and the student game had not been seen in the same way Bev, Hector and I saw it. I had my job in the game, but I still wanted a key involvement in the RLC, and I couldn't have both."

Bev Risman also resigned from the RLC executive committee, but both men continued their involvement at club level: Harrison with Leicester, and Risman at the newly revamped West London Sharks.

New blood was therefore needed at executive and administrative level. A replacement for Harrison was found in Trevor Moss, a CID officer at Cheltenham police station. Originally from Hampshire, Moss was a convert to the sport, a St Helens supporter and dedicated enthusiast well known to the Cheltenham Warriors. By the time the first RLC season proper commenced, two new faces were added to the management team. Phil Caplan, a noted rugby league writer and bookshop owner, had been invited to join a BARLA development sub-committee. One of the projects which that body focused on was the 1997 Southern Conference League, and Stuart Sheard began to assemble a team of specialists who were also committed expansionists aiming to develop the new RLC competition. Caplan's expertise in media and publicity made him an obvious candidate, and he became the RLC's first – and so far, only – media manager.

In April, a paper on a proposed youth league was presented to a meeting of RLC clubs in Bedford. The authors were Dave and Janet Berry. Originally from Hull, they had moved to Telford (where Dave was the deputy head of Thomas Telford School) and established a junior league affiliated to BARLA. In joining the RLC executive, their role was to administer a proposed RLC under-13 Youth League to operate on a festival basis.

Of course, clubs were also active leading up to May 1998. All the pioneering SCL outfits, with the exception of Kingston Warriors, were keen to continue, and a total of 24 interested clubs showed how the pilot season had captured the imagination. Those who had experienced SCL 1997 now knew what they had to do to maintain their impetus and some showed tremendous imagination in preparation for the second season of summer rugby league.

Ipswich Rhinos arranged a trip to Scotland in early February 1998 to take part in an International Festival of Rugby League and help rugby league development north of the border. Tragedy struck on the eve of their departure when their young captain, Iain King, was killed in a car accident near his home in Newmarket. King had been an inspiration to his club colleagues and a dedicated enthusiast, travelling considerable distances to attend training. He had also instilled an enthusiasm for rugby league in some of his playing compatriots at Newmarket Rugby Union club. His family set up a memorial fund to help young sports enthusiasts and in recognition of his achievements, the Rhinos established an annual memorial match between King's two clubs (league and union), as well as ensuring that the name of Iain King adorned the club's annual trophies for Player and Young Player of the Year. The club party still travelled north determined to fulfil their obligations in memory of their young captain, taking on a Scottish development side that included Graeme Thompson who went on to have RLC involvement with both Crawley Jets and Leeds Akademiks.

Internationalism was rife and a more exotic touch was added when the touring Russian champions, Strela Kazan, arrived in England in April to play three RLC clubs: Ipswich Rhinos, North London Skolars and Leicester Phoenix. The Russians, including leading players such as Robert Illyasov, won all three games, but the encounters were competitive nonetheless. The twinning arrangements that were so enthusiastically conceived in 1997 showed some signs of development. Bedford Swifts hosted Halifax Blue Sox for training and a friendly fixture in February and, following their admission into the RLC, Cheltenham Warriors successfully cultivated a relationship with their fellow Warriors from Wigan. Indeed, mention of the twinning resulted in a whole back-page spread in the *Cheltenham Echo*. The Cheltenham club were coached by Andy Haughton, the father of Wigan's international forward Simon, and included young James Haughton, Simon's brother, in their junior development programme. The family connection clearly helped. In the summer Simon, with fellow Wigan players Tony Mestrov and Gary Connolly, ran schools coaching classes in the spa town.

Of all the prospective new clubs for 1998, nowhere was there more ambition than at Northampton. Steve Newcombe, a long-standing proponent of the sport in the town, and also the leading Northampton figure in the East Midlands Knights adventure prior to the advent of the SCL, received the backing of his local MP, the town council and the local newspaper in a bid to bring rugby league back to Northampton. The aim was eventually Super League, though to begin with a place in the RLC was the objective. Impressive plans accompanied by an equally impressive initial budget certainly indicated optimism and ambition, but was there substance as well? Time would unfortunately reveal otherwise.

The RFL announced that both teams contesting the Grand Final at the end of the season would be invited to participate in the first round of the following season's Challenge Cup. In tandem with BARLA, the rugby league authorities held a forum on the new Rugby League Joint Policy Board at Bedford on 28 March as part of a national showcase of this significant move towards greater harmony in the sport.

The issue of the relationship between the new amateur flagship competition and what survived of other amateur leagues and clubs in development areas has been a perennial one throughout the duration of the RLC. Concern over whether the success of the summer conference would detract from the quality and quantity of teams in the London ARL seemed initially to be minimised as the latter ran a winter season with 11 clubs. This was a far cry from the heady days of some years previously, but it was a viable competition nevertheless. New teams that year included both Crawley

Jets as associate members and also the South London Saints, who would become more widely known in the future as South London Storm. The Saints featured in the LARL's Gordon Anderton Trophy Final on 26 April against Reading Raiders. On the same day, the Southern Counties Cup Final pitted together a Fulham Travellers side including Kieran Fitzgerald, who became a leading figure at Crawley Jets, and the London Skolars. Meanwhile in Hertfordshire, Hemel Hempstead RLFC continued on their mission to make their town a rugby league centre. An extensive development programme led by the club's development officer, Haydn Walker, ran in tandem with open-age preparations for the RFL Alliance season and an open expression of interest in playing in the proposed new RFL Division Two.

Rather than forging ahead at the expense of other development activities, the RLC happily co-existed with what else was going on. It was also increasingly obvious that the high profile of the new competition, as well as the lure of a structured league with an emphasis on good quality standards on and off the pitch, provided a magnet for others to join. An illustration of this status came on 21 April 1998 when the RLC launched the season in the prestigious setting of the Palace of Westminster.

Organised by David Hinchliffe MP and hosted by Sir Geoffrey Lofthouse, both of the All-Party Parliamentary Rugby League Group, club representatives, RLC executive committee members, other rugby league officials, journalists and some MPs from club areas, met to hear details of the forthcoming season. The RLC was to expand to 15 clubs, taking in Cheltenham Warriors, Chester Wolves, Crawley Jets, Northampton, South Norfolk Saints and St Albans Centurions. To accommodate this increase in numbers, an extra division was added, taking the number to three: East, North and South, with the winners plus the best second-placed club going through to the semi-finals prior to a Grand Final on 8 August.

Of the inaugural 10 who had started 12 months previously, Kingston had already left, and two others had made significant changes. West London Sharks came into being, replacing the old West London side that had started so promisingly and then failed to deliver at the 1997 semi-final. The new club had the support of the London Broncos. Also as a result of Super League influence, Worcester changed its name from 'Royals' to 'Saints' to reflect its burgeoning relationship with St Helens.

A memorable day culminated in an invitation to RLC representatives to make a presentation to the All-Party Parliamentary Group. Arguably, the biggest impression was made by chairman Lionel Hurst. In a speech that has come to achieve almost legendary status, Hurst referred to rugby league as a "Swiss finishing school" for rugby union players and he outlined the vision of a geographically all-encompassing game. In response to the idea of RLC clubs moving out of the competition into the professional arm of the game, Hurst said: "I can see that happening and if it does we will replace them with other new clubs coming through. It will be a conveyor belt which will go on and on until every sizeable town in the country has a rugby league team."

Open Rugby magazine accompanied Hurst's evangelical rallying call by succinctly summarising the RLC message: "...success is measured not in victories and trophies but in fulfilling all fixtures with a team well turned out and conducting themselves to a standard suitable for all to witness... The executive are keen to expand the RLC in both areas (traditional clubs and clubs based at RU clubs) and numbers but are still insistent that no matter how competitive on the pitch, a club must meet the criteria demanded off the pitch before they will be considered."

This message seemed to encapsulate the Northampton initiative on paper, but the reality was different. The club was not at the Westminster launch, and a scrutinising process revealed a less-than-rosy picture. After to-and-fro correspondence between club and RLC administrator Trevor Moss, the club took the decision to withdraw from the competition.

A re-vamping of the fixtures in the East Division was a necessary consequence, and it appeared then that the future of the game in Northampton had suffered another setback from which it might be hard to recover. Sadly, Northampton still lacks a rugby league club.

Nevertheless, there was excited anticipation as the clubs came to the starting line on 9 May to begin the first season of the Rugby League Conference. Eyes were primarily focused on the new boys and the first few weeks of the season were encouraging. St Albans Centurions set the pace with an opening day win in Oxford. In a classic encounter, the Hertfordshire outfit won 15-12, and followed that up with an equally impressive home victory against a side also fancied to do well: West London Sharks.

In East Anglia, the South Norfolk Saints answered those who had been sceptical about their feasibility. A narrow win over Bedford Swifts was followed by the team taking Cambridge Eagles apart, winning by a 60-point margin, scoring 82 points. The only side finding life in the RLC a bit of a struggle was Cheltenham Warriors. Though short of points, the team was competitive, gave seasoned campaigners Leicester and Birmingham a run for their money, and did not disgrace themselves against Chester Wolves in the second week of the season. Stewart Davies, scorer of the club's first ever try against Leicester, remembers the Chester fixture: "The game that stands out most for me has to be that first game against Chester. Only two of the Warriors side had played league before, but the final score was just 28-2. They hit very hard in the tackle but we showed them that we could hit just as hard and match it with the best of them. It was a good game to play in, but a real eye-opener."

Of all the new sides taking part, Chester Wolves were the major talking point in the first half of the season. On 9 May, they beat the previous year's finalists Leicester Phoenix 30-28 in a thrilling encounter that could have finished as a draw if Duncan Green's last minute attempted goal had drifted the other side of the post.

The Wolves were strong and difficult to beat. However, it wasn't this that drew attention to the club; it was who was turning out for them. Chester used to their advantage their close proximity to Warrington Wolves, and arranged for players with professional experience to bolster their ranks. Players of the calibre of Jason Roach, Gary Tees, John Thursfield and Paul Darbyshire all played for Chester, and not surprisingly some opponents felt this was an unfair advantage.

Chester were not, it must be said, infringing any competition rules. They were just using them to maximum effect and enticing the best available players in their catchment area, in much the same way as West London Sharks reaped the dividends of links with the London Broncos. For the first time, the RLC executive had an issue of potentially damaging proportions to deal with, but it was not an easy one to rectify given the fact that Chester – and West London for that matter – had operated perfectly legally within the rules. This also drew attention to the potential problems of accommodating clubs close to the game's heartland and professional areas, or clubs with ties to stronger outfits in the south. The executive decided that action must be taken and restrictions were imposed to prevent wholesale contributions from players with professional experience. While this pacified to an extent those who had been on the wrong end of the alleged 'unfairness', it would be apparent to all with the interests of the competition at heart that, in allowing clubs to compete from areas in which there was an abundance of players with greater experience - either at professional or leading amateur level - there would be perennial issues over equity.

There was development-a-plenty at Oxford Cavaliers. The departure of hard-working club official Mike Cunningham had preceded a new revamped administrative and coaching team under RLC chairman Lionel Hurst, who took over the club equivalent position. On the playing front, the addition of Oxford University player – and former Leeds University captain – Jeremy Shires, took the playing numbers up to the half-century mark, and the coaching staff was equally impressive. A coaching director, the vastly experienced Paul Johnstone, was complemented by a head coach in ex-Metropolitan Police coach Dave Doran, ably assisted by Alan Myler. South African Daryn Reeds, a former Worcestershire County Cricket Club player, was appointed as the club's first development officer with a remit to target four high schools to establish a schools league and Cavaliers under-13 and under-16 squads. Reeds and Hurst also set about forming close links with a network of twinned clubs, Villeneuve from France, Australian Super League's Adelaide Rams and – closer to home – the existing 'twin', Hull Sharks.

The inclusion of Jeremy Shires from the student ranks was a significant indication of the growing relationship between 'town' and 'gown' in Oxford. This was also shown by a coaching session held by Hull Sharks' Peter Walsh at the university club prior to the annual Varsity Match. Hurst's inspirational leadership and his talent at recruiting quality personnel to push the club forward would culminate in an explosion of interest and initiatives in Oxford, including the eventual appointment of a full-time RFL development officer.

Other clubs were also receiving a share of the limelight. As an integral part of the Super League season, on-the-road fixtures were played in a variety of venues across England, Scotland and Wales. While Northampton hadn't manifested as a team, it was a venue for one of these missionary games, and an opportunity arose to showcase the RLC as a curtain-raiser. On a sultry Friday July evening, Northampton Town FC's Sixfields Stadium hosted Halifax versus Sheffield Eagles, preceded by the RLC derby between Cambridge Eagles and Bedford Swifts. Halifax won 32-10, with Cambridge going two points better with a 34-10 victory. One week later, Cheltenham were similar

46

beneficiaries of Super League on-the-road. Wigan, on their way to Swansea to play St Helens, called in to see the home side narrowly defeated by Oxford Cavaliers. It was an uplifting performance from the Warriors (who had just registered their first victories in the competition), the side perhaps inspired by the presence of Andy Farrell et al.

Indeed, perhaps the experience of receiving a commemorative sword from his Cheltenham counterpart Ronnie Haines, provided a boost to Wigan captain Farrell and his troops who went on to defeat their arch rivals 36-2.

As the season progressed, it was clear that there were going to be new finalists in 1998. North London Skolars had focused their energies on the BARLA National Conference League and therefore the RLC provided a means of bringing through prospective players and giving them match experience. Leicester Phoenix kept their hopes alive for much longer as the semi-finals neared, but D-Day for them came on 25 July when they faced West London Sharks in a 'win-or-bust' fixture at Saffron Lane.

Despite a valiant attempt, the home side never really looked like achieving the necessary two points; the visitors won 42-22. The day was also notable for having three qualified match officials in attendance, a virtually unheard-of scenario, and all three were used.

Appointed match official Julia Lee suffered an ankle injury and was replaced by Steve Taylor, who can still be seen running touch-lines at Super League games. Leicester's own resident referee, Phil Jackson, provided further cover should a similar eventuality befall Lee's replacement. Leicester chairman, Julian Harrison, reflected on the number of occasions when obtaining one referee had proved to be a difficult – if not impossible – task. Now, using the London buses analogy, along came three at once.

At the end of July, the tables were complete. All had contributed to a magnificent first part of the season, with only Bedford Swifts remaining point-less. The final tables were as follows:

	Northern Division	Pl	W	D	L	F	A	Diff	Pts
1	Chester Wolves	10	7	0	3	280	147	133	14
2	Leicester Phoenix	10	5	0	5	250	304	-54	10
3	Birmingham Bulls	10	4	0	6	254	274	-20	8
4	Worcester Saints	10	3	0	7	208	306	-98	6
5	Cheltenham Warriors	10	2	0	8	163	253	-90	4

	Southern Division	Pl	W	D	L	F	A	Diff	Pts
1	Crawley Jets	10	8	0	2	359	229	130	16
2	St Albans Centurions	10	7	0	3	348	177	171	14
3	West London Sharks	10	6	0	4	250	228	22	12
4	Oxford Cavaliers	10	5	1	4	232	240	-8	11
5	North London Skolars	10	3	1	6	292	389	-97	7

	Eastern Division	Pl	W	D	L	F	A	Diff	Pts
1	South Norfolk Saints	10	8	0	2	461	264	197	16
2	Ipswich Rhinos	10	5	0	5	380	333	47	10
3	Cambridge Eagles	10	4	0	6	288	436	-148	8
4	Bedford Swifts	10	0	0	10	170	474	-304	0

Of the teams who impressed during the regular 10-game season, two stood out. South Norfolk Saints' early season promise never diminished and their eight victories from 10 games with a points difference of plus 197 kept them just ahead of their close rivals from the South Division, the Crawley Jets in the composite table. The Jets' success was perhaps not quite as surprising. They had, after all, beaten a London Broncos XIII in their preparatory round of fixtures in 1997, and with ex-professional and BARLA young-player-of-the-year Steve O'Reilly spearheading their play, they were confident of making an impression, even though they had lost their first game at West London.

Both sides contained players of flair and talent. For the East Anglians, the Greenhall brothers, Chris and Nick were particularly effective, as was the free-scoring full back James Shanahan, but the side also had a tremendous work ethic and a determination to prove themselves.

Crawley had some players with prior rugby league know-how in addition to O'Reilly. Australian Rod Hammond was particularly useful and Mark Henderson had played in the SCL for Worcester Royals and Kingston Warriors. The lure of the XIII-a-side code had been irresistible for some county-standard union players in both camps and with their talent and the coaching expertise of O'Reilly and his counterpart at South Norfolk, John Evans, they quickly developed into confident rugby league players.

South Norfolk had also made excellent use of BARLA coaching co-ordinator Brian Chambers. He had a remit to float between RLC clubs, launching new initiatives, holding coaching sessions in schools, meeting with key local authority sports development personnel, and generally providing practical advice and assistance to clubs.

In Norfolk, for example, he assisted the Saints in holding a BNFL Bronze Skills Awards session attended by 20 youngsters aged 11 years and over. He also helped put on a Level One Coaching course attended by players from the North Walsham rugby union club – the aim being to use this newly-acquired knowledge to form a junior side in 1999. South Norfolk Saints were intent on being in the game for the long run.

However, more immediately, the Jets and the Saints had to face the semi-finals and two equally determined sides in St Albans Centurions and Chester Wolves, all seeking inaugural season glory. That the four semi-finalists were all new entrants in 1998 vindicated the decision to accept their applications. They had undoubtedly been a significant asset for the RLC. Both semi-finals were keenly contested, but perhaps fittingly, the two most successful sides in the regular season reached the final. Crawley defeated St Albans 26-14, with two tries from Richard Billings. South Norfolk overcame Chester by a slightly wider margin with their five tries spread throughout the team, another indication of their all-round capabilities.

The Final was scheduled for Saturday 8 August at the Prince of Wales Stadium in Cheltenham. The prize was the new RLC silverware. Harry Jepson's role in promoting the cause of the SCL and rugby league in the London area for many years had led to a suggestion from Lionel Hurst to the RFL's Tom O'Donovan that this should be recognised. Thus, the Harry Jepson Trophy came into being, for the RLC Grand Final winners.

There was, however, drama prior to the Final and another test of the RLC executive's resolve. Unfortunately for South Norfolk's preparations, the day of the final coincided with the wedding of one of their players, Micky Byrne. More unfortunately – at least for the club – Byrne had invited some of his team-mates, making them unavailable for the Grand Final. If that wasn't enough, coach John Evans's wife was due to give birth that weekend, also putting him out of the picture at Cheltenham. Understandably, the club requested a postponement to an alternative date. While recognising the severe impact on the South Norfolk club and the possible consequences in terms of an equitable match, the RLC executive decided to stand firm and rejected the call to move the date, saying that arrangements should be adhered to, and a precedent for departing from them should not be set.

On a blisteringly hot day and before an encouraging crowd, the Saints produced a gutsy performance and at half-time were still in contention, trailing only by 12 points. The writing appeared to be on the wall when Richard Billings went over for Crawley after only two minutes. But South Norfolk hit back, not surprisingly through Shanahan, and although Steve O'Reilly scored a try a minute before the interval, hopes were still high amongst the Norfolk contingent – and probably most neutrals sympathetic to the underdogs – that they could perhaps cause a surprise.

When Trevor Bowles scored the first try of the second half for South Norfolk, hopes rose even further. It was not to be, however. Centre Rod Hammond came into his own after the break, scoring a 16-minute hat-trick of tries for Crawley, and with O'Reilly kicking eight goals, Crawley ran away with it to win 40-12.

The Jets were not the only winners on a triumphant day for the RLC and for the sport. The match had been well refereed by Rolf Hayes from Doncaster, a man who had officiated for many years and was well known in the East Midlands in particular. The organisation had been exemplary, and much of that was testament to the hard work of Cheltenham Warriors, and their enthusiastic administrative team of Stephen Rigby and Ruth Sigley.

The fact that the Warriors received the coveted 'Rugby Leaguer' RLC Club of the Year' trophy had much to do with their performance on an occasion when they weren't actually taking to the pitch themselves.

Crawley Jets: John Mercott, Mark Elliott, Richard Billings, Rodney Hammond, Simon Holms, Mark Henderson, Steve O'Reilly, Nick Dinsdale, Simon Kelly, Paul Sparkes, Simon Matterface, Charlie Tresser, Robert Dowling.
Subs: James Brannagan, Lee McDonagh, David Walker, Neil Mannifield, Brian Gander, Alan Nash

South Norfolk Saints: James Shanahan, Dave Tanner, Ian Maxey, David Horne, Trevor Bowles, Phil Friel, Brad Downes, Tim Groom, Hardy Johnson, Ken Dodds, Phil Minnett, Clive Vooght, Tim Malone.
Subs: Colin Fletcher, Neil Thynne, Andy Jupp, Andy Allen, Ken Griggs.

In times gone by, the end of the season meant relaxation for a few months. The advent of the summertime RLC had, subconsciously, changed this way of thinking for some players and clubs. For the former, there was always the option of either returning to rugby union for those who had come from that sport, trying rugby union for those who had put themselves in the shop window at RLC-host rugby union clubs, participating in the Student

Rugby League if eligible, or, if close to a suitable location, playing winter rugby league. From a club's perspective, those determined to better themselves realised that the off-season was a key period. It was a time for reflection and putting right any deficiencies in particular areas. This was very much within the ethos of quality standards advocated by the RLC executive.

The months immediately following the Cheltenham Grand Final were full of activity. To begin with, the RLC, under the management of John Nugent, formed a representative side and took on the North East at Chester and the Combined Services in Portsmouth in September. The squad reflected the playing strengths of the leading clubs and those new to the RLC. It was:

Marc Elwood (West London Sharks), Louis Ratapu (West London Sharks), Alex Sanerive (West London Sharks), Andy Brown (Cheltenham Warriors), Ronnie Haines (Cheltenham Warriors), John Mulraney (Cheltenham Warriors), Ian Riddel (Cheltenham Warriors), Leon Jammal (Worcester Saints), Jason Spafford (Worcester Saints), Rob Barraclough (Chester Wolves), Simon Hill (Oxford Cavaliers), John Williams (Oxford Cavaliers), Graham Crane (Oxford Cavaliers), Paul Daly (Oxford Cavaliers), Darrell Griffin (Oxford Cavaliers), Tony Williams (Birmingham Bulls), Ken Edwards (St Albans Centurions), Tim Groomes (South Norfolk Saints), Pete Webb (St Albans Centurions), John Sayers (St Albans Centurions), Ken Dunn (St Albans Centurions).

Two contrasting games saw the RLC defeat the North East 70-4 with Oxford's Graham Crane scoring three tries, and both Louis Ratapu of West London and Tony Williams of Birmingham claiming two apiece. The Cavaliers' Simon Hill scored 26 points. However, the Combined Services were a harder nut to crack, though a 20-12 defeat was far from a disgrace.

It was increasingly obvious to both the RLC administration and that of the match officials department at Red Hall, that a growing competition away from the heartland areas would require more referees. While immediately and for some years to come the RLC relied significantly on experienced officials from the north, it was preferable in the longer term to have a steady supply of local qualified referees and touch judges. A mixture of the two was ideal. The experienced northern-based officials, many of whom greatly enjoyed the refreshing nature of the RLC and the days out despite the distance, could pass on their knowledge to the players during games, and the newly qualified officials in development areas could learn in a mutually educational environment, away from the pressures of the BARLA leagues.

In 1998, the balance was heavily weighted in favour of the heartland-based match officials. There simply weren't many qualified referees in the south. To help, a referee recruitment course in Oxford in November aimed at qualifying officials for both the RLC and the student game. Twenty-five people took the laws exam, including Julian Harrison and Lionel Hurst.

A follow-up session in early December on a frozen Oxford pitch provided some important practical tips, but more importantly in the longer term, the initiative provided the impetus for the formation of the Southern Rugby League Referees Society (SRLRS), under the stewardship of two pre-existing match officials in the South: Alan Smith and Allan Steven.

Allan Steven was also called upon in November by the St Albans club to officiate in a three-way tournament at the Hertfordshire club on the afternoon of the Test Match between Great Britain and New Zealand at nearby Vicarage Road,

Watford. The event was memorable in so much as it advertised the potential of future RLC outfits Coventry Bears (who formed a merged team with players from Leicester Phoenix) and Nottingham Outlaws, as they contested matters with the Cheshire Police. The Nottingham team on this occasion was formed as a social rugby outfit by Nottingham Trent University graduates. They regularly attended rugby functions organised by the SRL Alumni, who were involved in the St Albans event, and as a result of growing interest in playing competitively key organisers Lee Gibson, Gavin Baker and Simon Charvet, among others, decided to form the Outlaws club and join the RLC.

The mention of Coventry and Nottingham is significant because it is interesting to note what future RLC clubs were doing in the interval between the 1998 and 1999 RLC seasons. In the North East, while Gateshead Panthers were making a clean sweep of all available trophies, the Teesside Steelers were taking a new geographical route by moving out of the North East League and joining Yorkshire League Division Five. Whitley Bay Barbarians reformed for the North East competition and their chairman and leading rugby league activist in the area, Ken Sykes, was elected to chair the North East Rugby League (NERL).

In Wales, the Cardiff Demons continued their participation in the RFL Academy competition, while the summer period also witnessed a re-launch of amateur rugby league activity with club sides formed in Cardiff, Swansea and the Rhondda, a potential 'Origin' fixture between East and West Wales and a planned fixture at amateur level against Scotland. In the Midlands, EMARLA continued to schedule games for Birmingham, who were playing winter and summer rugby, Derby City, the reserve sides from Nottingham Crusaders, Garibaldi and also a new club formed in Ilkeston and influenced by the Toyota car works.

A little further west, rugby league in Wolverhampton resurfaced with the Wizards taking on the mantle after the demise of the old Wolverhampton Borough operation. The driving force behind the new Wolves was former Kirklees RFL development officer Mike Rowan, and their ambition – and marketing potential – was illustrated by the announcement that the club's first signing was former Great Britain and Wigan winger, Henderson Gill.

For some of those mentioned, RLC participation would still be a little time away, but others had their sights set on joining the competition in 1999. The demand for places, anticipated as part of a successful venture, brought with it mixed emotions. On the one hand, there was sheer delight at the recognition that the RLC could make as significant a contribution to the national development of the sport as that achieved by Student Rugby League. Conversely, there was concern at whether the competition could cope organisationally both with an influx of new talent at club level, but also with the expectation that that national profile and responsibility might bring. There was also concern at the need to avoid losing clubs as fast as gaining them. The emphasis on minimum standards and the determination to retain and strengthen existing operations would prove valuable traits, but surely there was an extent to what could be achieved by an infrastructure based on talent, enthusiasm and dedication, but also based on volunteer contributions?

51

In addressing the short-term issue of how to accommodate those clubs vying to enter in 1999, Lionel Hurst provided some insights in *Open Rugby*. As we shall see, with the benefit of hindsight and the knowledge of subsequent developments, he also made illuminating comments on the geographical extent of RLC expansion: "I think the next question we face is how to develop the regional concept of the league to offset travel costs and difficulties, and so it is not out of the question that there might be four distinct groups next year. A northern group can't be ruled out, but we are keen to make sure that our development is on the fringes of and beyond the game's heartlands. Yorkshire, Lancashire and Cumbria are well catered for, and the development areas are the target for the RLC."

In the same article, Hurst talked of the need to learn the lessons of the Kingston and Northampton experiences of 1997 and 1998 respectively, by ensuring increased scrutiny of applications and of the vital role that junior development must play in providing depth, substance and longevity to the competition. The significance of publicising the RLC and its constituent clubs was also clear to the RLC management. As media manager, Phil Caplan ensured that the tremendous amount of volunteer work was recorded and promoted. Caplan reflected on its significance: "Nothing would have been possible without the tireless volunteers out there spreading the gospel and the least they deserved was to have their stories and successes told."

However, it was which clubs would apply and which would be admitted that focused minds as thoughts turned to 1999. The RLC executive committee had eight applications – from Manchester Knights (who had emerged from the old Tameside Borough club), Derby City, Nottingham, Newmarket, Wolverhampton Wizards, Crewe Wolves, Cardiff and Hemel Hempstead – with the possibility of further representations from Coventry Bears and a club in Bristol. When the committee met on 24 November 1998 at the Randolph Hotel in Oxford, it was apparent that there was a fundamental split that reflected the nature of the committee itself. The prevailing view from the 'volunteer' contingent (Moss, Caplan and Hurst) was that the impetus of 1998 should continue by further expansion, supported by a small increase in central investment from the RFL – their argument being that this increase was justified by the national profile achieved and that such a profile created a sponsorship opportunity that was easier to sell.

This view was not shared by the RFL's Tom O'Donovan. He said that Hemel Hempstead joining the RLC was fundamental. The club's application to join the professional ranks was rejected because their Pennine Way facilities did not meet the required standards, and the RFL had to find them a competition to play in. However, the matter of other additions was a non-issue. With the exception of Hemel, there was to be no RLC expansion.

This was unacceptable to the first camp. Lionel Hurst outlined their complete opposition to O'Donovan's position. Some tension ensued, with, in effect, an ultimatum being issued by Hurst and his colleagues. A compromise was reached with O'Donovan recognising the argument and statement of intent, and it was agreed to increase the number of clubs from 14 to 20.

6. 1999: Six new teams

The New Year started with the six new sides being unveiled at the Hilton Hotel in Leeds in January. There were no surprises at the new entrants - Nottingham Outlaws, Derby City, Crewe Wolves, Wolverhampton Wizards, Manchester Knights and Hemel Hempstead Stags – but eyebrows were raised at the omission of at least one other club. Coventry Bears had made an impressive case for inclusion. Formed by former Great Britain student captain Alan Robinson and with backing from Coventry Rugby Union club, the Bears had enlisted the assistance of Julian Harrison at the SRL Alumni in their efforts to join the RLC – the link being the significant student and graduate background to the club.

Despite efforts by the club to ascertain entrance requirements in good time, they were not forthcoming until the 11th hour. Thus, the Coventry application – despite its undoubted merits – was considered to be too late. Representations by the club were unsuccessful, but a measure of both league management strength in sticking to a decision already made and the determination and quality behind the club operation, resulted, ultimately, in satisfaction. The Bears heeded the RLC's advice and organised friendly fixtures with the armed forces, student and RLC clubs, in preparation for a future application. Their patience would be rewarded.

The background to Wolverhampton, Nottingham and Hemel has been outlined previously. Of the others, Derby City were formed in 1990 and played in EMARLA. With three schools in the city already playing the game and a new kit sponsorship deal with the local newspaper, the *Derby Evening Telegraph*, the club meant business. Indeed, the kit had made such an impression on a number of Derby County football fans when they saw it being modelled at a game, that some approached the wearer asking where they could buy it.

Crewe Wolves also had an EMARLA background, at least in the club's original guise, and with an experienced coach in Paul Clark, rugby league devotees in Cheshire could look forward to local derby fixtures against their fellow Wolves from Chester.

The last of the six was Manchester Knights. Though there may have been no surprise at their inclusion within the applications to join the RLC, their success provided a controversial talking point in some quarters. An application based on merit would have been unproblematic, such was the strength of their case in playing and organisational terms, especially considering the fact that they were largely a resurrection of the old Tameside Borough, and that they had leading journalist Peter Wilson behind them as club chairman. Controversy focussed on the fact that they were a rugby league club in Manchester, and whether that was compatible with a development league. Though their close proximity to league strongholds such as Oldham, Rochdale and Salford would obviously not be a disadvantage - the same argument could be levelled at Chester and Crewe to some extent - Wilson was quick to point out that the South Manchester area was 'predominantly football orientated', and the new club would fill a vacuum.

Attention was lavished on the new RLC entrants. However, there were developments happening throughout RLC territory. In the Eastern Division, Bedford Swifts made an important new signing when Tracey Greenwood, who had experience at operational level in Super League at Halifax Blue Sox, moved south and became the Swifts' new manager. Further east, South Norfolk Saints were working tremendously hard at junior development and using Brian Chambers effectively. They also secured a sponsorship deal with the Lincoln Financial Group, as did Gloucestershire Warriors in due course. Ipswich Rhinos too, were busy on the sponsorship front, and in Bellway Homes found a committed financial supporter over a number of years. The club were also paying considerable attention to the RLC message of 'getting the backroom right'. A new nine-person committee was formed, headed by the director of education for Suffolk County Council, David Peachey, an enthusiastic league supporter from Widnes.

Throughout the life of the competition, there were always calls for the RFL to appoint development officers to particular areas. A proper, viable, competitive structure to provide a flagship competition could only enhance development opportunities and between the 1998 and 1999 RLC seasons, long-awaited action in this area materialised. The catalyst was the new Rugby League Joint Policy Board, a working agreement and strategy involving both the RFL and BARLA, and a development that it could be argued came about from the example set by the Southern Conference League in implementing and promoting collaboration between the governing bodies to everyone's benefit.

In addition to appointments in Scotland of Ian Johnstone and Leeds of Julia Lee, officers came into post in West London and, interestingly, in Oxford. The former was John Hill who would dovetail nicely with London Broncos' developments in West London and who would have a particularly strong influence on local side, West London Sharks. Indeed, the club moved to Marble Hill Park, a picturesque setting in Twickenham and the West London RFL development operation's base.

In Oxford, Caro Wild was the successful candidate. Wild was a man who had already made a name for himself in the student game by founding and coaching the Luton University side. His appointment in Oxford was aided significantly by the input of Lionel Hurst and the Cavaliers, was supported financially by the local authority, and showed the flourishing state of the game then in the city of spires. His remit was very much based on the original development framework devised by Hurst and Daryn Reeds.

The appointments were not confined solely to development officers, though. Development managers were appointed in Yorkshire and in the London and the South region. The successful candidate for the latter post was John Kain. Originally from County Durham, Kain had played professionally at Castleford and then embarked on a coaching career that took in Keighley Cougars and also the Student Rugby League. It was perhaps his involvement with the students, in addition to his upbringing in another development area for rugby league, the North East, that enhanced Kain's enthusiasm for development. His new role with the RFL involved working with the RLC and overseeing the work of both Hill and Wild. He also had an important role in assisting the London ARL. The capital's amateur league was experiencing a few problems and had held an Emergency General Meeting on 3 January in the light of resignations leaving only seven viable sides.

One of Kain's first jobs in relation to the RLC, however, was to talk to a club delegates meeting in Oxford about the new development structure in the game and the possibilities that lay ahead.

The clubs formally gathered again in late April, in London, at the prestigious Rugby Club of St James. Principally concerned with the XV-a-side code, the club was keen to welcome rugby league and a collection of club representatives, officials, dignitaries and guests met to hear of the new structure of a competition now increased to 20 sides in four divisions. Each club would play 12 fixtures in the regular season including four cross-conference matches. For the first time an extended play-off system encompassing eight teams (the top two sides in each respective division) and then two preliminary and regionally orientated Grand Finals, would culminate in the final two sides who would compete for the Harry Jepson Trophy. In a major boost to the RLC, the preliminary Grand Finals (semi-finals in reality) were to be curtain raisers to Super League fixtures, although as it transpired only one (the South versus East contest) would actually do so – at The Stoop, home of the London Broncos. The Broncos' chief executive Tony Rea was present at the Rugby Club of St James, emphasising the interdependence of different aspects of the game in the South.

As was the case 12 months previously, optimism and expectations were high as 8 May dawned and the big kick-off approached. Rugby league in the southern half of England had arguably never been in better shape. The London Broncos were well established in Super League, and had just appeared in the last Challenge Cup Final at the old Wembley Stadium. The London Skolars had been successfully incorporated into BARLA's National Conference League. Though the London amateur league was a concern, the appointment of development staff would surely have an impact at open age level and provide a further boost to junior and youth development. As for the Rugby League Conference: three months of action would reveal all.

The customary sprint start to the season was enjoyed by a great number of clubs, with two areas in particular providing much interest. In the North West, Chester Wolves began the campaign in spectacular style and sent out a message to the rest of the league that they would be a force to be reckoned with again. Their defeat of near neighbours Manchester Knights in week two was particularly impressive given their opponents' performance on the first day. Wolverhampton Wizards were swamped by the fire-power of their fellow new boys, though of course that tag would be less appropriate to the Knights given their greater experience and rugby league education.

The game, sponsored by the *Daily Star*, was also memorable for the fact that Leeds Rhinos' international star Iestyn Harris performed a VIP kick-off. The Wizards could have done with some of Harris's talent as a gutsy baptism couldn't prevent a 90-0 defeat. The other area of interest was the South West and Cotswolds. The fact that Oxford Cavaliers swiftly clicked into gear was not surprising. Quality players with good coaching ensured that the club were the envy of most of its opponents and the side they wanted to beat.

Current champions, Crawley Jets tried to do just that on 15 May, but they and their expectant crowd at the superb Broadfields Stadium (venue for their first three home games of that season) were stunned as the Cavaliers were victorious. Though the Jets would eventually come good, they quickly fell into a pattern that was to characterise subsequent years. Early season defeats – possibly as a result of a slow re-acclimatisation to rugby league by their large number of county-standard rugby union players – were followed by having to win game after game to qualify for the latter stages, the team gradually building up momentum towards the business end of the season.

The other team in the South West area to impress was a major surprise. Cheltenham Warriors had, despite impressing as a club with their attention to detail and professional approach to administration, largely struggled on the pitch in 1998. 1999 was very different. They even had the longest unbeaten run from the start of the campaign, through until 19 June.

Their conquerors on that day, Chester Wolves, had already visited fortress Cheltenham and come away pointless. Inspired by former Leeds Rhino, Ronnie Haines, and the likes of Sonnie Williams, Andy Bird and John Mulraney, the Warriors created a lasting impression and were model ambassadors for rugby league in a rugby union hotbed.

These clubs – and others – were not the only ones to impress. Some players were attracting the interest of Super League clubs. In May, youngster Darrell Griffin, the RLC's young player of the year in 1998 after a series of stand-out performances for the Oxford Cavaliers, joined the London Broncos and quickly established himself in their Academy side. Parminder Tutt had been a leading local rugby union player before the emergence of the Wolverhampton Wizards gave him an opportunity to play a sport he had wished to try. The 90-0 opening day defeat at Manchester was perhaps not the ideal situation in which to shine, but he did. Iestyn Harris made Tutt the Wizards man-of-the-match that day and, incredibly, in a short period of time, Tutt and Harris would both be playing at the same venue on the same afternoon. While the latter starred for Leeds Rhinos in their Super League fixture at Wilderspool, Warrington, Tutt took part in the Academy game that preceded it as the Warrington Wolves swooped to invite the talented young man for a trial. With both the Wolverhampton defeat at Manchester and his Warrington Academy debut against Leeds also featuring on Sky Television, Tutt could be forgiven for thinking he was in rugby league heaven.

While Tutt's rapid rise to semi-stardom had perhaps come as a surprise, the number of players registering to play in the RLC, 750 by the beginning of June, was increasing equally rapidly and explained why RLC players were beginning to be noticed. A greater player base provided a larger shop window to scouts from the game's higher echelons. The RLC executive was also ensuring that this player chain continued in the long term. Under-13 festivals were a feature of the 1999 season, a reflection of the need to develop players early and to try to engrain into youngsters the basics of the sport and a sense of affinity towards rugby league. The recognition that the competition would perhaps stand or fall by whether clubs could produce talent from within rather than looking towards more short-term sources, was not lost on both management and clubs alike.

In mid-June more than 300 under-13s played, many of them for the first time on a competitive basis, at four different regional venues – Manchester, Worcestershire, Crawley and South Norfolk – the festival format being conducive to providing sufficient opposition and a great event as well.

Festivals in July attracted further interest with three more clubs hosting and some great talent emerging. It was also refreshing to see teams also forming at under-16 level and some clubs found that an abundance of open-age playing resources meant forming second teams. The RLC responded to this upsurge in player interest and John Kain's appointment by forming a coaching association and a development forum. That upsurge was also reflected as other clubs showed interest in joining the RLC. By June it was clear that there was keen interest from at least six clubs in participating in 2000. Such interest needed to be catered for, and thoughts behind the scenes turned towards the necessity of strengthening the RLC infrastructure to enable this expansion.

Lionel Hurst summarised the issue in *Rugby League World:* "We have a very positive problem, that the sheer level of interest is in danger of outgrowing the depth of the management structure at the top... We are not an elitist league looking to hive off the best clubs, we must bolster and look after the weaker ones. All of them start off with roughly the same geographical catchment areas and setting up resources. You would hope and expect that to start with the new clubs would not be quite able to match those who are more established. The expectations have already been raised for aspiring applicants. They will have to show a pedigree on the field prior to any decision on inclusion and that they have matching support and finance off it."

Media interest continued to grow. Phil Caplan's industry led to a full results service appearing on BBC Ceefax, and there was more television coverage. Leicester Phoenix and Oxford Cavaliers were covered locally. A bigger development was Sky Television beginning to feature regular updates from the competition. At the St Albans Centurions versus Oxford Cavaliers fixture on 10 July, Sky presenter Chris Warren interviewed Oxford and RLC chairman Lionel Hurst.

Hurst's enigmatic and passionate style and the ease of phrase for which he had already become renowned, proved perfect for the media, and the equally passionate display from the two teams complemented things perfectly. Though the Cavaliers continued towards the end of season play-offs with a clear victory, there was much to admire in the home side's display. The RLC was great viewing. The competition even inspired the launching of an unofficial – yet recognised – website, based at the Faculty of Art and Design at Manchester Metropolitan University and co-ordinated, as it is today, by John Haigh.

Of course, on the horizon for the sport was the 2000 World Cup, and preparations were beginning to gather pace, with key personnel addressing how the competition could be used to maximum effect. Members of the RLC executive contributed to seminars and joined relevant sub-committees concerned with event planning. The pioneers who started the whole bandwagon rolling only a few years previously, would have been staggered that those now running the competition were rubbing shoulders with professional personnel and planning for an international tournament involving the world's best players.

Back on the RLC pitches, the competition was hotting up, especially in the Southern Division. By the second month of the season, all five sides were still in with a realistic chance of making the play-offs. Though Crawley, Oxford and West London led the way, both North London Skolars and St Albans also chipped in. On 26 June, St Albans visited Marble Hill Park to take on West London Sharks. A fabulous contest full of skill and tension saw the game revolve around a drop goal from Andy Shaw which gave the visitors a 23-22 win. It was a fitting game to be played in front of Messrs O'Donovan and Hurst from the RLC executive who were there before a committee meeting that evening at The Stoop.

The Stoop's rugby fare that day featured London Broncos and Leeds Rhinos, and though the quality was better in the Super League encounter, most present at both games argued that for on the edge of your seat thrills, there was no contest. The RLC won hands down.

While the RLC was undergoing a honeymoon period of progress on the pitch, with no apparent problems or underlying issues that could hinder that movement, the reality was different. The truth was that the RLC was in danger of becoming a runaway train with a driver significantly under-resourced and under-supported. While the executive committee took overall collective responsibility, the day-to-day management of operations was principally focused on the volunteer triumvirate of Lionel Hurst, Phil Caplan and Trevor Moss.

With an already expanded competition and the prospect of having to cater for further club interest in 2000, an increase in profile, expectation and the development responsibility that went with the embryonic under-13 and potential under-16 situation, it was all becoming more than a part-time volunteer administration could be expected to handle, especially as they had to do much of their organisation by telephone. Increased investment was needed. This was obvious to Phil Caplan and he asked to meet RFL commercial director, Dave Callaghan, to put his views across.

They met on 22 June. Caplan outlined the scenario, and it was a big surprise to Callaghan who, as a result of the image he had gained from the media and the fact that the RLC had never been on any RFL agenda he had seen, had the impression that all was running smoothly. That the actual operation of a competition that carried with it the hopes of league expansionists everywhere could be so reliant on three individuals, who worked outside the game during the working day, astonished Callaghan. It was another key moment in the RLC story.

There was to be rapid movement within a month. On 28 July, Caplan, Hurst and Moss met with new RFL chief executive, Neil Tunnicliffe, to address these concerns at Leicester Forest East services on the M1. The result was firstly a formalised constitution which stated that the RFL directors would also become directors of the RLC, thus establishing a significant degree of governing body responsibility and accountability. It was also agreed that a full-time administrator would be put in place in time for the 2000 season.

During the space of five glorious July days, Leicester became a focus for rugby league activity. Leicester Phoenix secured a place in the end of season play-offs by thrashing a depleted Wolverhampton Wizards side. The game, of course, was crucial to the home side, but what had wider significance was the appearance in the Leicester ranks of full England international and former London Broncos, Leeds Rhinos and Featherstone Rovers player Ikram Butt. This was arranged through Gus Dinn, who worked for BARLA and had links to Bradford Bulls, where Butt was working in development. Of course, on a wider front, that the most prominent Asian rugby league player, was playing in a city similar to Bradford in its ethnic composition, should not be ignored.

After the meeting at Leicester Forest East to discuss the RLC, the participants went to watch the London Broncos take on Bradford Bulls in an on-the-road Super League fixture. The largest crowd ever to watch rugby league in Leicester witnessed a narrow win for the Bulls, but also the talent on display in the local area. Leicester Phoenix took on – and beat – the Coventry Bears in an exciting curtain-raiser and at half-time in the main fixture, under-13 sides from Leicester and Birmingham gave a demonstration of their progress in the XIII-a-side code. The match programme gave extensive coverage to local developments and the evening generally gladdened everyone who had the national expansion of the game at heart.

The Leicester versus Coventry game was, of course, a friendly fixture. But the RLC competition proper was reaching boiling point as the play-offs approached. Going into the last weekend of regular fixtures, only two clubs – Cheltenham Warriors and Hemel Hempstead Stags – had secured a definite play-off place. This showed the all-round competitive strength of the league. In three of the Divisions, Northern, Western and Eastern, three sides were in serious contention virtually from start to finish. In the Southern Division, as previously mentioned, that number increased from three to all five.

In July, the inaugural RLC player ratings were produced and the diversity of clubs represented further emphasised the wide spread of individual and club talent. Every game appeared to have numerous ramifications. The clash between East Anglian rivals Ipswich Rhinos and South Norfolk Saints on 3 July was a case in point. A one-point victory for the Rhinos effectively ended the hopes of the previous year's finalists, and through disappointing circumstances (relating, as we shall see, to Hemel Hempstead), it also ensured that the Suffolk side finished top of the Eastern Division. The final 1999 season league tables were as follows:

	Northern Division	Pl	W	D	L	F	A	Diff	Pts
1	Chester Wolves	12	10	0	2	603	155	448	20
2	Manchester Knights	12	10	0	2	526	172	354	20
3	Nottingham Outlaws	12	8	0	4	400	230	170	16
4	Derby City	12	2	0	10	128	431	-303	4
5	Crewe Wolves	12	0	0	12	132	690	-558	0

Western Division	Pl	W	D	L	F	A	Diff	Pts
1 Cheltenham Warriors	12	10	0	2	540	133	407	20
2 Leicester Phoenix	12	9	0	3	494	204	290	18
3 Birmingham Bulls	12	7	0	5	358	184	174	14
4 Worcestershire Saints	12	4	0	7	240	351	-111	8
5 Wolverhampton Wizards	12	0	0	12	46	907	-861	0

Eastern Division	Pl	W	D	L	F	A	Diff	Pts
1 Ipswich Rhinos	12	7	0	5	449	385	64	14
2 Hemel Hempstead Stags*	12	8	0	4	535	248	287	12
3 South Norfolk Saints	12	6	0	6	438	418	20	12
4 Cambridge Eagles	12	1	0	11	170	698	-528	2
5 Bedford Swifts	12	1	0	11	145	680	-535	2

* Hemel Hempstead Stags deducted 4 points for breach of rules

Southern Division	Pl	W	D	L	F	A	Diff	Pts
1 Crawley Jets	12	9	0	3	606	226	380	18
2 Oxford Cavaliers	12	9	0	3	458	224	234	18
3 West London Sharks	12	9	0	3	410	231	179	18
4 North London Skolars	12	6	0	6	344	395	-51	12
5 St Albans Centurions	12	4	0	8	314	375	-61	8

The play-offs took place over the course of three weekends from 1 to 15 August. The divisions were linked, with Northern and Western sides forming one half of the draw, Southern and Eastern the other.

The latter started with a convincing display from the Oxford Cavaliers, who went to East Anglia and defeated Ipswich Rhinos 31-16. On the same afternoon, real drama occurred in the other fixture where again the visitors – Hemel Hempstead Stags – took the spoils, but in a narrower fashion. Ultimately a try by Alex Murphy (not the St Helens and Great Britain legend), proved decisive as an 18-16 victory seemed to put the holders out and the Stags through. However, Hemel had already had four competition points docked for a rule infringement, thus allowing Ipswich to win the Division, and the playing – though inadvertently – of two ineligible players in the Crawley play-off game, meant that the RLC administration had another crucial decision to make: whether to expel Hemel from the competition.

The decision meant heartbreak for Hemel and a reprieve for Crawley. The Hertfordshire side were duly expelled from the 1999 competition, and Crawley proceeded to the regional semi-final to take on Oxford in a clash of mouth-watering potential at The Stoop. A close encounter was expected for the large crowd who gathered on 7 August to also view the afternoon's main contest between London Broncos and Salford City Reds in Super League.

Both RLC sides played attacking, attractive rugby and had already met in the league stages, so knew each other well. As it transpired, Oxford were never in the contest. Four Jets players – Henderson, Kemp-Gee, O'Reilly and Billings – scored two tries each, and individual scores from Fitzgerald and McDonagh coupled with the ever-reliable boot of Steve O'Reilly with seven goals, ensured a devastating 54-16 victory.

Crawley were therefore through to their second successive final. On the evening of 7 August, there were still four possible opponents for them to play on the big day because the Northern and Western half of the draw was still to commence. Twenty-four hours later there would be two. Cheltenham, the surprise package of the season, further astonished many by beating the much-fancied Manchester Knights by 35 points. A hat-trick of tries by Andy Bird led the way, and the arguably unprecedented transformation from one season to the next was another stage nearer completion.

On the same day, Leicester Phoenix could not match the achievement of the Cheltenham underdogs, and despite a brave performance, the more experienced and talented Chester Wolves won quite comfortably, 30-10. The regional semi-final between Cheltenham and Chester was, in similar fashion to its southern counterpart, scheduled as a Super League curtain-raiser. The venue was Wilderspool and the match was Warrington Wolves versus St Helens. For those looking forward to watching and playing at one of the game's great grounds, there would be massive disappointment.

One of the key reasons for moving rugby league to the summer was the weather. On that day, 15 August, conditions more akin to the old winter season came back to haunt the RLC and the two teams in particular. Wet weather meant the abandonment of any possibility of playing a pre-match game, and at the 11th hour, the RLC regional semi-final was switched to the renowned, but less prestigious, venue of Woolston. For Cheltenham this disappointment was compounded by defeat. The Warriors' outstanding season finished, though not without a demonstration of their vast improvement and talent. A 27-16 victory, with five separate try-scorers, saw Chester through to the final.

It was in many ways, a final of contradictions and opposites: Crawley, the more successful RLC team, versus Chester, the more experienced rugby league outfit. The Sussex side had players with great individual ability and flair. Chester, arguably, were a more functional side, reliant on collective effort. The venue had been chosen prior to the very first ball being kicked on 8 May. North London Skolars, winners of the first summer conference two years previously and now a developing force in the BARLA National Conference League as well as the RLC, had successfully applied to host it at their New River Stadium on White Hart Lane. They also provided some pre-final rugby league as the hosts took on prospective RLC entrants, Coventry Bears. The main feature provided possibly the most memorable and dramatic climax in the entire history of the competition.

In the first half, Crawley showed just why they were the reigning champions. Tries from Richard Billings and Lee McDonagh led the way, Chester's only response coming from two Duncan Curphey penalties. When Mark Henderson extended the Jets' lead with a try just two minutes after the interval, the writing appeared to be very much on the wall for the Cheshire side. Not a bit of it. Chester's revival was miraculous. Drew Povey, Matthew Bellamy and Giles Cook all scored tries and, with 13 minutes left, Chester, incredibly, had turned the game around.

Again, however, there would be a twist. Crawley would not give up their crown without a determined fight. With Chester's supporters still celebrating Cook's try, Richard Billings effectively silenced them. With 68 minutes gone, Crawley regained the lead. Significantly, Steve O'Reilly for once, was unsuccessful with his conversion attempt and the margin was just two points.

A compelling final was coming towards its conclusion and with virtually the last play of the match and with Crawley's ribbons being prepared for the Harry Jepson Trophy, a last-gasp Chester attack saw the ball land in the arms of Chester second-rower Richard Tyrrell. He touched down in the corner. Dramatically, referee Simon Cross from Castleford was unsighted. Consultation with both touch-judges ensued with everybody's eyes focused on the outcome. The decision was a try. The conversion attempt was immaterial. Chester had won 26-24 and the Harry Jepson Trophy was heading north.

Crawley Jets: Mark Henderson, Mark Elliott, Richard Billings, Justin Kemp, Guy Young, Steve O'Reilly (c), Scott Murphy, Simon Matterface, Ben Brookes, Nick Dinsdale, Kieran Fitzgerald, Rob Dowling, Dave Wattam.
Subs: Paul Sparkes, Neil Mannifield, Steve Holmes, Lee McDonagh
Chester Wolves: Duncan Curphey, Adam Giblin, Matthew Bellamy, Daniel Woods, Daniel Heaton, Nick Barnard, Mark Birmingham, Andy Penny (c), Drew Povey, Nick Glenn, Gareth Martin, Richard Tyrrell, Dave Tobin.
Subs: Colin Harris, Mark Cosgrove, Giles Cook, Alan Clare.

A wonderful summer of rugby had finished, though there would be a representative fixture against the Combined Services on 5 September at Coventry. There had been some lows and some awkward and depressing moments, but there had been a lot of highs. Many clubs had made significant advances, especially the club finishing highest in marks for minimum standards, Cheltenham Warriors. As a result of their success, their local appeal had begun to expand and the club decided to change their name from Cheltenham to Gloucestershire Warriors for the 2000 season.

The Warriors also had the Club Personality of the Year in Ruth Sigley, though she shared this honour with another talented figure, Tracey Greenwood of Bedford Swifts. For Chester, Crawley and Oxford, the post-season review would be one of great satisfaction. But that was also true for many others, including the administration and management as a whole. They had shown their ability to organise and lead, and on the horizon there was the prospect of significant central assistance, although this was still to be fully revealed.

On 28 August, the club met in Leicester to reflect and express their views on the way forward. Significantly, the gathering included RFL chief executive Neil Tunnicliffe. It was apparent that another junction had been reached. Some clubs were progressing faster than others. Some had different strengths and different needs. Some required greater guidance and support. Some were still to join the RLC and needed the reassurance of security and challenge. However, what the competition itself clearly did need was extra investment, in whatever form that could be organised.

While Chester's Grand Final victory and many great matches were the best memories, of greater significance for the short and long-term were the off-field meetings. As a result, the Rugby League Conference was about to step up yet another pivotal rung on the ladder.

7. 2000: Strengthening

That the Rugby League Conference had carved a telling niche in the sport was now undeniable. The competition was even mentioned in parliamentary debate in the House of Commons. When 'The Future of Rugby League' was brought before what remained of the House at 1.19am on 3 November 1999, David Hinchliffe MP – one of the champions of the sport's cause in Westminster – talked positively about the spread of the game, including the expansion of the RLC. He said: "The amateur game has spread throughout the country since the barriers in relation to union were lifted. The summer conference league, which has existed for the past two years, has spread like wildfire across central and southern England. Clubs are queueing up to join the league. Players who have played only union have not had the opportunity to taste the great game of rugby league. That expansion throughout the country is encouraging."

The timing of the reference was telling, for the RLC was about to undergo significant organisational change. The lobbying from the RLC's executive had been successful. A full-time administrator was firmly on the agenda, though it required the input of Super League (Europe) to enable the RFL to implement this. Much of the credit must go to the late Peter Deakin, a passionate advocate of the game and friend of Lionel Hurst, who at the time had a commercial and marketing role at the RFL. Deakin managed to persuade the Super League community that collective funding of an administrator for the RLC would be money well-spent. The position was advertised and interviews took place on 13 January 2000 at Red Hall. The successful candidate was Julian Harrison. He had come full circle and returned to the competition he had left in such a disappointing fashion two years before. Though his duties with the SRL Alumni (including helping to stage the 2000 Varsity match at Richmond) meant that he couldn't take up his appointment until 13 March, he had an early input into RLC affairs through attending executive meetings on 27 January and 24 February. It was agreed that Harrison's work base would remain in Leicester.

The 27 January meeting also focused on a new management structure to support Harrison's appointment. To provide a longer term focus on policy and strategy, a new three-man board of directors was established comprising RFL chief executive Neil Tunnicliffe, development executive Tom O'Donovan and RLC chairman, Lionel Hurst. Thus, the RLC became a limited company, with the company secretary based at Red Hall. In addition to the directors, a new secondary tier was also formed – a board of management that included the directors and previous administrator Trevor Moss, Dave Berry, John Nugent, Phil Caplan and John Kain. The latter's role was to be more hands-on, because he had line management responsibility for the new administrator and a leading input into the competition linked to his development position in the London and South region. Caplan continued to be responsible for all media matters, and while it wasn't so definitely specified, Berry was primarily concerned with junior and youth development.

With the new management structure in place, the January meeting focused on the 2000 season, and specifically, the outcome of the club application process. Potential new entrants would have to fit into a workable competition structure and John Kain had put some thought into a number of possible frameworks. His final suggestion – and the one adopted by the RLC hierarchy – was four groups of six clubs each, which allowed some cross-conference games within an overall total of 12 regular fixtures, to be followed by an eight-team play-off weekend, two regional finals and a Grand Final to be staged at a venue in the Midlands area in mid-August. Four groups of six, of course, meant the addition of four new clubs to the existing 20 who were successfully re-admitted. The successful quartet were South London Storm and Kingston Warriors from the London ARL, Coventry Bears and the Pennine League's Rotherham Giants. The southern duo were included on the basis of their all-round club strength. Both had thriving junior sections, with the Storm having more than 100 registered players from under-11 level upwards. Kingston were a very different prospect from the club that had started, but not finished, the 1997 pilot season, and in addition to their much-heralded junior policy, they could also boast a number of representative players.

Coventry Bears' accolades were undisputed. They had fulfilled all the requirements asked of them 12 months previously and were expected to make a significant impact. The case for Rotherham was put very strongly by BARLA's Ian Cooper. Mindful of the fact that – similar to Manchester and Chester – they were close to heartland areas, the club was still classified as 'developmental'. The Giants had been successful in four consecutive promotion campaigns in their BARLA league, but their expansion into the RLC was intended to provide additional rugby league opportunities to newcomers to the sport.

Of those not included, Newmarket's application was not sufficiently supported, and while attention was directed towards important developments occurring in North Yorkshire and the North East, it was decided that clubs in these areas should be encouraged to organise things internally and become a self-sufficient league entity, with a view to incorporation into the RLC in the future. Developments in the South West, likewise, were to be monitored. A club in Bristol was envisaged, though the Buccaneers moniker and Avonmouth link that appeared to be the way forward at that time, did not come to fruition. Rugby league in Bristol would arrive, but not in 2000.

The 24 clubs competing for the Harry Jepson Trophy in 2000 were divided into four regional divisions:

North: Chester Wolves, Crewe Wolves, Manchester Knights, Nottingham Outlaws, Derby City, Rotherham Giants.

West: Gloucestershire Warriors, Leicester Phoenix, Birmingham Bulldogs ('Bulldogs' replacing 'Bulls' as the suffix due to name duplication with the city's American Football team), Coventry Bears, Worcestershire Saints, Wolverhampton Wizards.

East: Ipswich Rhinos, South Norfolk Saints, Bedford Swifts, Cambridge Eagles, St Albans Centurions, Hemel Hempstead Stags.

South: Crawley Jets, South London Storm, North London Skolars, West London Sharks, Oxford Cavaliers, Kingston Warriors.

While this distribution of clubs put tremendous pressure on the new entrants in the South Division and also meant difficult prospects for others, such as Crewe and Derby, for geographical reasons – as opposed to competitive ones – the groups were perfectly matched, because they recognised and encompassed Sport England regions.

Of course, the RLC was now about much more than open-age rugby. In an extension of the previous season's work and as part of a youth development strategy, Dave Berry proposed – and had ratified – the scheduling of under-15 fixtures as well as the under-13 festivals begun in 1999. Representative rugby had also been a feature of the previous two post-seasons, and the desire to step up the operation and broaden the involvement to include club representation at management, coaching and support level was also laid down at the meeting table. The RLC would lose the services of Brian Chambers as his BARLA contract was coming to an end, and so the idea was to provide his replacement and other people's input from within the club network. With the World Cup looming, ideas for opponents included a possible fixture against an Emerging Nations side as well as the more obvious candidates from the services and student sectors.

For Julian Harrison, it was a very different RLC from the one he had left at organisational level at the end of 1997. While there was the natural difference in terms of scale, the intricacy and attention to detail had grown. Emphasis was given on issues that had only fleetingly come to the surface during the 1997 pilot season, or at the very least, had been previously organised on an *ad hoc* basis. There was now, for example, a registration database with clear procedures and regulations on matters such as player quotas and play-off eligibility. There was also a basic, but structured, disciplinary system, and the general rules and regulations had now been formulated and were operational. Harrison himself had previously started this work by putting together the first draft constitution, but the input of time and expertise had moved this piece of work to a new level. As has been shown throughout this book, the onus on clubs meeting centrally set minimum standards had been a constant priority, but whereas this had meant a brief verbal feedback session during the pilot season, the expectation was now that clubs would receive formalised marks and a report, and that there would also be some monitoring – resources permitting – during the season.

The subject of resources was now much more prominent, and to Harrison's slight surprise there was an onus on him to come up with itemised figures in an overall budget of £40,000. As a reasonable portion of this figure was taken up with his own salary and office expenses and considering that a maximum of £750 per club was available, subject to conditions, it was clear that the RLC still operated on a limited budget. An early illustration of this was an edict from Tom O'Donovan that, if possible, a venue for the pre-season clubs meeting should be found at no cost to the RLC.

A source of potential income was sponsorship. This was the responsibility of all in the new management structure and accordingly a number of feelers were sent out. As an increasingly high-profile competition with an ever-expanding national dimension, confidence was high that backing could be found. That a major sponsor, leaving aside the Super League (Europe) input, was not found until League Publications emerged on the eve of the 2001 season was surprising. One saving grace for the limited budget was that the cost of match officials continued to be met elsewhere within the RFL coffers. Again, the difference between the appointment procedure in 1997 and that in 2000 was immense. Responsibility during the pilot season had fallen on Niel Wood and Student Rugby League, and the task had been problematic. In 2000, the RLC appointments operation came under the umbrella of the RFL and the match officials department headed by Greg McCallum. A designated appointments officer was found, and David Lowe began an involvement that has lasted to this day.

In 1997, it wasn't uncommon for games scheduled for Saturdays to occur not only on Sundays, but also to be arranged, re-arranged and to kick off at different times. While recognising summer travel – and congestion – as an obstacle, there was a much firmer feel to the scheduling arrangements three years on. Very occasionally, this bordered on extreme inflexibility. The precedent set at the 1998 final continued to be enforced and though clubs could request alterations to the fixture list at any time, realistically the best chance of getting changes was very early on when the draft fixtures were released. Even then, there was no guarantee of acquiescence from the RLC board of management as Crawley Jets found out when they wanted to move their home game against West London Sharks to enable them to play in the relative luxury of the Broadfields Stadium. Other factors had to be considered and the request was turned down, much to the chagrin of Mark Richardson, the Crawley chairman.

The influence of BARLA was apparent in the new organisational arrangements. Indeed, during the course of the next two years or so, moves towards rules established and enforced by the amateur governing body could be seen, especially in the areas of registrations and disciplinary procedures. Clubs by this time were using the insurance arrangements organised centrally by BARLA with Bartletts and Company of Leeds. However this trend towards uniformity with BARLA had one significant proviso. The RLC, as an associate member of BARLA with a link also to the RFL and Super League (Europe), was free to take the most appropriate rules on offer and to reject others, while obviously retaining those necessary under legal and constitutional stipulations. For example, the rules on registration and player quotas were different and tailored to meet RLC requirements, as were the stipulations of unlimited interchanges and the option of quarterly breaks at the discretion of match officials when the weather was unbearably hot.

The ability to develop rules and procedures within a high degree of flexibility helped to keep the competition relevant to its constituent clubs and their development backgrounds.

Harrison's most immediate task was to arrange for venues for the clubs meeting, the official season launch and the Grand Final. The former was quickly sorted out through the generosity of the Wolverhampton Wizards club with their then home ground in a complex at Castlecroft that also included a hotel. Various venues were considered for the launch and the final with the preference being not only somewhere central, but the same venue doubling for both, thereby providing symmetry to the season. Two possibilities stood out: Welford Road, home of the Leicester Tigers rugby union club, and Coundon Road, home to Coventry RFC, but also, of course, Coventry Bears. The decision to take the launch and final to the latter was not only cost effective, but also built on the formal links the ground had to rugby league and the RLC. It was also a fitting way to applaud and reward the Bears for their patience and professionalism in the way they had handled rejection 12 months previously.

On 1 April, the clubs meeting took place in Wolverhampton. It was a depleted RLC leadership that spoke to the representatives present at Castlecroft. None of the directors could be present, so it was left principally to Harrison and Kain – with input from Dave Berry, Phil Caplan and Trevor Moss – to inform the clubs on various matters. These included RLC input into events surrounding the World Cup (including the possibility of RLC representation at a prestigious event planned for Rugby School) and encouraging further applications to the Awards for All funding scheme.

Indeed, some clubs had already been successful applicants. Cambridge Eagles had received £800 for coaching support, for example, and both Oxford Cavaliers and St Albans Centurions managed to obtain even higher awards - £2,500 and £4,000 respectively. Berry spent some time outlining the 'RLC for Youth 2000' scheme. Caplan reminded clubs of their responsibilities regarding match reporting, while urging everyone to instigate promotional opportunities, and to inform him of successful outcomes. He stressed the necessity of a widespread media portfolio in order to maximise the potential of securing lucrative sponsorship for the competition. John Kain also touched on the longer term and the policy and strategy work that was to be covered by the RLC directors.

It was a lot to take in for both clubs and RLC administrator alike. Julian Harrison had been left with a lot to do prior to the start of the season. His relatively late start to the job (he had less than two months from starting date to the big kick-off on 6 May) hadn't helped, and in many ways a whole pre-season's preparation coupled with the need to familiarise himself with numerous issues, had to be crammed into a matter of weeks. This was not ideal and the pressure told into the season. John Kain's support was invaluable, and between them, things were rapidly put into motion and priorities agreed.

Ten days after the gathering of clubs in Wolverhampton, predominantly the same personnel met up at Coundon Road, Coventry, for a very different occasion. While in Wolverhampton, the topics for discussion were 'nitty-gritty' affairs; in Coventry the purpose was to showcase the competition and the season to come for the benefit of guests and the media. The official launch of the season included the customary flamboyancy of Lionel Hurst, the great wit and humour of Harry Jepson, the official rugby league input from Tom O'Donovan and Peter Deakin, and more reflective words from Keith Fairbrother, the chairman of the Coventry club (both union and league), who had played rugby league professionally.

The usual photo and interview opportunities were taken in an atmosphere of celebration, but also anticipation of hard work to come. There was a business side to the day as well. The 12 regular fixtures for each club contained two weeks of cross-conference games. Though the divisional pairings were known, the exact composition of those two weeks of fixtures was still to be decided. Accordingly, a draw took place conducted by Phil Caplan and Julian Harrison in the solemn and dramatic fashion much loved by radio listeners. Using the balls from the old Regal Trophy draws, club representatives came in turn to delve their hand into the bag and reveal their opposition. Derek Millis of Hemel Hempstead Stags and Mark Richardson of Crawley Jets could be forgiven for thinking that luck had deserted them as they drew each other in a repeat of the previous year's play-off.

With the fixtures now scheduled and the big kick off just weeks away, time was taken up in sorting out the various pre-season details. For Julian Harrison this meant a number of matters, including attempting to sort out a disciplinary matter from a pre-season friendly between Worcestershire Saints and Derby City, and voicing the concerns of the board of management upon learning that both Manchester Knights and Rotherham Giants were changing their home venue following their initial applications. The reality was – and is – that changes of venue happen, but it was slightly more of an issue for Manchester because the move took the club away from the development base in the city, and into neighbouring Oldham, which was not in the same category. A move of two or three miles wasn't going to make much, if any, difference to the team the club would turn out. Rather, the move had symbolic ramifications and the board – while recognising the limitation of its powers to prevent it – felt that the club should know its concerns.

There was also focus on affairs of a much broader nature. With a new infrastructure in place at the RLC, it seemed sensible to examine the relationship between the flagship competition and the London ARL. This was particularly relevant with the direct involvement of John Kain in both. While the RLC powers-that-be were keen to reinforce the sovereignty of their competition, some co-operation could be encouraged. Some RLC clubs could field second teams and where these fell into the catchment area of the London competition, it was appropriate that they play their reserve grade matches in it.

That the London League could produce quality clubs and players was without dispute. The two current RLC examples were showing their capabilities. South London Storm had launched a range of merchandise via their club website, and three Kingston Warriors players, Ian Morrison, Doug Rodman and Glen Osborne, were making an impact at a higher level at the London Broncos. Julian Harrison was keen to monitor the relationship between the two competitions and look for opportunities for mutually supporting developments.

Harrison was quick to discover that the twinning relationships between RLC and Super League operations were not quite as rosy as he had thought. However, there was ample opportunity to rectify this. Meetings involving – among others – Harry Jepson and Gary Hetherington, had occurred in the past and these were to be reconvened to move things forward. There were further matters working in favour of this, one of them being, of course, the financial input from Super League (Europe) that had enabled the RFL to appoint a full-time RLC administrator.

For the RLC to continue making an impact in the game there needed to be clear guidelines on future development and expansion. This was fundamental to the rhetoric espoused when the new management structure was put into place and at the clubs meeting in Wolverhampton. The responsibility for policy and strategy was in the hands of the directors, with practical input from the operational team. For Tom O'Donovan, one of the keys to making a success of this was the direct input of Lionel Hurst and Trevor Moss. Under the new management and operational arrangements, their role had become much less hands-on, and this was seen as an opportunity to direct the energies and talent of both men into a more focused area.

Hurst, as was widely known, had a gift for conceptualising the bigger picture. Human beings will always differ in their vision of the future. As far as the RLC was concerned, the Randolph Hotel meeting in November 1998 had already revealed different perspectives on how the competition was to develop. A resolution was found then that prevented significant damage to the management structure. Eighteen months further on and differences were bubbling beneath the surface once more. Different — and perhaps divergent — views compounded by organisational change with consequent modifications to individual roles, can be a challenging combination of factors.

As far as the RLC was concerned, there were significant differences between a volunteer contingent comprising Lionel Hurst and Trevor Moss, and the RFL perspective headed by development executive Tom O'Donovan. This time, however, there was a third party in the form of the hands-on operational team and at the core, RLC administrator Julian Harrison. Harrison recalls: "I was becoming increasingly confused as to which line I was supposed to be following. Who was in control? As an employee of the RFL, my hands were tied, but I couldn't ignore one of the RLC directors and the current chairman of the competition. At the beginning, this conflict manifested itself in small ways, and these could be overcome, but I began to realise that this was a much bigger animal and one that firstly I didn't have time to address, and secondly, it wasn't my responsibility to do so anyway."

Harrison sought advice from John Kain, his line manager. However it was a matter for the entire board of management to address, and this was recognised by other members, including John Nugent, Phil Caplan and Dave Berry, who voiced to Harrison their support and desire to look at the issue. Nevertheless, it was a headache that Harrison could have done without and it was to prove a particularly difficult one to solve.

Harrison had intended to visit South London on 6 May, the first day of the 2000 season. However, just before the weekend he was contacted by Jamie Walsh the secretary of Birmingham Bulldogs to say that he and chairman Jim Eccles were stepping down from the committee at the Midlands club. As they had been the administrative cornerstone of the club for many years, this concerned Harrison so much that he decided to visit the club's game at Wolverhampton instead and talk to those concerned. Any problems off the field were certainly not mirrored on it as Birmingham, in a new playing kit, produced a devastating display to inflict an 86-4 defeat on the plucky Wizards. The Wolverhampton team were not disgraced and the visit and other current developments demonstrated their considerable progress. Wolverhampton were possibly the only side in the RLC then to have a fanzine in addition to a match-day programme. The club were also embarking on an ambitious scheme in collaboration with a local college to establish a rugby league Academy. Though ultimately this proved unsuccessful, their enthusiasm and vision made a lasting impression, and was covered by the local BBC television station.

There were fluctuating results for the new boys on the opening day. Coventry were convincing winners at Worcestershire Saints and Rotherham saw off Crewe by a much narrower margin, 34-30. However, the two London sides fared less well. Both couldn't have had tougher baptisms. South London Storm gave Oxford Cavaliers a game, but lost 62-4, and match day south of the river was a positive experience to those present, including RLC chairman Lionel Hurst, and Dave Hadfield, from *The Independent*.

Kingston travelled to Crawley and, potentially on a hiding to nothing, got precisely that as the Jets won 86-0. Elsewhere, the most impressive display of the day came from Manchester who defeated champions Chester Wolves 28-20. A depleted Gloucestershire Warriors side were also impressive. In a topsy-turvy game at Leicester, the Warriors eventually triumphed 32-25, and the South West outfit's performance was all the more creditable considering they were severely depleted and even had to rely on coach Andy Haughton making an appearance as substitute.

These games seemed to point to a higher level of intensity and quality in the Conference. There were clearly some talented, determined, yet still developing teams around. Two in that category met in the second week of the season. Despite their close proximity and consequent rivalry, the relationship between Hemel Stags and St Albans was extremely positive. Mutually supporting initiatives and close friendships were the order of the day. The first Hertfordshire derby of the season was as fierce an encounter as any in the competition. Home advantage was decisive as the Stags won 19-10. Two other leading lights met at Marston Ferry Road that day. Oxford beat Crawley, gaining some revenge for their heavy defeat in the previous season's regional final. The Oxford team had panache. A notable student presence in the form of Jon Flatman (Birmingham University) as well as Jeremy Shires, was mixed with local talent, representation from the forces and a French contingent.

Allowing for the natural club rivalries and fierce competitive spirit inherent in any league in the sport, the RLC has always been characterised by a collective goodwill and co-operation. With the World Cup now just months away, there were opportunities aplenty for the RLC family to demonstrate this to the sport in general as well as helping themselves in the process. With John Kain having a specific remit both for the RLC and for developing initiatives for the World Cup, club representatives gathered in Bedford on Sunday 14 May to consider their role. The aim was to introduce rugby league to a new audience and channel people's energies into generating new participation at all levels.

Some RLC clubs had the advantage of larger coaching and administrative numbers available with others such as Gloucestershire and St Albans having World Cup games in their area. Nevertheless, opportunities were open to all, and the showpiece tournament also offered the potential of greater collaboration between different rugby league sectors – involving the students in particular – and of using the National Lottery Awards for All funding scheme. Some clubs had already done this, but the production of a template for grant bids offered the chance for all RLC clubs to obtain financial support for development purposes, providing that they had the human resources to take advantage.

For some clubs, there were occasions when having the necessary number of players to complete fixtures was problematic. This affected Derby City in mid-June and prevented the East Midlands derby fixture at Nottingham from taking place. To their credit, the club quickly got over the embarrassment caused and, despite problems on the eve of their fixture at Chester later in the season, the team did play. Coach Ray Wilson had voiced concerns to Julian Harrison about his team of relatively inexperienced players having to regularly tackle more experienced sides from Chester, Rotherham and Manchester. This may have had an impact on player availability at times, with injuries in mind, and it emphasised the difficulties inherent in a structure where a balance was needed between the desire to avoid mis-matches and to maintain local fixtures.

That the balance wasn't right at present was apparent, particularly in the Southern Division where geography dictated that the two new entrants from the London League had to be included alongside four of the strongest sides in the entire competition. However, there appeared to be little choice. The board of management felt that the competition wasn't yet mature enough to encompass stratification along player capability and talent, rather than geographical, lines. The former would have meant the formation of Premier Leagues and greater travel demands.

The RLC was perhaps split into three club categories. First, there were sound clubs which did not necessarily have strong teams; second, the converse, and last, clubs that were a mixture of the two without being particularly dominant in either. Enforcing a Premier League format too early risked the viability of clubs and posed challenges that could be detrimental if not disastrous. It was in 2000 that this debate over how the RLC should be divided really began to gather momentum. The debate continues into the present, and though there may well be moves afoot for change in 2005, the RLC still retains the same solely geographical format (with natural modifications season-by-season) as it has always had.

Prior to Derby's non-fulfilment of their match at Nottingham, two other clubs had suffered the same problem. Kingston was one of these, providing a brief moment of concern and *déjà vu* when, for various reasons, they did not travel to West London in the third week of the season. The other was Leicester Phoenix the previous week. On the same day that Bedford Swifts travelled to Thetford short of a full team of XIII players and got walloped by South Norfolk Saints, conceding more than 120 points, the Phoenix side failed to fulfil their game at Birmingham.

The RLC board had to take action, but also keep things in perspective. In both cases, the experience turned out to be a one-off for this season, and while it was considered prudent to issue warnings, more draconian action

71

might have precipitated lasting damage to club operations. A new scoring mechanism was initiated should there be repeats in the future. The traditional BARLA score for a non-fulfilled fixture was 18-0. To follow suit could penalise both the non-offending team and others in the respective division should points difference be important at the end of the regular fixtures. The decision was made to award victory in line with the offending team's previous league performances and points differentials with a score of 18-0 being the minimum score that could be applied. For Leicester, this meant an 18-0 defeat, but for Kingston, heavy defeats by Crawley and North London Skolars took a heavy toll. Under the new arrangements, their margin of defeat to West London was 73 points.

Exacerbating matters was the problem of scheduled youth festivals not taking place. While the festival format was fine in principle, problems quickly surfaced if clubs in a region dropped out for whatever reason. To address this, a degree of flexibility had to be given, with clubs with available teams but no opposition from within their division, encouraged to join other festivals or even, in some cases, such as Birmingham and Gloucestershire, arranging fixtures among themselves. This was a rapid departure from Dave Berry's plans, but at least it allowed those clubs who had managed to attract and retain interested youngsters to field them in matches, even if increased travelling was the unavoidable by-product.

Absent players, however, was not the only problem. Despite the appointment of a highly-efficient match officials appointments officer in David Lowe, he could not prevent the regular re-scheduling of allocated officials to matches in other leagues or even the professional game when withdrawals occurred due to injury or re-appointment. This became a regular weekly occurrence, often with Thursday or Friday becoming a time for urgent and pleading phone calls. The problem was often exacerbated by the distances referees had to travel to some fixtures and it was no surprise that East Anglia and the South East region often presented the most difficulty for Lowe when providing replacements. However, the problem was not always confined to those regions. Swift action and the luck of a friendship helped Rotherham Giants, for example, on 13 May. The appointed referee, Andy Stelfox, found himself stuck in traffic in Preston and unable to get to South Yorkshire. Giants coach Darryl Osborne, unable to get hold of Julian Harrison on his mobile because Harrison was in virtually constant discussions with Birmingham, Leicester and board members as it was the same afternoon as the cancelled match in the Midlands, resorted to ringing a refereeing friend himself, and Ian McGregor took up the whistle at late notice.

The rapid development of the Southern Referees Society did help matters. They were called into action on the morning of Saturday 1 July when Kingston's appointed referee found himself on the wrong side of the English Channel. Again, decisive action by Julian Harrison and Shelley Drewett, the Kingston secretary and the society's Allan Steven, ensured that a qualified match official was found in local referee Daniel Valverde. A month previously, Harrison had almost had to pull off one of the appointments of this and many a season when again Kingston's official had to withdraw from his engagement. With David Lowe struggling to find someone able to fill his shoes from within the official list, Harrison – on the spur of the moment – asked a representative from a sports medical company whom he just happened to be meeting at the time. That sales rep was Allan Agar, a legendary figure within rugby league, especially in Featherstone, as a result of their triumph against mighty Hull in the 1983 Challenge Cup Final. Agar, ever the true enthusiast, was willing to pull on his boots and find a whistle. This would have been a memorable coup and fantastic publicity, but unfortunately the story did not have a fairy tale ending. After checking, Agar found that regrettably he couldn't make it, so Lowe's list was the last resort. Happily for the game, Lowe came up trumps and Australian David Sharpe was given the fixture.

Harrison's working week was following a regular pattern, as Fridays in particular seemed to bring with them a regular diet of anxiety over refereeing appointments, club predicaments and possible non-fulfilled fixtures and a myriad of other administrative disputes. The RLC administrator felt he was coming to the end of his tether. Friday 30 June turned out to be a watershed. After yet another last-minute change to a refereeing appointment at St Albans, consequent issues over procedures, coupled with a refusal to sanction a request from St Albans chairman Gary Tetlow to transfer players from North London to St Albans to specifically play against South Norfolk, Harrison and Tetlow (who were actually great friends) had a heated conversation. For the competition's administrator, this nearly was the straw that broke the camel's back as the pressure intensified and he talked to John Kain about resigning.

While the possible absence of a match official on a Saturday afternoon was an obstacle, it wasn't one that was impossible to overcome. This was seemingly becoming less and less true of the RLC management situation. After only one week of the season, Sir Rodney Walker called the board of management and the RLC administrator together to discuss the situation. Regrettably, not all board members were present. Harrison openly admitted to Sir Rodney that he felt stressed by his current predicament, his mental state not helped by the burden of having to get the season up and running with very little lead-in. When reservations were then expressed by Lionel Hurst at the point of holding board meetings when actions hadn't been resolved from previous gatherings, Harrison angrily contacted the RLC chairman and heated words were spoken. It was clear to all that there needed to be both a clearing of the air, and some practical action taken.

Sir Rodney's input was sought and freely given, and board members again met with him in Leicester at Leicester City FC. By this time, new faces had entered the fray.

Neil Tunnicliffe had departed from the RFL, his place as chief executive being taken temporarily by Peter Haworth, a management consultant from Surrey. Sir Rodney Walker had appointed Haworth to assess the situation at Red Hall and make recommendations on efficiency and organisational development. After reviewing affairs at league headquarters, his conclusion had meant the departure of development executive Tom O'Donovan, and the elevation to the positions of executive directors of Greg McCallum, Dave Callaghan and Peter Webster. All three also became the directors of the

73

Rugby League Conference and McCallum, in particular, was to oversee operational matters in his new position as director of rugby.

O'Donovan's exit was a particular shock. He was a long-standing employee and a key individual in the rise of the summer Conference competition. Though he had his critics, it would be fair to remember him for succeeding in pushing through the formation of the Southern Conference League at RFL headquarters. When Trevor Moss called Julian Harrison on Saturday 3 June to break the news (Harrison was at Nottingham attending the Outlaws home fixture with Leicester Phoenix), it was a major surprise, though the prospect of working more closely with Greg McCallum was a significant boost for Harrison's faltering morale.

Ironically, Haworth himself didn't last much longer in his new position. The lure of working for 'a major European company' proved too strong, and he quickly left the game. He was around long enough, however, to attend the afore-mentioned meeting with Sir Rodney Walker and the RLC board of management in Leicester on 13 July. The discussions reinforced the RFL commitment to the RLC as a key development initiative, with the prospect of more resources being available both centrally and via commercial involvement. In return, Haworth indicated the necessity for stringent monitoring, with financial control saying at Red Hall. Sir Rodney was keen to explore the links between the competition and developments in Wales, Scotland and Ireland, but he also advised consolidation over the next year.

Sir Rodney also spoke positively of the developing relationship between the RFL and Super League (Europe) (SLE). The RLC was, of course, a significant part of this, and in this period there were meetings to examine how the arm representing the elite professional clubs could further assist the now-established, but still in some ways, fragile, amateur competition. On 10 June, Super League's Gary Hetherington met RLC president Harry Jepson, Julian Harrison, John Kain, Lionel Hurst and Dave Berry in Chester. A number of important areas of collaboration were discussed. These included assistance in finding sponsorships and SLE providing further support for the RLC. Linking into the marketing and commercial expertise of the likes of Gary Tasker, Ian Robson and Hetherington himself could prove beneficial to the grassroots league. However, it was the brainstorming session around the development of the twinning relationships that really caught the imagination. That the existing arrangements had only had limited success was pretty clear. They were based primarily on a one-to-one club basis. With a geographically and numerically expanded competition, such arrangements were no longer appropriate. Thus, it was proposed that Super League clubs could ally themselves to whole regions, allowing the possibility for enlarged 'Service Area' type structures with the professional clubs having specific spheres of influence all within a general twinning framework. Suggestions were made. Leeds were to link with the Eastern region, Castleford with the East Midlands, Bradford with Scotland and St Helens with Wales. The difficulty, as always, was practical implementation. History shows that the idea largely went no further, at least as far as anything impacting centrally and uniformly on the Rugby League Conference was concerned. Nevertheless it is interesting to note that in 2004, for example, St Helens have made a link with Wales and that Warrington have made inroads into the West Midlands.

The reason for meeting in Chester was also so the officials could see a match, the Wolves versus Nottingham Outlaws, and a practical demonstration of the RLC's progress. This showed the potential for a grassroots competition to grow. The Wolves' home ground at Chester Rugby Union club is one of the best available to RLC sides, with a covered stand, well-appointed clubhouse and beautifully prepared pitch. Everything worked well that day. The Chester club were perfect hosts, and the game represented all that was refreshing about the competition. Though the home side won 46-12, the quality of rugby league from both teams was outstanding. Gary Hetherington was impressed and reflected on this in *Rugby League World*, writing: "Everything about the event – the facilities, the presentation and the quality of play was first class. I suppose that my vision beforehand was coloured by what I had experienced in Sheffield where there was a lot of work done coaching people who were new to the code but exceptionally enthusiastic about it. We put together a kind of pub level touch and pass just to get things going, a sort of crude form of rugby league and I was expecting to see a similar kind of keenness without necessarily a high skill level. There was a lot of quality on display in a hard match played in a tremendous spirit. There is no doubt that many of the players on view can play at a high level and half a dozen or so were very good. What tends to strike you straight away is the total commitment and concern everyone has for the sport."

Always an advocate of development and firm supporter of the competition, Hetherington's words were a terrific boost to all involved in the RLC. They reflected reality. The 2000 season was living up to expectations in quality and excitement. July saw some tremendous rugby league as the tension heightened with the advent of the play-offs, and it started off with a sensation. Hemel Hempstead Stags were the convincing leaders of the Eastern Division and they travelled to the unusual venue of Waterbeach Barracks just north of Cambridge, to take on an Eagles side that promised much but rarely delivered.

What followed was probably the performance and the surprise of the season. Cambridge produced 80 minutes of tenacious, virtually flawless rugby and the Stags had no answer, relying on glimpses of quality from Chris Caws and Phil Aiken, but not coping with the collective might of Cambridge. For stalwart Barry Butterfield it was a proud moment – his face a picture of absolute delight as he reflected on what his side had produced. Hemel quickly recovered their composure and poor Bedford were the recipients of a backlash of immense proportions the following week, with the Stags triumphant by 72 points to a solitary field goal.

In the Northern Division, Manchester Knights and Rotherham Giants were having a great fight for top spot. The Knights' 25-12 triumph on 22 July was the key result and, with Chester and Nottingham not far behind, it was compelling viewing. Even at the wrong end of the table, there was pride at stake. Derby's recovery from the season's low in not fulfilling their fixture at Nottingham illustrated their character. Having failed to register a point in defeats against the two top sides, they rediscovered scoring in defeat at Birmingham and then, in a superb battle against Crewe, won 26-16.

North London Skolars were the undisputed entertainers of the regular season. They averaged 45 points a game, and to come out on top of a division that included Crawley Jets, West London Sharks and Oxford Cavaliers was no mean feat. They were well fancied going into the play-off series, coming second only to Manchester in the composite table. In their division, the fight for second place went down to virtually the last kick of the final league game. Symbolically and fittingly, it was Crawley's Steve O'Reilly who managed a touchline conversion to steal a victory – and second place - from the despairing West London Sharks, who only a minute previously were in the play-offs courtesy of an 18-18 score - the drama of sport.

The Western Division was less dramatic. Despite glimpses of quality from all sides, it was always going to be Birmingham and Coventry qualifying for the end-of-season knockout phase. The only question was in which order they would finish. By a quirk of the fixture list, the final regular season game was Coventry versus Birmingham at Coundon Road.

In a fantastic advertisement for Midlands rugby league, the Bears came out on top, but the winning margin was not enough for them to pip the Bulldogs to top spot. Birmingham had emerged from the disappointment of previous seasons and had assembled an impressive line-up with stalwarts combining with new talent and a pack of ferociously large proportions featuring the renowned Sigley brothers. They had also recruited well from Moseley rugby union club. Considering their traumatic start to the season off the field, their achievement was all the more laudable.

One fact showed the progress that had been made and the success of the league as a whole: every side managed at least one win. In two of the four divisions, the gap between the first and second teams was two points, and in the Western Division the title was decided on points difference. Hemel Hempstead Stags had the biggest winning margin over the team in second place, four points ahead of their rivals from South Norfolk.

The final league tables after the regular season were as follows:

	Eastern Division	Pl	W	D	L	F	A	Diff	Pts
1	Hemel Hempstead Stags	12	10	0	2	521	172	349	20
2	South Norfolk Saints	12	8	0	4	520	284	236	16
3	St Albans Centurions	12	7	0	5	366	221	145	14
4	Ipswich Rhinos	12	5	0	7	320	375	-55	10
5	Cambridge Eagles	12	4	0	8	203	450	-247	8
6	Bedford Swifts	12	1	0	11	146	748	-602	2

	Northern Division	Pl	W	D	L	F	A	Diff	Pts
1	Manchester Knights	12	11	0	1	442	176	266	22
2	Rotherham Giants	12	10	0	2	452	187	265	20
3	Chester Wolves	12	9	0	3	405	183	222	18
4	Nottingham Outlaws	12	6	0	6	327	261	66	12
5	Derby City	12	2	0	10	90	386	-296	4
6	Crewe Wolves	12	1	0	11	180	486	-306	2

	Southern Division	Pl	W	D	L	F	A	Diff	Pts
1	North London Skolars	12	10	0	2	552	195	357	20
2	Crawley Jets	12	9	0	3	525	186	339	18
3	West London Sharks	12	8	0	4	531	127	404	16
4	Oxford Cavaliers	12	8	0	4	522	172	350	16
5	Kingston Warriors	12	1	0	11	93	725	-632	2
6	South London Storm	12	1	0	11	106	750	-644	2

	Western Division	Pl	W	D	L	F	A	Diff	Pts
1	Birmingham Bulldogs	12	10	0	2	486	157	329	20
2	Coventry Bears	12	10	0	2	496	178	318	20
3	Gloucestershire Warriors	12	6	0	6	457	201	256	12
4	Leicester Phoenix	12	4	0	8	323	342	-19	8
5	Worcestershire Saints	12	2	0	10	202	439	-237	4
6	Wolverhampton Wizards	12	1	0	11	70	934	-864	2

The RLC had always been concerned with introducing new blood and talent to the sport. Indeed, that was its primary *raison d'être*. So, not content with fresh local converts from rugby union and other sports, the RLC had an international dimension. Certain clubs, principally in the London area, had a long history of antipodean players, and Oxford had added a Gallic flavour to their playing roster. However, Cambridge Eagles had found the most exotic and surprising overseas player. The Eagles had attracted a player from Japan, Masohiro Komori. He represented the RLC in an end-of-season fixture against a Welsh amateur side, and was then selected for his country in the Emerging Nations World Cup. Linguistically, this might have posed one or two problems for an average mortal, but not for Barry Butterfield. Between coach and player, they discovered a common language. Team talks therefore occurred twice at the Eagles: a collective effort in Butterfield's blunt – and occasionally colourful – Yorkshire dialect, and a one-on-one session in a more sedate and flowing Spanish.

Broadening its horizons in club and player terms was an RLC priority, with potential areas for expansion and development identified. The most obvious was the North East. With a new rugby league development officer in Lisa Jagger and continuing support of her predecessor Mick Hogan, the North East summer competition was active and flourishing. Running in parallel to the Rugby League Conference, it was surely only a matter of developing finance and administrative capabilities at both club and central operational level to bring about a marriage in the future. Harrison was also talking to Jagger's equivalent north of the border, Mark Senter, about the possibility of one-off matches between Scottish and English teams.

At the end of June he spoke to Jeremy Shires. He was a leading figure in Oxford rugby league, both town and gown, but he was well known in Leeds University circles and enthusiastically outlined the feasibility of a Leeds University graduates side. While this took time to come to fruition, the evolution of the Leeds Akademiks in the RLC is one of the most significant developments of recent years, bringing together the student and amateur games in a northern model of the London Skolars concept.

Despite many problems during the three months of the regular season, overall the RLC had moved forward apace, with the possibility of future growth. While discipline at matches had become much more of an issue in

2000 with some unsavoury incidents that the competition could have done without, a system was now in place and working that could deal with disciplinary cases relatively efficiently. This was progress, as was the development of the representative team system.

The rise of the competition had registered with the BARLA selectors looking to implement as wide a selection process as possible for the Great Britain and Ireland side that would compete in the forthcoming Emerging Nations World Cup. Accordingly, a gap week had been introduced prior to the Grand Final for the RLC to focus solely on representative team training to identify possible candidates to take the step up onto the international stage. Realistically, it was highly unlikely that anyone from the RLC would make the squad, though another developing arm of the game, the armed services, were ultimately to be represented in the final BARLA squad. However, that it was now possible for a player from Worcester or Derby, Crewe or Gloucester, Ipswich or Crawley to gain selection for Great Britain at amateur level was a development of immense symbolic proportions.

Following nominations for both the RLC squad and coaching and management team, the RLC representative operation now took shape. The head coach was Dave Doran, with assistance from Marcus Tobin (North London Skolars) and Shane Crellin (Gloucestershire Warriors). The manager was Bedford Swifts' Tracey Greenwood. A further support team also included Andy Lindley (Oxford Cavaliers) and a whole host of Gloucestershire Warriors' backroom staff: Stephen Rigby, Ruth Sigley and Nigel Wachs. Hemel's Pennine Way ground was used for training, and the Stags – in particular, Derek Millis – became involved. The support from such a variety of clubs was encouraging and the response from the players was equally positive and impressive. A productive working relationship developed between Doran, Greenwood and RLC administrator, Julian Harrison. This harmony and determination arguably permeated down through to other staff and players alike.

Back to the competition for the Harry Jepson Trophy, and the play-offs on 29 July had an astonishing outcome. All four away sides won with the consequence that all four divisional winners went out. The encouraging thing for the competition was that, in all cases, with the possible exception of South Norfolk at North London, an away victory was not that much of a surprise. Coventry Bears were worthy winners at Manchester, and Crawley carried on their remarkable unbeaten run of victories in all-or-nothing contests by triumphing at Hemel Hempstead. The Birmingham versus Rotherham fixture was a classic with the Giants' prop forward, Gary Archer particularly impressive as the South Yorkshiremen won 29-27.

Two points was also the margin of victory at White Hart Lane, though a much more dramatic transformation occurred in this game. At half-time, the Skolars were leading 20-8 and looked certain to reach the regional final. There may have been some complacency in the second half, but that would diminish the response from the South Norfolk Saints who, realising that it was time to go for broke, produced an outstanding recovery. Their winger Ian Reynolds grabbed a hat-trick of tries. Tony Neutze also achieved this for the Skolars, but it wasn't enough, and the Saints won 34-32.

With the regional finals coming at the end of it, the week beginning Monday 31 July was a busy one. For one morning at least, match preparations were put aside as Julian Harrison and Phil Caplan attended a SLE meeting in Leeds on Tuesday 1 August to state the case for ongoing support for the RLC. Ever since the day at Chester nearly two months previously, there had been rumours of possible developments in SLE's support for the RLC, with supposed confirmations of director and operational positions in the RLC being taken by Super League personnel. It was time to find out just where the land lay. The meeting certainly clarified the SLE standpoint. Support in financial and practical terms would continue, though the matter of direct personal input into formal positions was not considered to be necessary at present. Rather, it would be the role of the RLC management to seek support whenever needed, with Gary Tasker identified as a particular source of assistance.

While this method of involvement was not discouraging and the assurances of support greatly encouraging, it was a disappointed and a bemused duo that left the Super League offices after the meeting, as Julian Harrison explains: "It was clear when we went in to meet the assembled gathering that with one notable exception in Gary Hetherington, familiarity with the competition and what it had achieved was remarkably low. I had forwarded a background document to Super League beforehand which I thought clearly stated our position. I then found myself having to repeat much of what was in it, which considering the limited amount of time we had to state our case, was frustrating and in a sense a 'waste of time'. Of course, it dawned on Phil Caplan and me that some had simply not read it. The questions asked demonstrated a real lack of knowledge, and while it was good to establish actual dialogue and develop our relationship, much of the anticipation at exploring possibilities that we had begun to raise at Chester, quickly evaporated."

Any disappointment was quickly put to one side as preparation work for two regional finals took precedence. The plan had been to stage these games as pre-match curtain-raisers at Super League fixtures that coming weekend. However, there were a number of problems, some of which were insurmountable. Firstly, RFL Academy games were the official introduction to the main fare, and despite representation to the RFL to move them to accommodate the RLC fixtures, this request was not granted. Secondly, only one of the targeted venues was accommodating. The possibility of Wakefield Trinity Wildcats didn't materialise, and St Helens did not respond to Julian Harrison's attempts to discuss the matter. That left Warrington Wolves, and here there was good news. Peter Deakin, ever the RLC supporter and genuine devotee of rugby league expansion, offered the chance to play the Rotherham versus Coventry game at Wilderspool – the only option being (as a result of the Academy game situation) to stage it after the Super League clash between the home side and Salford City Reds. His offer was accepted.

However, that left the RLC having to enforce the contingency plan for the Crawley versus South Norfolk fixture in the event of Super League grounds being unavailable. That game was to take place at the home venue of the club finishing higher in the composite table, which meant Crawley.

The games were spread over two days, the Saturday fixture being the Southern/Eastern Final. On a gloriously hot day in Sussex, the Jets marched into the grand final though they were pushed all the way by a determined South Norfolk side resplendent in their change shirts - the yellow Bradford kit worn by the Bulls at the 1997 Challenge Cup Final. The Saints took the lead. And though it was quickly overturned by the home side and never regained, Crawley could never comfortably shake off their opponents and it was a relieved and delighted Jets management and team that celebrated at the final whistle. The local paper triumphantly whooped it all up, as reporter Andy Wilson recounted on the *Play the Ball* website: "I happened to be in Brighton on Monday, and Crawley's victory over South Norfolk received full-page coverage in the *Evening Argus*, which claimed that Sussex could now boast 'Britain's best amateur rugby league team'. Wonder what the chaps at Skirlaugh and West Hull would make of that?"

The Northern/Western Final was a much closer affair. Playing on the hallowed Wilderspool turf seemed to inspire both teams to produce accomplished performances, without the flamboyancy that had characterised the game the previous day. It was rugby league in its rawest sense, arguably a throw-back to yesteryear and, at the end of the day, it proved heartbreaking for Coventry, desperate to book a final place on their home pitch at Coundon Road. Rotherham's powerful front six provided the backbone of a narrow victory and set up another clash of styles for the Final against Crawley.

RLC Grand Finals are not solely a contest for the Harry Jepson Trophy – though that, of course, is the main attraction. Rather, they also focus on celebrating the competition as a whole and rewarding the achievements of clubs and individuals throughout the season. At Coundon Road on Saturday 19 August, a large crowd of supporters and guests also included the winners of the *Rugby Leaguer* awards chosen by Ray French, who had reported on the competition all summer. The Club of the Year was a popular choice, particularly among the locals, as Coventry Bears came out on top. Personality of the Year was Derek Millis of the Hemel Hempstead Stags, just recognition of his abilities as an organiser and administrator. The playing awards went to young Manchester Knights winger Ryan Knight (Young Player of the Year) and seasoned campaigner from finalists Crawley Jets, Steve O'Reilly. Knight had had a fantastic season, attracting the attention of Salford City Reds where he went post-season to see how he would adapt to playing at a higher level. Ironically, O'Reilly wasn't in the RLC 2000 Dream Team. The line-up was based on man-of-the-match nominations during the season, and comprised:
Graham Batty (Rotherham Giants), Ryan Knight (Manchester Knights), Phil Aiken (Hemel Hempstead Stags), Damian Greene (North London Skolars), Victor Owagboe (North London Skolars), James Cathcart (Coventry Bears), Caro Wild (Oxford Cavaliers), Jack Howieson (Hemel Hempstead Stags), Jake Holmes (Birmingham Bulldogs), Gary Archer (Rotherham Giants), Glyn Thomas (Ipswich Rhinos), Tony Neutze (North London Skolars), Raoul Simons (St Albans Centurions).

Following a pre-match under-13 fixture between Coventry Bears and Nottingham Outlaws, the teams for the Grand Final lined up as follows:

Crawley Jets: Alex Meredith, Mark Elliott, Richard Billings, Mark Henderson, Ed Dowling, Ian Kilgannon, Steve O'Reilly (c), Paul Sparkes, Andy Shaw, Simon Matterface, Kieran Fitzgerald, Tony Platt, Dave Wattam.
Subs: Nick Dinsdale, Rob Dowling, Justin Kemp-Gee, Steve Holmes.
Rotherham Giants: Dean Jackson, Chris Jasinski, Nicky Colley, Graham Batty, Mark Walker, Craig Weston, Sam Moore, Michael Chadwick (c), Craig Woolley, Gary Archer, Richard Skidmore, Steve Duckenfield, Darryl Jackson.
Subs: Chris Walls, Nigel Short, Dan Lynch, Paul Scott.

An atmosphere of feverish excitement abounded and dignitaries there to witness the event included the customary RLC brethren and representatives from various rugby league governing bodies and organisations including RFL technical director David Waite. The Sky Television cameras were present to film a feature for their weekly magazine programme. Much of the pre-match discussion focused on whether the larger, more rugby league-experienced men from Rotherham could nullify and gain dominance over the more agile, but smaller, former champions from Sussex.

When Crawley raced into an early 18-0 lead, the answer seemed apparent. O'Reilly began the scoring, charging down a Rotherham clearance and racing half the length of the pitch to gather the ball and score. Loose-forward Dave Wattam then scored twice in three minutes to extend the lead. A quick riposte was needed from the shell-shocked Yorkshiremen and it came in spectacular fashion. Tries from Craig Weston and winger Chris Jasinski put Rotherham back in the game, and discredited the preconceived notion that the Giants were simply big and forward-orientated. The Jets were not to be denied, however, and their more expansive and controlled play reaped the ultimate reward, winning 38-22. Kieran Fitzgerald went over twice and further scores from Tony Platt and Alex Meredith finally laid the Giants to rest, though they scored the game's final try through outstanding centre Graham Batty. The game had everything – including a streaker – and was well officiated by Blackpool-based referee Richard Morris.

David Waite was visibly impressed, pointing in particular to the shoulder-first tackling technique of both sides. As Harry Jepson presented the trophy to victorious Jets' captain Steve O'Reilly, his counterpart Mick Chadwick also demonstrated the true sportsmanship that served the RLC so well. His dignity in defeat was one of the defining moments of the season.

The remainder of the summer and into autumn saw the issue of RLC expansion firmly on the agenda. With the conclusion of both the mainstream Conference and that in the North East, it was appropriate to discuss whether there could be a natural incorporation of the latter into the former. The first step was for Julian Harrison and John Kain to sit down with Lisa Jagger and Mick Hogan. Before August was out, this meeting had taken place and the RLC contingent were updated on the capabilities of the North East clubs as well as being left in no doubt that the running of any operation in the North East had now outgrown the time Mick Hogan could devote to it. While nothing could be decided immediately – logistical factors, mainly financial ones, needed to be addressed first – a further meeting with club representatives was the next step. That took place a month later. Only Julian Harrison was there from the RLC, but representatives from Teesside Steelers, Sunderland City, Bridlington Bulls, Wetherby and Durham joined Jagger (also representing

Newcastle) and Hogan to examine further the possibility of RLC admission. Harrison realised that the clubs would be an asset to the RLC. It was a whole region that could be embraced as opposed to a single town or city, and that was very much what the RLC management – aware of the need to avoid outpost clubs – wanted. In addition, the advantage of the presence of a dedicated development officer was now apparent. A number of the clubs had junior sections, some – Sunderland City being a good example – were thriving. What was really needed was assimilation into a national framework that could boost club operations, enable structured competitive fixtures to attract new players and provide a much-needed profile enhancement. All the factors that had combined to create and sustain a successful Rugby League Conference were present.

Although unable to make any promises, Harrison was tremendously excited as he drove back to the Midlands. Geographical expansion was there to be grabbed. The prospect of a 'club in every sizeable town or city' was that bit nearer.

Harrison's delight was fuelled by interest from elsewhere. He received enquiries about possible clubs in Bournemouth, Luton, Blackpool and Guildford and had also discussed with London ARL secretary, Louis Turner how to achieve better liaison between the two competitions. At the northern extreme, Scotland Rugby League were looking at the feasibility of a competition that would eventually become the Four Nations tournament. While at amateur level, Wales, Scotland and Ireland were already playing fixtures against each other, the matter of England was less clear cut. The obvious solution was for the English team to be the RLC representative side – at least initially. The implementation of this would take time and detailed work, involving liaison with BARLA and the RFL, but for now the principle was accepted. The other suggestion from the Scots was much easier to conceive and implement – a challenge fixture between the Scottish Champions and the winners of the Harry Jepson Trophy.

Not to be outdone, the Welsh too entered the fray, through the Welsh development officer, Stuart Singleton, with a proposal for the inclusion of a Welsh club side in the Rugby League Conference.

It was likely at this stage that the Welsh side would be Cardiff Demons. Coincidentally, observers got an inkling of what sort of side could emanate from the principality very early in the post-season period, when a Welsh Amateur XIII, containing a significant number of Cardiff players, took on the RLC representative side on Sunday 10 September at Gloucestershire Warriors' Chosen Hill ground. This was the first test of the new RLC representative structure. The squad assembled the previous day to go into camp in preparation for the match. The management and coaching staff had the task of organising a meaningful weekend's rugby league activity with a strong purpose. Not only was there the matter of beating the Welsh, but a train-on squad of 30 players was to be picked at the end of the weekend to meet regularly for training over the winter to prepare for some high profile fixtures in 2001. An encouraging crowd gathered on the Sunday afternoon to see the fruits of Dave Doran's labours the previous day. Both sides featured some outstanding individuals and an effective Anglo-Welsh clash – notwithstanding the appearance in the former ranks of a Kiwi, a Japanese and indeed, a Welshman – inevitably fostered a high degree of determination and rivalry. The teams were as follows:

RLC: Matt Cannon (Hemel Hempstead Stags), Andy Brown (Gloucestershire Warriors), Phil Aiken (Hemel Hempstead Stags), Richard Billings (Crawley Jets), Masohiro Komori (Cambridge Eagles), Martyn Hilton (Nottingham Outlaws), Chris Caws (Hemel Hempstead Stags), Richard Tyrell (Chester Wolves), Richard Smith (Hemel Hempstead Stags), Darryl Jackson (Rotherham Giants), Rob North (Rotherham Giants), Ronnie Haines (Gloucestershire Warriors), John Mulraney (Gloucestershire Warriors).

Subs: Rob Johnson (Crewe Wolves), Mick Scargill (Oxford Cavaliers), Paul Fairhurst (Oxford Cavaliers), Dave Wattam (Crawley Jets), Richard Whitehouse (Worcestershire Saints), Damon Mari-Metuarii (Hemel Hempstead Stags), Gareth Martin (Chester Wolves).

Wales: Brendan Bowen, Wayne Williams, Paul Tollson, John Brackbury, Martin Thomas, Pete Gooding, Nigel Edmunds, Paul Davey, Mark Bush, Jeremy Moody, Mark Dando, Neil Lewis, Scott Heirene.

Subs: Anthony Hughes, Alex Buchanan, Anthony Loxton, Tom Midgeley.

In the event, the strength of the RLC side and their extra day's training was too much for the Welsh. It was the 69th minute before the visitors got on the scoreboard. By then, the RLC side already had seven tries. The final score was 40-8. A delighted coach Doran put together his train-on squad and also added Rotherham Giants' Rob North as a nomination for the BARLA Great Britain and Ireland under-23 squad. With a specific RLC selection day for the Emerging Nations World Cup also having taken place, these were exciting times for representative football in the Conference. Excitement was exacerbated by the news that as Crawley had declined to take up their allocated place as grand final winners in the 2000-2001 Challenge Cup competition, there was a place for the RLC going spare.

The proposal that the representative side replaced Crawley in the draw was acceptable to the organising authorities, and one high profile game in Dave Doran's plans was guaranteed.

It was now four years since the real roots of the competition had been sown. During the course of that period, the name of Lionel Hurst had become largely synonymous with the Rugby League Conference. Hurst's personality, in particular his speeches and persuasive rhetoric in debate, had helped the RLC achieve a high profile and ensured that the voices of many grassroots people in development areas had now been heard and would continue to be so. Those abilities had not been lost on those in authority in the game at elite level.

This included London Broncos, the south's sole Super League outfit. The club approached Hurst to become their new chief executive. He thought about the opportunity and eventually decided that it was too good to refuse. Although it meant relinquishing most of his current input into the RLC, he was not lost to the competition altogether. Hurst retained his position on the management board and set about the task not only of strengthening the Broncos operation itself, but in improving the relationship between the professional rugby league club and its extensive catchment area in the South of England. Though it is outside the remit of this book to go into Hurst's achievements at the Broncos in any significant detail, his time at the club included a number of initiatives that directly impacted on the RLC. These will be considered later.

While Hurst's appointment at the Broncos was a further illustration of the impact of the RLC, the inclusion of the administrator and others with RLC experience on the new RFL development strategy board was another. Set up to provide a collective focus on development, this board was a product of the new regime at Red Hall under director of rugby - and RLC director - Greg McCallum. His style of management was refreshingly open and co-operative, formal and businesslike while retaining a friendly demeanour. This was a breath of fresh air for Julian Harrison, who recalls: "Greg was a tremendous supporter of the competition, but also of the individual. He was extremely busy, yet always found time to get back to me if I needed him. I remember him phoning me on my mobile late in the evening to let me know of things impacting on the RLC at a meeting he had just attended. He even called me from Heathrow Airport en-route to a wedding when he realised I was awaiting some important information. He was definitely the kind of guy you really wanted to work for and, under his stewardship, the RLC, I believe, was not only safe, but going forward as a competition."

Though memories of the 2000 season were still relatively fresh, it was time to look ahead and begin the task of implementing those vital and necessary amendments to a whole host of administrative and organisational procedures affecting registrations, the representative system, match official appointments, sponsorship and financial affairs. In the past the RLC had not always focused on procedural arrangements for friendly fixtures, for example. Now, especially with the possibility of a winter programme of matches in the Midlands, it became vital to have these in place. Furthermore, as a way of centrally incorporating and utilising the skills, knowledge and enthusiasm of club personnel, the formation of operational task groups (some more advisory, others with more direct involvement) was an early priority. These built on the rationale and early workings of the old development forum and coaching association. Despite being open and receptive to ideas and comments from the grassroots, the RLC had never been a 'democratic' entity with clubs having the ability to vote and be directly represented at league management level. This was deliberate and is still the case today. However, as a means of furthering inclusion, the involvement of volunteers to look at and guide particular areas, ranging from minimum standards to general development, was a positive step forward, even though for practical reasons, real achievements were limited.

There was an additional reason for getting on with things. The World Cup was taking place in the UK and France in October and November, and it was all hands on deck for rugby league employees. John Kain was heavily involved in some development initiatives based around particular game locations, and Julian Harrison was to be team liaison officer for the qualifying group that included Wales. As a consequence, both men's time for RLC matters during the month of the tournament was limited. There was one joint initiative that involved the RLC. On 25 October, a symbolic event took place at Rugby School as part of the lead-in to the competition. A number of mini-games were played involving a range of sides, including the RLC's Coventry Bears, and these were followed by a celebratory dinner to commemorate the first appearance of rugby league on the famous Close at the School, where mythically the game of rugby football was started. Of course, with Gloucestershire Warriors home ground at Chosen Hill also used as the training base for the New Zealand squad during the group stage and with Kingsholm, home of Gloucester Rugby Union club, the venue for the Kiwi's opening game against Lebanon, rugby league in Gloucestershire was big news. The New Zealand coach Frank Endacott freely gave his time during his team's stay in the South West to give coaching advice to both John Evans of South Norfolk Saints and Gloucestershire's Shane Crellin, but there was a feeling that consultation with the local rugby league club might have yielded even further dividends.

One of Harrison's key tasks before the World Cup got under way was to get application forms for the 2001 season distributed, including clubs in the North East and London areas. All the expected replies were received – some with very impressive 'curricula vitae' – though some forms required either chasing up or greater elaboration. Interest in the competition was still widespread, with Cliff Spracklen requesting details and a form on behalf of the Bramley club only recently departed from the professional game and looking for potential comeback avenues.

In the meantime, the new RLC representative management and coaching team were preparing themselves for the Challenge Cup. On 14 November, Julian Harrison and Shane Crellin travelled to Manchester for the prestigious first round draw. Work was well underway to find a venue should the team be drawn at home. As it happened, the issue was academic as the RLC were drawn to play at Eccles, one of amateur rugby league's most renowned clubs and the scene of Great Britain international Adrian Morley's early time in the sport. While there was disappointment at the difficulty such quality opposition would present, it was an opportunity to showcase the RLC's elite talent in heartland territory. The team did not disappoint in the match on 2 December. With a little more composure, and better product from the boot of the usually reliable Chris Caws of Hemel Hempstead Stags, the RLC side would have secured a sensational victory. A late Eccles try cemented a 26-16 win, but for a time in the second half, hopes were high that progress in the competition could be made.

2000 RLC Grand Final Awards: Manchester Knights' Ryan Knight
(Young Player of the year), Coventry Bears' Ron Banks (Club of the Year)
and Hemel Hempstead Stags' Derek Millis (Personality of the Year)

2000 RLC Grand Final:
Crawley Jets' Steve O'Reilly receives the Harry Jepson Trophy from Harry Jepson

8. 2001: The North East

During the early years of the RLC the competition had remained largely independent while drawing upon the resources and influence of a wide range of organisations and areas of the game. This was the strength of the new venture and a fundamental reason for its success. The first years of the new millennium were also characterised by tremendous advances in the development of the game in general. There was a similar summer Conference in Scotland and the continuation of amateur international fixtures. The new service area concept, a key part of the game's development strategy, opened up rugby league to potentially vast new markets, particularly in previously virgin territories. It was clear to Greg McCallum and development staff in such areas that the RLC needed to join wider initiatives that would be mutually beneficial to the game and specific RLC clubs. Thus, management and operational groups were founded in the London and the South areas. Julian Harrison represented the RLC in both.

This meant he could ensure that support was gained for RLC youth development. This was easier said than done, though for 2001 agreement was reached to continue the mandatory ruling on under-13 participation, but to make under-15 and under-16 sides optional.

The legacy of past separatism was not entirely conducive to easy assimilation. The RLC had gone it alone for some years. To incorporate and be incorporated was not going to happen overnight. Greater contact with the London ARL and the student game was more straightforward, as they both focused on the open-age game, though the latter offered scope for development from under-16 age upwards. But for Harrison, there was a need to manage potential problems caused by a developing relationship between the still ongoing RLC youth strategy, and general rugby league development in the South and North East regions, and in Wales.

This proved to be a bit of a challenge and Harrison was quite angry on more than one occasion at the apparent lack of understanding of the RLC's wider position – and his own one of intermediary – from colleagues who were development officers for specific areas.

One of the remedies for greater cohesion was to appoint Caro Wild to the new RLC strategy board, the latest body charged with the operation of the RLC competition. He was joined by fellow development manager Andy Harland, and Ian Cooper, the BARLA chief executive as new additions to the team that also comprised Harrison, Caplan, McCallum and Hurst. Cooper's involvement was, according to Julian Harrison, pivotal in moving things forward as both his ties with the amateur governing body, as well as his extensive knowledge and capabilities as an administrator, made him an outstanding acquisition for the RLC. McCallum, of course, provided the operational link with an RLC directorship that also approved another significant addition to the competition's backroom. David Lowe had achieved an enormous amount as administrator of the BARLA National Conference League and already had experience of the RLC as its match officials appointments officer. When Harrison broached the subject of the need for administrative support for the summer Conference with the directors, he knew the man he wanted for this role. Lowe, likewise, needed little deliberation when asked if he would be interested in helping out on an additional and more formalised basis. His ability as a meticulous organiser was virtually second to none and he took over key roles and responsibilities for matters such as registrations, discipline and insurance, as well as continuing to appoint referees throughout the summer months.

Not that such organisational developments were a straightforward process. Persuading the RLC directors of the advantages of such advances at management and operational level was one step. McCallum considered that wider support was needed, and consequently Harrison – following on from the previous Super League meeting in August – now faced a similarly daunting (and larger) audience when addressing a full meeting of the Rugby League Council on 26 January 2001. Though the gathered assembly included people well versed in the RLC story and purpose (such as Bev Risman and Ralph Rimmer, for example, in addition to RFL personnel), Harrison probably did as much educating as he did preaching on that January afternoon.

The main event of the winter period in any RLC close season is, of course, the announcement of the results of the application process for the forthcoming summer. Speculation was rife that a North East clubs division was to be added, but would that happen and would there be other additions? A club in Wales had also been mooted and the RFL were keen – as they had previously been with Hemel Hempstead Stags – to find a more appropriate playing vehicle for the Cardiff Demons side. Drawing on the rugby talent of South Wales in general, but particularly the student rugby league set up in Cardiff would virtually guarantee a competitive outfit. There would be no shortage of capable administrators either, and the support of the Wales Rugby League and the Welsh development officer was also a massive advantage. Nevertheless, the incorporation of an extra club in addition to the possibility of the North East clubs entering the competition en masse caused a potential problem with fixture scheduling. Julian Harrison had again enlisted the Paul Johnstone's assistance, and the latter spent many hours going over various permutations. The next meeting of the RLC leadership on 14 December discussed a variety of issues, including the future of Cardiff Demons. With Welsh development officer Stuart Singleton waiting anxiously outside, a decision was reached. Cardiff were admitted, though how they were to be incorporated was still to be decided. A North East division of five clubs, comprising Teesside Steelers, Newcastle, Bridlington Bulls, Sunderland City and Gateshead Panthers, was also to be included, thereby increasing the number of RLC clubs from 24 to 30.

While the clubs were all informed individually of the decision, the usual press embargo came into force and it was not until 8 February that the announcement of the 2001 season line-up was made public. Journalists, including the Sky Television cameras, assembled at Red Hall to hear McCallum, Harrison and Caplan outline the composition of the league and bring the audience up to date with the off-field winter developments. With the significant expansion northwards and westwards, both Stuart Singleton and

Lisa Jagger were present to summarise the implications for the game in their respective regions.

The new 30-team competition comprised six divisions of five clubs each, with each club committed to playing two opponents from two different divisions in cross-conference fixtures. The line up was:

North East: Bridlington Bulls, Gateshead Panthers, Newcastle, Sunderland City, Teesside Steelers.

North: Crewe Wolves, Chester Wolves, Derby City, Manchester Knights, Rotherham Giants.

Midlands: Birmingham Bulldogs, Coventry Bears, Leicester Phoenix, Nottingham Outlaws, Wolverhampton Wizards.

East: Bedford Swifts, Cambridge Eagles, Ipswich Rhinos, South Norfolk Saints, St Albans Centurions.

South: Crawley Jets, Kingston Warriors, North London Skolars, South London Storm, West London Sharks.

Central South: Cardiff Demons, Gloucestershire Warriors, Hemel Hempstead Stags, Oxford Cavaliers, Worcestershire Saints.

However, on the eve of the press conference, news reached Harrison that was not included in the official announcement. Mick Hogan had told him, apologetically, that Gateshead Panthers were withdrawing their application. Concern over the viability of the operation and any consequential discrediting both of the RLC and of North East rugby league was behind the decision. Pre-season nerves and doubts had manifested themselves previously within new clubs – Reading Raiders being the earliest example from 1997 – and while understandable, in some cases they could be alleviated and prove to be unfounded. However, when such an assessment came from a man with considerable experience both of the North East and grassroots rugby league, it was clear that the assessment was realistic. On the plus side, Gateshead's withdrawal allowed the RLC three months to find a replacement – though the need for that club preferably to be in the North East was obvious – and the remnants of the Panthers set-up switched their allegiance and involvement to Newcastle, which was a relief to Harrison who had had some concerns about the strength of the Tyneside club.

Search for a replacement meant help from Lisa Jagger. She came up with a number of options, with a preference for Durham. Durham Tigers had been a stalwart member of the North East set-up and a representative from the club had attended the clubs meeting with the RLC the previous year. Nevertheless, an application had not materialised and the club had ceased to function as a competitive unit. A Durham club would therefore have to be formed afresh, and through the energy of North East pioneer Phil Selby, a local schoolteacher, this happened, with a late emergency application to join the RLC for 2001. The club was Durham Phoenix.

Throughout the long winter and spring months, activity was not just off the pitch. An Eastern Counties Cup competition was organised, principally by Cambridge Eagles' Barry Butterfield, and reached its conclusion at Bedford at the start of April. As far as the representative team was concerned, it really was all systems go. The side had a new name, the RLC Lionhearts, new kit, a new training system (including use of fitness testing in Llandudno with

Student Rugby League's Craig Twist) and a new competition in which to participate: the Scottish Courage Cup. It was also the focus of some new ideas, many of them from the visionary Lionel Hurst. Among other things, Hurst was keen to develop international links, particularly with the French, and also explore the possibility of participation in a Nines or Sevens tournament. Hurst's vision eventually became reality through the inauguration of the York Festival Tournament during the Queen's Jubilee Year of 2002, though it involved RLC club sides rather than the Lionhearts.

The previously voiced issue of the Four Nations again came to the surface when Scotland Rugby League chairman Clive Mason circulated a formalised proposal to also include the French. This was eventually submitted to the RFL's policy board international sub-committee, though for the moment for the Lionhearts the need to honour the commitment made to the Scottish Courage Cup organisers took precedence. For this to happen, two gap weekends were incorporated into the season proper to cater for home fixtures against the Great Britain Police and the RAF. A friendly, preparatory fixture was also needed. On 25 February, at Hemel's Pennine Way, a London Broncos side containing Andy Johnson, who had Super League experience, and some home grown familiar faces in Jono Jones and Chris Thair, the new development officer at the Broncos, provided an excellent test for the Lionhearts prior to their inaugural campaign in a tournament which catered for a variety of development and amateur sources. Though the team was beaten, head coach Dave Doran was satisfied with the progress made and confident that his squad would equip themselves well against the policemen, airmen, and the students when the cup commenced.

Lionel Hurst had wasted no time in exercising his influence on the London Broncos and increasing a commitment to support the RLC and grass roots rugby league. That the Broncos were already sympathetic and actively engaged in assisting the competition was without doubt – they even took their Fourth Round Challenge Cup tie against Batley Bulldogs to the home of RLC champions Crawley Jets – but the new chief executive was determined to ensure that positive and lasting connections were made. The Broncos' Graeme Thompson gave extra development support to the RLC and he urged local clubs to get involved in collaborative initiatives such as a Nines Tournament at Greenwich University. Arguably, Hurst's lasting legacy to the competition while at the Super League club was his promotion of a local amateur side in Greenwich. This became the Greenwich Admirals. Playing initially in the London ARL, the club was formed from by Broncos supporters in the area with help from Thompson, and soon became successful.

As the season loomed ever closer, problems began to mount for the RLC organisers and particularly for Julian Harrison who faced some difficult health problems in his family. Britain was also hit by a foot and mouth epidemic with serious consequences for rural areas and the farming industry. The RLC was not immune. Oxford Cavaliers' base, for example, was temporarily closed.

Other matters affecting player compensation payments from professional clubs focused the attention of club and league officials alike, as did the outstanding issue of the World Cup kit promised to Gloucestershire Warriors as a result of their assistance the previous year with the New Zealand camp.

This time of year habitually threw up preparation problems affecting insurance, registrations, match official appointments and the like, but Harrison also had the added issue of Lionel Hurst's position in the RLC. Hurst's obligations to the London Broncos affected the time he could devote to the RLC, and regrettably he was often absent from meetings of the new RLC strategy board. After considering resigning, Hurst decided to decrease his input, but not withdraw from RLC activity completely.

The Gateshead saga had been resolved with the elevation of Durham Phoenix, but Harrison faced more problems. Kingston Warriors and South London Storm had successfully entered the competition in 2000 following their acknowledged and healthy experiences in the London League and their tremendous progress in junior and youth development. Now, only a year on, both were experiencing problems at open-age level that threatened their participation in the 2001 season. For Kingston, this proved to be only cautious concern and, following close monitoring, the difficulties that they feared when they spoke to Julian Harrison in February, never materialised to any large extent. For their near neighbours, the Storm, however, it was a different scenario.

In 2004 with the benefit of seeing the tremendous progress made at the club, it now seems remarkable that South London Storm came very close to relinquishing their position in the RLC only three years before. Had they done so, questions would have been posed on their viability as an open-age set-up. Yet, for a fortnight or so in early April, there were real fears that they would become a one-season only RLC operation. Julian Harrison was informed by Paul Johnstone, who coached the club as well as performing miracles with fixture lists; that the club would not be competing. The problem appeared to be off the field rather than on it, and so Harrison enlisted help from the London Broncos' Graeme Thompson, and the London League to keep them running and fulfil their RLC commitments. Long-standing club stalwart Julian Critchley, now a referee in the competition, took much of the responsibility. The club came back from the edge of disaster and played at Bedford a little over a month later on the new season's opening day. A heavy sigh of relief was breathed all round.

April is traditionally when the competition is launched. The debate over venues is always lively, and this was the case in 2001. However, following a suggestion from Greg McCallum, it was decided to develop the interest from the town of Rugby in Warwickshire that had been stimulated by the World Cup event, and look at holding both launch and grand final there. The attraction was obvious – a pre-existing involvement, a central location and the offer of central assistance in the staging of both from the RFL. Moreover, two well-appointed and ideal venues suggested themselves – Rugby Lions' rugby union ground at Webb Ellis Road for the final, and Rugby School for the launch. As a result, the usual array of club delegates, guests, officials and the media gathered in the Old School Hall on 11 April for a memorable day of formal presentations, informal networking and practical workshops.

The presentations included the unveiling of the first ever formal title sponsor of the RLC, in the shape of League Publications Ltd and their managing director, Martyn Sadler, who had, of course, been present at the very first match in the former Southern Conference League. In rebranding the competition, the Totalrl.com Rugby League Conference a connection was immediately made with LPL's website which now encompassed the previously recognised, but unofficial RLC site hosted by John Haigh. The success of the sponsorship can be gauged by the fact that it is still going strong in 2004.

The significance of the off-field developments at management and operational level were re-stated, as was the importance of both representative and youth football to the future of the RLC. Attention was drawn to the achievements of both Matt Cook (Bedford Swifts) and Desi Williams (North London Skolars), who had been selected for the forthcoming Great Britain under-15 international against France in Hull and were also destined for the London Broncos junior development squads. Cook is now at Bradford Bulls and Williams at Wigan Warriors.

The afternoon's workshops were devoted to coaching and organisational matters and were conducted by David Waite and Gary Tasker. Their enthusiasm and recognition of the importance of both their input and that of the competition as a whole, was not lost on those present who benefited enormously from the vast experience of the two speakers. The magnificence of the venue marked another new dawn for the RLC. It was now up to the clubs – and specifically the players – to demonstrate a product befitting the profile that the competition now almost took for granted. They would not let anyone down.

As a preview to the action to come, Sky Television's programme *Rugby League World* featured two of the new clubs, Cardiff Demons and Bridlington Bulls. One of the reasons for the latter's inclusion was that their director of rugby was former Leeds and Great Britain legend Les Dyl. He owned a restaurant in the town and his rugby league energies were devoted to coaching and organising his players into an outfit that could perform well in the RLC. They started the season with a bang. Playing at Bridlington Rugby Club and with a passionate following behind them, the Bulls began by narrowly defeating fellow RLC new boys Sunderland City 46-45 and then travelling to Durham and defeating more comprehensively the even newer Phoenix. Optimism was rife and though defeats would come at the hands of some of the other North East clubs, Bridlington established themselves well. The same was also true of Cardiff and Teesside, while the old guard showed that whatever the competition threw up in new opposition, they were still ambitious and hungry for success.

Two of these met in the South Division on 5 May, the opening day of the season. North London, now solely focusing on the RLC following their withdrawal from BARLA's National Conference League, proved that this approach was going to be to their advantage, as they travelled to Harry Jepson Trophy holders Crawley and won 26-12. The Jets were always relatively slow starters, so an early season loss was no surprise. Their recovery, however, was immediate. The third in the triumvirate of South Division championship contenders, West London Sharks, couldn't match the Sussex men's fire-power a week later, and the Jets' 29-10 victory was comprehensive. When Crawley met the Skolars again, on 16 June, the tables were turned. Again the away side won, but this time it was the Jets.

Throughout the regular season, there was little to choose between the two and when the 12 league fixtures were up, they were locked on the same number of points, with only Crawley's greater points difference, just 40, providing the edge. This would have been academic had a decision gone the way of the Skolars in their clash at West London on 2 June.

Travelling home from another derby fixture – a classic encounter between Ipswich and South Norfolk that ended in a draw – Harrison took a phone call from West London coach and secretary Mike French to say that there had been some confusion and argument over the final score of their game, and to expect a call from North London's Hector McNeil. Sure enough, moments later, McNeil called to proclaim that while the referee had given the score as 36-34 to the home side, he had actually missed – or at least not recorded – a Skolars goal that would, of course, have tied the score. On arriving home, Harrison contacted the referee for his version. Honestly, but frustratingly, he was not certain whether he had missed the vital two points or not. After considering the official scorecard, the protests and arguments of the North London club, and lengthy deliberation between Harrison and David Lowe, Harrison decided that there was no alternative but to follow the official score as given originally by the referee and as recorded on his scorecard. The 'case of the missing goal' was over, but in addition to costing the Skolars the game and the divisional championship, it highlighted the increasingly competitive nature of the competition. Every point – and indeed, every kick – was vital.

Elsewhere, the North Division was interesting because, although still finding it difficult to take points off the top sides, there were signs that both Crewe Wolves and Derby City were raising their playing standards to complement their excellent work off the pitch. Teesside and Hemel were a class apart in their respective divisions, the only sides not to drop a point in the first part of the season. Coventry Bears were not far off emulating these performances, their sole defeat in the league stage coming, surprisingly, at Leicester Phoenix. On one of those magical days when the form book goes out the window, Phoenix drew comparisons with yesteryear and their inaugural season success, by convincingly despatching a Coventry side short of a few regular players, but nevertheless still expected to triumph over their near neighbours. The 36-26 victory was one of the results of the season.

In many ways the East Division was the most fascinating. No one side dominated, illuminated by the composite table at the end of the season which had the divisional winners, Ipswich Rhinos, in 13th place and behind teams who had finished third in other divisions. The Rhinos' 32-20 victory at South Norfolk in July was the significant result.

Unfortunately, there were occasions during the course of that summer when the many positive aspects of the competition were overshadowed by the negative one of non-fulfilled fixtures. This had been a feature of all seasons stretching back to 1997, but 2001 was, in many ways, a watershed. The problem began on the first day, as Gloucestershire, previously ever-present performers, were unable to raise a side to travel to Cardiff, despite the strenuous efforts of administrator Stephen Rigby. For the Welshmen, it was a portent of things to come. Only two of their scheduled six home fixtures took place – the remainder succumbing to the same problems that had befallen Gloucestershire. Possibly the most controversial cancellation occurred when Birmingham failed to fulfil their West Midlands derby game at Coventry on 16 June. The issue wasn't just the non-fulfilment itself, but that with some available players carrying injuries, there were 11 players at hand. This posed a dilemma and produced diametrically opposed standpoints – the integrity of the competition versus the risk of injury. The suggestion was made by one member of the strategy board that Birmingham should be ejected from the competition, the argument being that clubs, including Leicester on that day, had travelled with 11 or fewer players in the past. Nevertheless, with the summer heat and the consequences of a depleted team facing the league leaders, it was hard to blame the Birmingham coach for putting the safety of his players before anything else.

For Julian Harrison, who had experienced life at both club and league level and realised the inherent pressures, it was a difficult decision. He felt sympathy for both clubs, but also realised that Coventry had been seriously disadvantaged. The timing of the withdrawal, late Friday afternoon, only compounded Coventry's sense of being hard done by.

Harrison referred the issue to the strategy board, who decided not to suspend or eject Birmingham Bulldogs from the competition, but simply to let the laws of the competition as they related to non-fulfilments come into play. As the season unrolled, more and more games fell the same way. Was this a sign of impending doom or decline? Or was it a reflection of the increased intensity of the competition, leading to more injuries and thus more unavailability? Had the RLC overstretched itself? Was it placing too many demands on clubs? Or was it simply a case of bad luck? There simply wasn't time for systematic analysis, but issues of travel, work demands and holidays had to be added to the list of causes.

There was also the rugby union factor to consider. The RLC season had been gradually lengthening from one year to another, if only by a matter of weeks. This was also true with the rugby union season, especially at leading amateur level. A longer playing season and an increased pre-season affected the availability of many RLC players who played both sports, some of whom were contracted to their rugby union clubs. The consequence for an RLC club faced by such an eventuality was clear. A regular side wasn't going to materialise. Players were going to come and go according to circumstances outside the control of the club, and this would manifest itself in what, if any, side could turn out on a Saturday afternoon. That Leicester Phoenix could beat Coventry one week and then put more than 80 points past Bridlington the next, during the course of a season in which they failed to travel to the latter and Cardiff, illustrates the problem. Those two magnificent performances came at a time – the middle of the summer – when they had all their players available, including those with rugby union commitments.

On 8 August, four games failed to take place. Already questions were being raised concerning the commitment of some clubs and also of the fairness of the rules for calculating the results of non-games. Cross-conference games, and especially the fact that clubs were expected to play four during the regular season, were also pointed to as a contributory factor. On 19 May, the first occasion in the season when all the games were of this type, difficulties were experienced in travelling by Cardiff going to St Albans and Oxford at Ipswich. Both games nevertheless took place. Despite setting out, Leicester didn't make it to Bridlington at all, their mini-bus breaking down on the motorway. That some clubs could overcome adversity as well as logistical and geographical headaches and plan ahead was admirably demonstrated by Wolverhampton Wizards and Rotherham Giants who both stayed overnight before their clashes at Newcastle and Crawley respectively. It didn't seem to serve them well. The Wizards went down 84-0 and the Giants were thumped 68-18.

It was mentioned earlier that Lionel Hurst was responsible for a number of initiatives while at the London Broncos that had a direct bearing on the Conference competition. The formation of the Greenwich Admirals was one. Another was the much vaunted and now operational 'pyramid structure'. Hurst, alongside Graeme Thompson, presented this to an assembly of rugby league personnel representing all sectors of the game at a meeting at UK Sport in London on 16 May. In essence, the vision was of a unified competitive structure with Super League at the pinnacle and regional grassroots amateur rugby league – as characterised by the RLC – at the bottom, with means of progress through the system depending on ability, aspiration and off-field organisation and resources.

Alongside a unified structure – and responsible for its implementation and development – there would be a new unified administration for rugby league, taking the policy board step to its logical conclusion. The meeting provided an opportunity for discussion, and the RLC representatives Julian Harrison and Phil Caplan outlined the reasons for the competition's successful formation and progress. In many ways the RLC provided a perfect case study, of the vision that was being presented. Following the 16 May meeting, the strategic review of the game was carried out by Nigel Wood, former chief executive of Halifax Blue Sox and now employed by the RFL for that purpose. An implementation committee oversaw the entire organisational transformation that ensued.

As we shall see, that process had significant implications for the RLC. Part of Wood's remit was to gather information and opinion from the various sectors of the game. Accordingly, he travelled to White Hart Lane for the classic encounter between North London Skolars and Crawley Jets. Harrison felt he should have gone to at least one other game to get a broader picture of life in the competition. Nevertheless, Wood also met Harrison to discuss the RLC and how it might fit into a revamped league structure for the sport.

So began a lengthy process of dialogue over a period of months with Harrison determined to ensure that all the RLC issues would be both understood by his RFL colleague and then acted upon.

The topic of the RLC also came up during Wood's conversations with both Lionel Hurst and Bev Risman, and difficulties arose because of their difference of opinion with Harrison over a fundamental issue – the timing of change. Harrison's opinion was that the RLC needed a further season of preparation before the advent of a National League that would include RLC clubs. This view was not shared, and Wood was initially keen to go with the contrary opinion and implement the change from the 2002 season onwards. Harrison, supported by key colleagues, stuck to his guns and continued to argue his case. His view, though personal, was shaped by conversations with club personnel who outlined the pressures that they would experience through and as a consequence of such a dramatic transformation.

The debates over the National League system under the professional game carried on for many months. Various permutations were considered and there appeared to be swings between the favoured choice almost on a monthly basis. Should there be a unified National League Three encompassing both RLC and BARLA clubs, who would, of course, have to change their season to play in summer – at least for one of each clubs' open-age teams? Should there be two parallel National League Threes? Should a BARLA National League sit above an RLC National League? Should the RLC league, whatever that may be, become open immediately to clubs from outside the competition, such as from Scotland? What would the promotion and relegation system be? Indeed, would there be one? What about minimum standards? Who would be responsible for generating ideas, making decisions and implementing them? Clubs debated the issues, as did Harrison, the RLC strategy board and interested observers and supporters. So did the national strategy committee that met at the beginning of July in Leeds. It was an ongoing saga of great significance.

In the meantime, of course, the RLC competition continued. Harrison found that the daily grind of the season was wearing him down - 26 May was a particularly difficult Saturday. Ipswich versus West London kicked off late. That was unfortunate, but not really a problem. A similar fate befell the North London versus Kingston fixture. With the result standing at 102-0 to the Skolars, Harrison was informed – by a home side concerned about points difference - that the game had been cut short. Nevertheless, the result stood. Of greater concern were events at Cambridge, St Albans and Bridlington. Disciplinary issues affected the last two games, with complaints over refereeing also being voiced in relation to the St Albans versus Bedford fixture. At Cambridge, a competitive game didn't even take place. Come kick-off, the Eagles didn't have a full side and the visiting South Norfolk team's policy of never asking for, or offering, loaned players, meant the fixture was not fulfilled.

It was a weekend of seemingly constant mobile phone conversations with people in various states of anger, annoyance and reflection, and for Harrison, spending the weekend in the North East with his wife after taking in an incident-free clash between Durham and Newcastle, it not only spoilt a weekend break, but came on top of problems with insurance and registrations. When personal criticisms appearing on the 'Fans Forum' section of the RLC website were made known to him, Harrison wondered whether the stress and situations he was expected to resolve made it worth continuing in the job. For the moment, he decided to persevere, and received a welcome boost by the enthusiasm of the RLC representative side.

The Lionhearts had opened up their Scottish Courage Cup campaign with defeat by the Great Britain Students in April. It was therefore imperative that they took maximum points from their two home fixtures against the British Police on 24 June and the RAF on 29 July. At half-time in the first encounter, things didn't look promising. The score was 6-4 to the Police, who were well organised by former Bradford Bulls player Jon Hamer. It needed all the attributes assembled by Dave Doran and his coaches to turn things around. Tries by Phil Aiken and a last minute 30-metre solo effort by North London Skolars' winger Mike Okwusogu gave the Lionhearts a 17-12 well-deserved victory. The second game produced a much more comprehensive win, though again the side were trailing at the interval, 18-12, and played superbly in the second half. Rotherham's Darryl Jackson and Ryan Knight of the Manchester Knights both scored twice, and for Knight it capped a scintillating performance on the wing and continued the fine run of form that had also seen him make his debut for Salford City Reds Alliance side.

It was a good period for individual achievements and representative honours in the RLC. Gavin Gordon, a player with considerable experience at many levels including the London Broncos, North London Skolars and West London Sharks, became the competition's second full international representative following Masohiro Komori, when he regained his place in the full Ireland team against France in Albi.

Throughout this busy period, negotiations were taking place with both Rugby Borough Council officers and staff at Rugby Lions RFC over the Grand Final scheduled for Saturday 1 September. A problem developed: Rugby Lions had a scheduled home fixture on that date, against Bedford. In order to accommodate the rugby league fixture, a double-header was necessary, though the offer from the host club was to schedule the RLC Final after, and not before, the rugby union match. The RLC Grand Final would, in effect, be the main match and the union game the curtain-raiser. After some debate with the RFL and the competition's sponsors, League Publications, it was agreed to play the game at Rugby.

There were no problems securing help from clubs and volunteers. Coventry Bears, Bedford Swifts and Wolverhampton Wizards provided essential manpower for the big day. Stefan Hopewell, the former media manager of the Rugby League World Cup in 2000, was a willing PA announcer, and Tracey Hirons (née Greenwood) ordered the medals. Coupled with the support of RFL staff and the usual hands-on work of the RLC duo of Caplan and Harrison, it was a formidable working team that was assembled for the showpiece of the RLC season.

Who would compete in that final was, of course, still to be decided. The last two months of the 2001 season produced some gripping rugby. Some games spring immediately to mind, such as Crawley's narrow but deserved victory at Rotherham in a repeat of the previous season's grand final. Equally narrow and significant triumphs came for South London and Kingston over Crewe and Derby respectively.

In a sensational game at Chosen Hill, where Hemel Hempstead Stags had their unbeaten record threatened by a determined Gloucestershire Warriors, the Stags eventually won 30-27. Durham Phoenix won their first game in the competition, beating county rivals Sunderland City, and leaving it to the last weekend in the regular fixtures to do so. This victory was significant not only for the Phoenix, but the competition as a whole because it ensured that all clubs won at least once during the summer. For some players too, milestones were achieved. Gloucestershire's Andy Brown was honoured by his club for appearing in all but eight of the Warriors' first 40 fixtures, and Sunderland City registered possibly the oldest player, at 59 years, to appear on the RLC official registration list – up until then at least. For one club as well, performances had received the attention of a leading brand name. Wolverhampton Wizards were courted by Red Bull.

After 12 rounds of fascinating and keenly contested battles on – and off – the pitch, the final divisional tables were complete:

	Northern Division	**Pl**	**W**	**D**	**L**	**F**	**A**	**Diff**	**Pts**
1	Rotherham Giants	12	9	0	3	514	234	280	18
2	Chester Wolves	12	8	0	4	423	315	108	16
3	Manchester Knights	12	6	0	6	404	251	153	12
4	Crewe Wolves	12	4	0	8	243	461	-218	8
5	Derby City	12	3	0	9	188	452	-264	6

	Southern Division	**Pl**	**W**	**D**	**L**	**F**	**A**	**Diff**	**Pts**
1	Crawley Jets	12	10	0	2	643	165	478	20
2	North London Skolars	12	10	0	2	610	172	438	20
3	West London Sharks	12	9	0	3	542	253	289	18
4	South London Storm	12	3	0	9	207	555	-348	6
5	Kingston Warriors	12	3	0	9	173	710	-537	6

	Eastern Division	**Pl**	**W**	**D**	**L**	**F**	**A**	**Diff**	**Pts**
1	Ipswich Rhinos	12	7	1	4	380	255	125	15
2	South Norfolk Saints	12	6	1	5	266	347	-81	13
3	Bedford Swifts	12	4	0	8	298	387	-89	8
4	St Albans Centurions	12	4	0	8	249	402	-153	8
5	Cambridge Eagles	12	1	0	11	146	448	-302	2

	North East Division	**Pl**	**W**	**D**	**L**	**F**	**A**	**Diff**	**Pts**
1	Teesside Steelers	12	12	0	0	667	147	520	24
2	Newcastle	12	10	0	2	585	199	386	20
3	Bridlington Bulls	12	4	1	7	323	473	-150	9
4	Sunderland City	12	1	1	10	207	541	-334	3
5	Durham Phoenix	12	1	0	11	126	666	-540	2

	Central Division	**Pl**	**W**	**D**	**L**	**F**	**A**	**Diff**	**Pts**
1	Hemel Hempstead Stags	12	12	0	0	537	121	416	24
2	Gloucestershire Warriors	12	9	0	3	422	202	220	18
3	Cardiff Demons	12	8	0	4	393	210	192	16
4	Oxford Cavaliers	12	5	0	7	236	424	-188	10
5	Worcestershire Saints	12	2	0	10	167	507	-340	4

	Midlands Division	**Pl**	**W**	**D**	**L**	**F**	**A**	**Diff**	**Pts**
1	Coventry Bears	12	11	0	1	652	84	568	22
2	Nottingham Outlaws	12	8	0	4	418	309	109	16
3	Leicester Phoenix	12	5	0	7	371	428	-57	10
4	Birmingham Bulldogs	12	3	0	9	279	457	-178	6
5	Wolverhampton Wizards	12	1	0	11	152	655	-503	2

At the end of the final league game at Coventry, where the home side defeated Nottingham Outlaws, Julian Harrison sat down in the club house and conducted the draw for the play-offs. Four days later, and prior to the play-offs commencing, Diane Colley, chief executive of Rugby Borough Council, was asked to draw the teams out of the hat for the semi-finals. The purpose of this was two-fold: first, to give all eight competing play-off sides an indication of their possible route to the final, and also to help in arranging semi-final venues.

On Saturday 11 August, the remaining eight teams took to the field with a Grand Final place for two of them less than three hours of rugby away. Two games were close; the other two were straightforward home victories. A depleted Ipswich Rhinos had to travel to reigning champions Crawley, and never looked likely to cause a shock. Two tries each from Cartwright and Kruger helped the Jets to a 48-4 victory. Teesside's demolition of Newcastle was even more impressive. Julian Harrison's second visit of the season to the North East saw an outstanding home performance. A 56-8 triumph before an appreciative crowd and reported on – as had been the case for most of the season – by BBC Radio Cleveland and their enthusiastic journalist Bob Deans, provided the perfect antidote for the home side who had been desperately disappointed the previous week when Manchester had to cancel their visit due to player shortage. The 'Steel Machine', as Deans had nicknamed them, were well-oiled and efficient to a man. Though a hat-trick from McCallum took the headlines, the seven other try scorers epitomised the Steelers' team contribution and talent.

The other two games were very different affairs. Despite trailing at half-time, Coventry Bears gained revenge for their semi-final defeat the previous season by knocking out Rotherham Giants 28-21. Doubles from Francis Slater and Carl Southwell put paid to the Yorkshiremen's aspirations of going one step further than in 2000, though with John Dudley also scoring two for the Giants, it was a close affair. The final game was closer still. For the first time in the competition's five-year history, extra-time was necessary to separate Hemel Hempstead Stags and North London Skolars. An extra-time try from Hemel's Andy Curtain was the definitive moment of a memorable match. It was a shame that somebody had to lose and devastating for the Skolars who had contributed so much to the season, but Hemel's winning ways continued and they looked a good bet to go all the way to Rugby.

In a season when there seemed to be problems fated to occur at every step of the way, the semi-finals were no exception. Following investigation of a number of venues across the central area of England, Nottingham's home seemed to be the ideal choice for a potential double-header feast of rugby. However, inevitably there was a snag. The ground was only available on a Sunday. Crawley's Steve O'Reilly, thinking of the need to avoid Saturdays, had arranged his wedding for a Sunday, and his big day coincided with the semi-final. Should there be no room for manoeuvre, both O'Reilly and most of the Crawley team would be missing.

Memories of 1998 came flooding back. Julian Harrison, however, saw differences this time around. The game had been fixed for a Saturday throughout the season. Only recently had the option of a Sunday fixture been communicated to clubs. In addition, he felt that there had been too many cancelled fixtures already that summer without having, literally, to enforce another one. Hasty phone calls provided a remedy that satisfied both Crawley and opponents Coventry Bears. Bedford's Athletic Stadium was available on the Saturday and could accommodate this match, with the Hemel versus

Teesside game remaining, as initially arranged, at Nottingham on the Sunday. With things resolved, although a kit clash still had to be sorted out, action could commence.

The semi-final weekend provided arguably the best illustration of RLC rugby up until that time – and possibly ever since. All four sides were equally matched, though Teesside, notwithstanding their unbeaten performance over the season so far, were considered by some to be the rank outsiders. They were the top sides in the composite table, there was so little to choose between them and everything pointed to two games of intensity and quality.

The first contest surpassed all expectations. Crawley's defence of their trophy had been dogged at times, thrilling at others, but always determined. All these traits were drawn upon to combat a Coventry side hungry for success. That Crawley did everything possible apart from win is testament to their own attributes, but more so their opponents. Inspirationally led by skipper Alan Robinson, but followed by every player in a Bears' shirt, it was a field goal from the talented Irishman James Cathcart that separated the sides, Coventry hanging on to win 17-16.

If that wasn't sensational enough, the second semi-final 24 hours later, if anything, eclipsed it. Again, a field goal was important. Phil Gowing's success for the Steelers gave the North East side a 3-2 half-time lead. In the second half, tries came and the game, and the lead, ebbed and flowed. Revill and Bedworth scored for Teesside, Curtain and Willoughby for the Stags. Fittingly, it was Steelers' player-secretary, Lloyd Darby who scored the try that took the Steelers to the final. Teesside won 19-14 and they would meet Coventry on 1 September.

Darby had spent many years at the club and had experienced some low points, but here was his moment of glory and no-one deserved it more. Elated, he paid tribute to Hemel after the final whistle, a deed replicated with the same sportsmanship by Hemel's disappointed manager, Derek Millis.

All the previous RLC finals had been relatively high-scoring affairs. Teesside and Coventry's 2001 match was an exception, but still a gripping spectacle nonetheless. With the disagreements over the choice of venue now in the past, it was the choice of day that now affected the attendance of those either reporting on the game or attending as guests. Initially there was no clash with Super League fixtures. However, a Super League game was switched to that Saturday afternoon, and a relatively routine match between Huddersfield and Hull attracted a number of reporters and Nigel Wood among others, who would otherwise have been at Rugby.

Another notable absentee was Lionel Hurst though this was for a very different reason. The London Broncos were in turmoil after the announcement that Richard Branson wished to pull out of his investment and chairman's role in the club. Rumours were rife that the Broncos would be relocated and the position of Hurst as chief executive was uncertain. Honourably, Hurst felt that to attend the RLC Grand Final would detract attention from the occasion, and thus he kept away. This didn't stop a protest from London Broncos supporters at the game. A 'Keep Broncos in London banner' was picked up by the Sky cameras and other media and shown on television and in the rugby league press.

With the Rugby versus Bedford rugby union fixture out of the way, the gladiators from the North East and just down the road entered the Webb Ellis Road arena. The two teams were:

Coventry Bears: Rich Pepperell, Andy Lewis, Russ Saltmarsh, James Causey, Francis Slater, James Cathcart, Alex van der Walt, Carl Southwell, Matt Allsop, Alan Robinson (c), Ian McGregor, John Nicholls, Matt Wright.
Subs: Rich Davies, Struan Murray, Ben Biss, Rich Draper.
Teesside Steelers: Ian Boyd, Ben Kerr, John Stewart, Mick Kent, Gareth Kerr, Duane Revill, Phil Gowing, Sean Taylor, Jason Dunn, Anthony Slee, Andy Garside, Adrian Crowe, Lloyd Darby (c).
Subs: Chris Mattison, Paul Metcalfe, Phil Orr, Stewart Evans.

It was soon apparent that this was going to be a game of attrition, drawing on every ounce of energy and skill. It was difficult to gauge on past form how the contest would develop. In the event there were only two try scorers. Coventry's Richard Davies went over from close range twice, the second on the hour seemingly tipping the scales in the Midlanders' favour. However, throughout the season, the presence at centre of the Steelers' resident policeman, Mick Kent, had proved to be a valuable asset. He was devastating when running onto a ball from 20 yards out, and twice during the final he had sufficient space and a quality pass to make his momentum and bulk count. The second time with eight minutes left on the clock was the conclusive score. Phil Gowing's deadly boot did the rest, and the Bears were left to rue their misfortune – James Cathcart had seen a long-range goal attempt hit the post – as Teesside hung on for a 12-10 win.

Darby, sporting a broken jaw, received the Harry Jepson Trophy from the great man himself, and proclaimed his side's victory as testament to the quality of the game in the region. His awareness of the need to promote North East rugby league at a moment of personal triumph demonstrated the appeal of the RLC and the visionary nature of its personnel.

Players, supporters, officials, sponsors, guests and the media assembled in the superb bar area to officially draw the season to a close with acknowledgements of thanks and for the presentation of the End of Season awards. In another example of partnership support, these trophies had been supplied by Rugby Borough Council and were presented by Diane Colley to their grateful – and in some cases, surprised – recipients. Dave Wattam of Crawley Jets and Hemel's Grant Hathaway were worthy winners of the Player and Young Player of the Year awards respectively. For their outstanding enthusiasm, organisational skills, attention to detail and their performance in hosting the two semi-finals, the Club of the Year award was shared by Bedford Swifts and Nottingham Outlaws. The Club Personality of the Year was Duncan Merrill of the Wolverhampton Wizards, a man whose dedication to the Wizards cause was almost legendary. He even has a Wizards tattoo.

The performance of the match officials was also recognised. Referee David Merrick received words of encouragement from Greg McCallum and the young official outlined his debt of gratitude to the competition for giving him opportunities to display his talents.

The 2001 season had, despite its problems, been a great success. Fifteen games didn't take place, but 171 did. The competition had expanded, lengthening its boundaries and encompassing whole new areas with potential for further growth. From Plymouth to Bolton, Telford to Greenwich, expressions of interest in RLC 2002 were received, though Harrison was cautious about any idea of automatic expansion. Speaking to *Rugby League World* magazine, he said: "The question we've got to pose is are we going to expand next season at all, and as ever, that's dependent on resources."

Preliminary discussions had begun with the Scottish Conference about the development of closer ties, and internally, the move towards a 'Premier League' style format was a bit closer – though lessons had to be learnt from non-fulfilled fixtures.

There had been an increase in media interest. Their end of term questions were concerned with how the competition intended to proceed and fit into the ongoing strategic review of league structures and such like. It was this issue that focused the mind as the season drew to a close. For Julian Harrison, the opportunities offered by the current analysis of the sport, were there to be taken. In the same edition of *Rugby League World*, he said: "To a certain extent the review should be a Godsend for us because it will help shape the future for the next few years, whereas in the past the RLC has unavoidably gone on a year-to-year basis."

It was an opinion shared by the magazine which one month before had concluded its section on the competition with the words: "The next stage of development has been reached which should cement the footings and secure the long-term future of one of the most exciting projects Rugby League has initiated in its illustrious history."

The overall vision of the RLC becoming inextricably linked to the wider structural review appeared to be agreed upon. It was now just a question of practicalities and method. Providing the 'flesh to go on the bones' would now be the immediate task for the competition's organisers and those with positions of power and influence over the RLC. It was possibly the most important piece of work relating to the competition since the initial pilot season of 1997.

Action from the 2001 RLC Grand Final: Coventry Bears versus Teesside Steelers

2001 RLC Grand Final: The victorious Teesside Steelers team

Above: Action from the
2004 Shield Final:
Cardiff Demons versus Thorne Moore
Marauders

Right: Cardiff Demons
– Shield winners 2004

Harry Jepson Trophy final 2004:
West London Sharks
versus Widnes Saints

Below: The winning Widnes
Saints team

9. 2002: Looking Ahead

Though the bigger picture was prominent, the realities of post-season work could not rest on implications of strategic reviews and images of National Leagues. More mundane, but important, matters still required attention. The fine-tuning process began immediately after the final.

The RFL team at Red Hall was not the only body undertaking a strategic review and considering the RLC in future plans. BARLA had initiated its own analytical proceedings. The larger strategic review had acted as a catalyst to the amateur governing body, and BARLA had an input to the main work. The RLC were invited to participate and provide a different amateur perspective to the gathering of northern county, district and member leagues. Julian Harrison and Phil Caplan attended the initial meeting on Sunday 9 September 2001, with Harrison the lone RLC representative at the second meeting a month later. BARLA chief executive (and RLC Strategy Board member) Ian Cooper had the task of promoting some controversial proposals to his BARLA audience. These focused both on the possible change of season at elite level so it would become an integral part of the new pyramid structure, but also on the fundamental issue of an 'open' game free from any delineation on amateur or professional lines. Of course, this struck at the core of BARLA's *raison d'être*, and there were strong views on both sides. Cooper saw the necessity of addressing these matters if BARLA was to remain a key player within the overall structural transformations affecting the whole sport. At a practical level, both an open game and summer rugby were issues directly affecting the future of a National League in which BARLA was expected to exist, possibly alongside, but at least in tandem, with the RLC. The RLC, of course, was both open and summer-orientated. These issues also had implications for future promotion into the semi-professional ranks.

Ian Cooper and Maurice Oldroyd were both keen to involve the RLC in the discussions. Cooper and Julian Harrison were liaising regularly on the proposed National Leagues, and both were members of the National Development Strategy Board and therefore could see their own work in the wider domain of the development of the sport overall. Oldroyd also expressed his and BARLA's support for junior and youth development within the RLC. The process of assimilating the Conference within a wider development framework now gathered pace. The revised Rugby League Development Strategy, for example, was circulated to RLC clubs for comment, and the London and the South operational group input into competitive structures and age focus increased considerably. This would affect matters such as coach education and links to Service Area frameworks, and resulted in an exciting new development focus for the RLC 2002 season – an under-18 RLC academy competition. Through links with the London Broncos and Sheffield Eagles in addition to using the expertise and resources of both the RFL development team and Niel Wood at the Student Rugby League, Caro Wild developed a proposal for a competition aimed at bridging the gap between youth and open-age rugby. It was a significant breakthrough and demonstrated the importance of partnership work.

The application process for 2002 took up time and thought. Harrison's list of possible applicants had grown considerably over 12 months, and now included the Leeds graduates, Bolton le Moors (the fruit of National Development Strategy Board member John Kidd's efforts), Telford, Luton Vipers (fresh from a successful season in the London League) and Bramley, among others. Interestingly, and posing a new dilemma for the RLC organisers, expressions of interest were also received from a number of services-based sides and also from Scotland. Blandford Bulldogs, who were army based, and the Metropolitan Police were both viable operations, but with obvious limitations for junior development. No such problem existed with Glasgow, but their inclusion would make extra demands on their opponents (obviously from the nearest RLC region, the North East, but wider afield for the play-offs). The Cardiff experience of 2001, with four cancelled trips to the principality was a recent lesson. The competition also seemed set to lose two clubs. South Norfolk Saints had experienced difficulties in 2001, even suffering the embarrassment of not fulfilling a fixture. As a consequence, and possibly also due to coach John Evans' student rugby league commitments, the club decided not to re-apply for 2002, but to arrange friendly games to maintain interest and to strengthen the club infrastructure. The finalists of 1998 would not be lost forever to the RLC.

The London Skolars were looking in a different direction. Never short of ambition, and with a sound financial base and potential, they were looking towards the semi-professional ranks of National League Two. Julian Harrison visited London in mid-October to meet with Skolars' Hector McNeil and Mark Croston to hear about their plans. Harrison knew McNeil well, and was certain that McNeil would not enter into any scheme that did not have a realistic chance of success. The club organised a meeting of interested people, including Bev Risman, in November to outline their plans and elicit support. Their preparations would be well worthwhile.

There is never a close season for players involved in the RLC Lionhearts, and as the competition's representatives in the Challenge Cup, their preparation began early. It was also clear that pressure was growing for the team to become England's representatives in a future Four Nations tournament. Yet, before all that came a visit from the New South Wales Police team on 17 October. This game took place midweek and was well handled by the management, coaches and players. Though the Australians won, the game was another feather in the RLC's cap.

The stature of the game and the potential playing talent was also recognised by Sheffield Eagles player-coach Mark Aston, who came to Bedford to watch the contest. The Eagles were firm supporters of the competition, seeing its significance as a breeding ground for players and clubs. Their chairman Ian Swire had a genuine interest in grassroots rugby in development areas and Phil Caplan ensured that he was up-to-date with the RLC's progress because Swire was a frequent visitor to his bookshop. If proof were needed, the Eagles 2004 squad had four players (John Breakingbury, Aled James, Jack Howieson and Greg Hurst) with RLC experience.

Following the NSW police match, attention turned to the Challenge Cup. The first round draw proved both kind and cruel to the Lionhearts. A home draw was a real boost, though the opposition, Featherstone Lions, would ensure that the team would be tested to its limits. Coach Dave Doran felt confident going into the game at Hemel that victory could be achieved to add further credence to the side's growing stature. However, it was not to be, with the Featherstone team securing a narrow win. They would not know it then, but the Lionhearts would not get another stab at the famous trophy.

With the Strategic Review omnipresent, club delegates congregated in Coventry on Sunday 4 November to discuss various issues including possible structures for the RLC 2002 season and the impending move towards a unified competitive structure for rugby league. It was a beneficial exercise for Julian Harrison and Phil Caplan. The opportunity to give presentations on national development and the growing links between Sheffield Eagles and other aspects of the game in the Midlands, particularly the student sector, in addition to RLC affairs, complemented the discussions on structural issues. The comments that were received helped to clarify the RLC competition for 2002, and also to guide Harrison in his talks on the National Leagues. On the latter, it was very clear from the views expressed on that Sunday that there was considerable concern about parallel BARLA and RLC divisions.

With applications for the RLC now beginning to come in, including a video from Cambridge Eagles, a clearer picture of what the competition would – or more accurately, could - have to work with in the way of clubs and geographical spread - began to emerge. Ron Banks at Coventry Bears had continued his track record of submitting the first application and, in addition to the established clubs, there were confirmed intentions of participation from the Metropolitan Police, Luton Vipers, Blandford Bulldogs, Glasgow and Randlay/Telford. Though not new, Durham was changing its name to that of its predecessors, the 'Tigers'.

The clubs had been presented with alternative formats for the season to come at Broadstreet on 4 November. All the options introduced an extended play-off series involving all clubs. Following the completion of the regular fixture rounds, clubs would be divided depending on their league position and would then compete for either the Harry Jepson Trophy - for those finishing higher in their respective divisions - or a new Shield - for those finishing lower. Also, Harrison was convinced, despite strong arguments to the contrary, that it was too early to think of Premier Leagues for the RLC. The series of non-fulfilled fixtures in 2001 was a factor, and his view was that stability was the first priority to prepare for the emergence of a National League involving RLC clubs that could become –in effect - a RLC Premier League, in 2003. In any case, the stratification on playing ability lines central to any Premier League would occur in 2002 through the division of the competition in the play-offs.

Despite receiving comments on the proposed structure, nothing could be finalised until there was a budget for the competition. Harrison had submitted a proposal to the RFL, and Nigel Wood was invited to attend the RLC Strategy Board meeting on 15 November. Unfortunately, he could shed no light on the financial resources available and so no final decision on club applications and structures could be made. This was a period of great uncertainty and opportunity for rugby league. Such a radical review of the game had the potential to overhaul established procedures and initiatives. Though the RLC's success as a competition and development tool was clear to see, that was no guarantee of future increased investment or organisational reform. In such a climate, it was agreed within the strategy board that a detailed budget was required before commitment could be given on the number of teams and the structure.

At the same November meeting, Mark Senter and Clive Mason from Scotland Rugby League gave a presentation on the merits of a Glasgow club in the RLC and also of the Four (or perhaps Five) Nations tournament. Harrison had been liaising with Mason on these matters and the Challenge Match between Teesside Steelers and the Scottish Conference winners, Edinburgh Eagles, which was provisionally scheduled for the eve of the 2002 Challenge Cup Final at Murrayfield.

The non-decision on 15 November frustratingly proved to be an enduring one. Julian Harrison also made representations to Nigel Wood on various RLC issues, the Strategic Review and National Leagues that also proved difficult to resolve. For the RLC administrator, this was more than a minor inconvenience: "Clubs were wanting answers and decisions made on their future participation and development path. They were expecting me to provide these answers, but my hands were tied. I could appreciate the complexities involved and the pressures on the decision makers who had the whole sport of rugby league to think of, but that didn't really help me. At times there didn't seem to be an indication of when things would be finalised and with an off-season as well as a competition to plan, that led to considerable difficulties."

The Strategy Board met again on 11 December, and again deferrals on outstanding decisions had to be made. An exception was made for the Luton Vipers application. With South Norfolk Saints withdrawing from the competition that year, there was a gap in the Eastern Division that needed to be filled to maintain the competition's current quota. Luton fitted the bill perfectly. The Vipers had resurrected themselves and had great potential. Formed in 1991, they had effectively folded at the end of 2000 due to difficulties in establishing themselves and problems over a home ground. Now an offer of accommodation at Stockwood Park RU club had provided a tonic and the club's progress was astonishing. In addition to the RLC, the Vipers had plans for a second team in the London ARL and a youth and women's set-up. They could look forward to RLC football in 2002.

Financial uncertainty prevented closure of the other applications, though further information was also needed in some cases. Only the Metropolitan Police were dismissed from the reckoning at this stage, because of the lack of a youth development framework. The RLC policy at that time meant their exclusion, but the door was left open for them should there be a change in the future.

Within a day of the December meeting the number of potential additions had reduced again, but this time as a result of a club decision, rather than one by the RLC. The Glasgow bid had considerable merit. The formation of what was a super club to participate in both the RLC and the Cumberland League had much going for it. Unfortunately, it didn't have time. The absence of a decision on 11 December with the prospect of another month of waiting, effectively made up the minds of those behind the Scottish initiative, and they reluctantly withdrew their application. Of course, there was no guarantee of a positive result to their application in any case, but for the absence of information at league level to be such an important factor was disappointing.

Though the RLC was still in limbo to some extent, there was movement on a wider front. The RFL implementation committee produced its interim report to the RFL member clubs and it was startling reading. The report focused on the financial situation at rugby league headquarters at Red Hall and pointed to problems in financial management. It suggested that personnel changes might be forthcoming and an executive chairman from outside the game could be appointed. This explained why no decision on the RLC budget was revealed. Though there would be no immediate news regarding this RLC matter, there were considerable implications for the directorship of the competition. Nigel Wood became the RFL's operations manager alongside the triumvirate that comprised the executive committee (and of course the RLC directors), Messrs Webster, Callaghan and McCallum. Yet, within a very short period, Wood was to be the only member of the quartet to remain in office. Dave Callaghan resigned to pursue other interests in sport and Peter Webster was put on extended leave on health grounds. Greg McCallum went to spend the festive period with his family in Australia. In his absence, there were rumours concerning his future. He would return to England, but not to his office at the RFL.

The next scheduled RLC strategy board meeting was on 17 January. Little did Harrison know when he drove to Leeds that morning that he would be walking into D (decision) Day for the RFL. He had requested that a decision be made on the budget prior to the time of the 11am meeting and, on arrival at Red Hall, he immediately sought out Greg McCallum to find out if it had been. He was greeted by the news that McCallum was on the verge of officially departing, was not in the building and with rumours that his desk had been cleared. The pattern for the day had been set. A number of other staff were informed of the termination of their contracts. Amid turmoil, tears and recriminations, Harrison sat down with the rest of the RLC strategy board and attempted to deal with what matters they could in the continuing absence of a budget figure and with uncertainty over who would assume responsibility for the RLC at Red Hall. The most important agenda item was the applications process. Glasgow and Blandford were ruled out for 2002, leaving Telford Raiders and Bolton le Moors still in the pot. It was agreed that, although their interest would still have to be gauged as a result of the delay, both clubs would have to agree to participate, or neither would be admitted. The need for even numbers was decisive.

At the end of an unforgettable day, Harrison's presence was requested by Nigel Wood. After what he had witnessed in the preceding few hours, a nervous and pessimistic RLC administrator made his way towards the boardroom, concerned over his own job. Amazingly, Wood informed him that the competition budget was to be increased to more than £60,000. In a day of much sadness and bitterness, the RLC had got a result, though the loss of some RFL staff considerably dampened any enthusiasm.

For Julian Harrison, the loss of Greg McCallum was a shattering blow. An understanding and mutual respect had developed between the two and the Englishman greatly valued the input and personal support he had received, as well as the massive contribution the Australian had made to the competition. To lose him was a setback from which – in rugby and professional terms – Harrison would not really recover while at the RLC.

Following the cataclysmic events of 17 January, the immediate dilemma for the RLC was the admission of Telford and Bolton. The best option was for both to agree to participate and the second best would be for neither to do so. The worst scenario was for one to say 'yes' and the other 'no'. But this occurred. While John Kidd proclaimed the Bolton le Moors club ready to take their place, Dave Berry reluctantly informed Harrison that Telford were not quite in a position to do so. Kidd took the news that his club would not be offered a place with great courtesy and stoicism. He knew it was not the outcome that anyone wanted, and appreciated the difficult position that everyone was in. His – and Bolton's – time would come.

Another difficult decision that would involve inevitable let-down was also on the cards regarding the RLC Lionhearts. A verdict on the Scottish Courage Cup versus Four Nations quandary had been long-awaited. To enter both would have meant too many representative matches. It could not wait any further as the Lionhearts had already been entered into the former with at least an expectation that they would represent England in the latter. It was felt that the Scottish Courage Cup had provided an appropriate test of the side's capabilities. Yet the lure of wider representation, international recognition and a higher profile could not be ignored. Neither could the pressure from the other nations for the inclusion of an English team. With the possibility of opening up avenues at club level across national boundaries also needing to be considered, the scales tipped in favour of the Four Nations. Julian Harrison contacted organiser Vic Musgrove to withdraw the Lionhearts from the Scottish Courage Cup.

The RL policy board (to whom the matter had been referred) agreed to the Four Nations proposal presented to them by the RLC administrator, via BARLA's Ian Cooper, and the process of ensuring conformity and agreement over tournament rules and eligibility criteria began. This was not easy. There were different rules on eligibility to consider, different motives for participation and different ideas on organisational matters. What was paramount was to provide games of a meaningful nature, with prestige and, if possible, an equitable competition with no dominant force. The RLC obviously had the largest playing base and, for the Lionhearts, it now meant switching from eligibility via club participation to eligibility based on nationality. The team had in the past contained players from various nationalities, but it would be inappropriate to continue to do this and call the side 'England'. It was clear that while the nations could work collectively together and still come up with an operable series of games, a central co-ordinator would assist considerably. That person – the first tournament director – was Graeme Thompson, and it was he alongside RFL colleague Nick Halafihi who would chair the first Four Nations meeting on 19 March.

These decisions apart, more everyday RLC matters continued. The usual pre-season preparations, this time embracing structure, rules of the competition, minimum suspensions/fines, medical and health and safety information, youth and Academy administration and the challenge of gaining increased sponsorship as well as the perennial issues were there, though the absence of a centralised RFL contact with a specific RLC remit (as had been the case with Greg McCallum) did cause concern. Were there to be changes to matters arranged by the RFL in previous campaigns, such as the match officials operation? With the implementation committee's focus being on finance, would the cost of appointments still be met under the match officials budget and who would resolve any issues, minor or major? Both Julian Harrison and David Lowe did not work at Red Hall, and this meant that everyday information and updates were not necessarily communicated to them. Harrison often travelled to Leeds to talk to Nigel Wood and other key individuals in an attempt to gain answers to niggling concerns. Sometimes this was productive, at other times not. Rugby league's organisational reform was not always conducive to dealing with nitty-gritty issues.

But the appeal of the competition was still magnetic. The list of potential entrants to a future RLC now included Sheffield-Hillsborough Hawks, Blackpool Sea Eagles, Rugby and Heysham (though the club that materialised in this area would be Lancaster). The Sheffield club were currently playing in the BARLA National Conference League but were turning towards summer opportunities. Their Hillsborough Arena home had been transformed into a marvellous facility and the RLC organisers were keen to hold semi-final fixtures at the ground in 2002. The Hawks had close links with their near neighbours, Sheffield Eagles, and John Kain's role as development officer was a massive plus for the RLC and clubs in the Eagles' own sphere, such as Derby City. The RLC outfit were quick to take advantage and pursued discussions on the subject of Service Area possibilities and youth development.

With one semi-final earmarked for Sheffield, a southern venue was needed. The RLC turned to familiar territory. Through the influence of Lionel Hurst, Cheltenham was to stage that game, the Finals Day and the forthcoming home amateur international fixture between England and Wales. An all-embracing Festival of Rugby was a more ambitious idea than simply a one-off game and appealed to Hurst's wider vision and the local authority's intention of attracting visitors to the spa town.

In January 2002 the full proposals of the RFL implementation committee were revealed. In a significant boost to rugby league development, the department at Red Hall was to be upgraded and strengthened. This culminated in a new development executive position, to be filled by Gary Tasker, and two national development managers. Andy Harland would focus on the 16-and-under age bracket, while Niel Wood would move from Student Rugby League to take responsibility for the game from age 16 upwards. This included the RLC. An independent board of directors, free from club involvement, had been another of Lionel Hurst's clarion calls, and this was now duly ratified by the implementation committee. The board would come into operation in November, at which time the implementation committee would relinquish their role.

For the unified competitive structure, there was little surprise in the embracing of a National League structure for 2003, though there would be modifications to the initial conception of five divisions (including Super League) as the original plan was for separate BARLA and RLC-orientated National Leagues. This was dependent on both producing an appropriate number of clubs. Though this was not going to be straightforward for the RLC, it proved impossible for BARLA in that time framework. The problems related to the BARLA clubs playing in the summer and the associated prospect of withdrawal from the elite BARLA National Conference League.

This was still a year away, however, and the way the RLC was to be structured in 2002 still had to be announced. In February, all was revealed. The Broadstreet meeting the previous November had helped to clear the way, and the format for the season was one that was pretty much in the club – if not the public – domain anyway. There were to be three phases – divisional fixtures lasting 10 weeks, a four week play-off series, followed by semi-finals and a Finals Day – and two trophies to play for: the Harry Jepson Trophy and the new RLC Shield. The clubs lined up in six divisions:

North East: Bridlington Bulls, Durham Tigers, Newcastle Knights, Sunderland City, Teesside Steelers.

North: Chester Wolves, Crewe Wolves, Derby City, Manchester Knights, Rotherham Giants.

Midlands: Birmingham Bulldogs, Coventry Bears, Leicester Phoenix, Nottingham Outlaws, Wolverhampton Wizards.

East: Bedford Swifts, Cambridge Eagles, Ipswich Rhinos, Luton Vipers, St Albans Centurions.

South: Crawley Jets, Kingston Warriors, North London Skolars, South London Storm, West London Sharks.

Central South: Cardiff Demons, Gloucestershire Warriors, Hemel Hempstead Stags, Oxford Cavaliers, Worcestershire Saints.

National League places were now at stake, depending on both clubs' off-field and playing performances, and that was very much an underlying emphasis for the new season, as Julian Harrison outlined in *Rugby League World:* "We have deliberately aimed at consolidating the competition in 2002 in an effort to raise the intensity and standard in preparation for National League entry. A number of new applicants from all parts of the British Isles have been deferred as a result, with aspiring clubs encouraged to re-submit in 2003 when we anticipate being able to significantly increase regional feeder leagues to underpin Division Four (the RLC 'National League'). All the clubs are tremendously excited at the prospect of where this summer's competition will lead to and that should ensure even greater profile for their outstanding efforts."

The prospect of a conveyor belt of clubs, with the RLC making a massive contribution in turning new, local operations playing in regional feeder leagues, into strong and healthy organisations vying for places in a National League, was an appealing one. Clubs could see the way and the challenges that lay ahead.

There was a hive of activity around the nation. In the Black Country, Wolverhampton Wizards were focusing on the future. They held a meeting of club personnel on the last day of January, inviting RFL officers Julia Lee and Steve Fairhurst down to talk on youth development, schools work and the advantages of linking into Active Sports. But more pressing was their ground situation. They had moved from the Castlecroft complex, so to prevent the nomadic existence that had plagued others, the answer was quite straightforward to club secretary Duncan Merrill. Wolverhampton would produce their own ground. Merrill's employment at Banks' Brewery was an advantage, and with their assistance, the Four Ashes venue that remains their home today came into being as a new focus for rugby league action.

Securing their long-term future was also the concern of Crewe Wolves. Through the tireless energies of club stalwart and local schoolteacher Phil Johnson, a partnership had developed between the club and a local sports college. In later years this grew to include Warrington Wolves and Manchester Metropolitan University in a pioneering concept that promises to produce a steady stream of new rugby league talent in South Cheshire.

Elsewhere, a number of moves were afoot. Birmingham Bulldogs also moved grounds and indeed out of Birmingham, by switching to Walsall RFC. Arguably the most influential player in the history of the competition, Steve O'Reilly, announced his retirement from Crawley Jets. He was replaced by former St Albans Centurion Glenn Tyreman who ironically had masterminded the Jets' worst ever defeat to date when his St Albans side defeated Crawley 56-4 in 1998. Cambridge Eagles also announced a new coaching appointment in Tony Cooper, a former Swinton, Kent Invicta and Fulham professional and former Eagles player as well.

At both extremities of player experience, Sunderland City's junior team set up a new girls under-14 side to complement their boys teams at under-12, 14 and 16 level, and two Coventry Bears players, Alan Robinson and James Cathcart, were in the Ireland team that took on the USA Tomahawks in the annual St Patrick's Day clash at Glen Mills in Pennsylvania. Robinson scored a try and Cathcart kicked three goals in a 24-22 triumph for the Irish.

In February, Harrison was told by Nigel Wood that he wanted him to be the RLC representative on a National Leagues sub-group. This body was to comprise all the integral constituents of the new playing structure and ensure that ideas and work progress were co-ordinated and consistent with the overall schema. As it happened, Harrison never attended any meetings. His input was primarily through Ian Cooper of BARLA, and covered matters such as minimum standards, application processes, criteria and forms. Cooper had more to cover because of the particular circumstances regarding BARLA clubs and the National League concept and there were also a more pressing concern as matters needed to be resolved before the 2002 winter season commenced. Consequently, information emerged from BARLA's headquarters before anything concrete could be agreed about the RLC. Nevertheless, this didn't stop Harrison fielding interested enquiries about the National League from Derek Millis at Hemel and Darryl Osborne at Rotherham.

Julian Harrison had come close to leaving his post as RLC administrator on a number of occasions. But events since the turn of the year had led him to once again question his involvement. The departure of Greg McCallum had been a blow, and the ongoing saga regarding the budget, and delays and confusion in decision-making had increased his sense of disappointment and despondency. Working in Leicester, away from the RFL headquarters in Leeds also added to his sense of alienation, and this combination of things conspired to make him seriously review his position. Though – indirectly – reassurance had been given about his own employment through the increase in the RLC budget, Harrison privately speculated on the new national development posts and how they would impact on his own job. He had seen valued colleagues and friends disappear virtually overnight from their positions within the game. To the RLC administrator, the transition to the new set up at Red Hall had not translated into the personal contact, liaison and interest that he had experienced and enjoyed under the old regime. He wondered whether this was symptomatic of the changes, whether it was personal or, more seriously, if this signalled a sea-change in the development of the RLC. Was the competition now turning towards greater centralised control and away from the ethos of the Southern Conference League and RLC which had proved so successful?

Eventually, Harrison came to a decision. He could not let these feelings continue and potentially damage forever his love of the competition and the game. It had begun to do so already. He began to dread day-to-day dealings and the prospect of attending meetings and games, and even found it difficult to watch matches on television. He therefore decided to look for alternative employment and found it in the building in which he had been housed for the previous four years running his rugby league office. On 27 March 2002 he was offered the post of Social Inclusion Officer at the Rural Community Council (Leicestershire and Rutland). He accepted it and the next day tendered his resignation from the RLC. It was to be some weeks later before the RFL made the news public. A press release quoted Harrison as saying: "The decision to leave the Rugby League Conference at such an exciting and challenging time in the competition's development was not taken lightly but, having seen the Conference develop significantly during the last two years, I now believe it is the right time for me to undertake a new personal direction."

Personal reasons were therefore cited for the decision, and this was true. However, as revealed publicly for the first time here, they related to much more than a simple change of career.

Other people were moving on. Scotland Rugby League Chairman Clive Mason and his wife Karen revealed that they were not seeking re-election to their volunteer posts. Closer to home, Tracey Hirons and Dave Doran advised Harrison that they would be relinquishing their roles with the RLC Lionhearts, though retaining their other involvement in the sport. Their eventual replacements would be Duncan Merrill and Connor Gissane. With Harrison's resignation received and accepted and an agreement made to limit his notice period to four weeks, ensuring that he could oversee the Edinburgh versus Teesside Challenge Match on 26 April, the RFL moved quickly to ensure that there was adequate cover at least for the interim. With David Lowe continuing to provide administrative support, the overall responsibility for the competition was given to Niel Wood. Though he began a new role with the RLC earlier than he might have anticipated, this was the logical appointment given his remit as national development manager and his superb track record at Student Rugby League. He could call on the support of others, notably Phil Caplan, and the RLC could not have been more favourably represented.

April 2002 was, therefore, Julian Harrison's last formal month of involvement with the competition. It opened with the annual launch at the Broadstreet facility that had hosted the clubs meeting in November. Coventry Bears were planning to play their first league match of the season against Ipswich at the ground. Workshops and seminars were conducted on development (Julia Lee and Steve Fairhurst) and on the future, including the National League structure (Julian Harrison and Phil Caplan). Other speakers included Harry Jepson, Gary Tasker, Graeme Thompson, Caro Wild and Lloyd Darby, the last three relating to international, youth and club issues respectively. The RLC set the scene for the season: A Four Nations tournament, an under-18 academy competition for eight clubs with some regional festivals, and an open-age championship that would be as eagerly contested as ever, but with perhaps more significance as a result of the National League situation and structural reform. Disappointingly, Sky Television's cameras could not be present and Harrison was grateful to Gary Tasker for not only his input into proceedings, but also for ensuring that there was a formal RFL presence.

The day also provided an opportunity for further consideration of the implications for RLC clubs of a move to National League status. These included player and club development, minimum standards, potential future semi-professionalism and the length of season. Clubs were able to raise issues of concern and informally register interest. The 2002 launch therefore fulfilled a number of purposes, but for Julian Harrison it was a personal struggle. "I can remember in my speech referring to the privilege of working with all those assembled in front of me and the many hundreds (if not thousands) of others at clubs the length and breadth of the country. The majority of those in the audience didn't know I had resigned and I could feel tears in my eyes when I said those words knowing how short a time I had left. I spoke rather more from the heart than I had previously planned and I put myself through an ordeal as a consequence. Afterwards, addressing and discussing issues that I would not personally have to deal with was, in a sense, surreal. I was very glad when the day was over."

A month of fine-tuning was ahead for clubs and administration alike. The pre-season friendly highlights included Hemel's home game against Paris Chatillon and Bedford Swifts' coup in attracting the Leeds Rhinos Academy side to Bedford. The Greenwich Admirals, due to begin competitive life in the London League, also made their debut against St Albans Centurions. Off the field, Bridlington's development plans received a welcome boost through a National Lottery grant and the appearance of Castleford assistant coach Gary Mercer at the club's launch night. Development was also afoot on merchandising and sponsorship. Rotherham Giants secured the support of the *Rotherham Advertiser* for a further three years, and Bedford saw the benefits of producing a comprehensive brochure on the club in an effort to attract financial investment and sponsorship deals with local companies.

Now with a handover to arrange as well as a season commencing, Julian Harrison was busy ensuring that everything was in order for his successor. Moreover, there were a number of matters that Harrison was determined to see through. BARLA had issued an invitation to address their Open-Age Committee at Fartown, Huddersfield on 16 April and, considering the extensive support he had received from Ian Cooper and other BARLA staff plus the recognition that links between the RLC and BARLA were likely to get closer as a result of national developments, Harrison made this appointment a priority. However, barring a last-minute scare when Phil Selby informed him that there were problems at the Durham Tigers club that might prevent their participation in the season (they didn't), the principal concluding task for the outgoing administrator was the challenge match in Scotland.

Work on this game had been ongoing since the start of the year. Initially part of a festival of rugby league entertainment scheduled to also include a nines tournament, it ultimately proved to be the sole focus of attention on the eve of the Challenge Cup Final, unless pre-final liquid celebrations are included. The enthusiasm of both teams was matched by that of Scotland Rugby League who had promoted the venture wholeheartedly and arranged for the presence of Sky reporter Angela Powers and the television cameras. With the RLC also succeeding in drumming up considerable interest, a large crowd gathered at Broughton FP Rugby Club to see Scotland's best take on the Teesside 'Steel Machine'. Though Edinburgh Eagles started the stronger and established a 12-8 lead, the Steelers' power and pace was the decisive factor. A quick three-try riposte before half-time sealed their dominance and though the second-half was more even, there was only going to be one victor. The match ended with a 30-20 triumph for Teesside, and Harrison was left with the final task of presenting the trophy to Lloyd Darby. It was a superb conclusion to a fulfilling two years' work as the RLC administrator.

The RLC was now in new hands, as indeed was the RFL under the stewardship of new executive chairman Richard Lewis, and one week after Edinburgh, the 2002 season kicked off. The opening day's games whetted appetites for the new campaign. For once there were no severe thrashings - though Oxford did put more than 50 points past Worcestershire Saints - testament to a quirk of the fixture list that seemed to match teams by strength and geography, but also perhaps due to the rise in playing standards at some of the traditional strugglers. There were some notable performances. North London Skolars impressively defeated a strong West London side 38-10. Coventry too made headlines by despatching Ipswich Rhinos 40-6. Crawley saw off their old adversaries from Hemel, but in a much closer fashion, 28-26. Champions Teesside carried on where they had finished at Rugby and Edinburgh, by sweeping away Rotherham Giants 48-8.

New boys Luton Vipers also started with a win. A plucky Cambridge Eagles side provided a relatively gentle opening to their RLC inaugural season. However, the Eagles proved again that they must never be taken lightly. A Luton side that would go on to become one of the season's big successes duly won, but only after a spirited display from the visitors.

The Vipers, inspired by their triumph on the opening day, then proceeded to see off both Wolverhampton and, perhaps unexpectedly, Ipswich. Their rivalry with close neighbours St Albans Centurions was one of the most compelling sub-stories of the season. With little to choose between the two sides, with players well-known to each other and officials as dedicated and as ambitious as they come, it finished with a title decider on the last day of the regular season.

There were encouraging signs of progress throughout the competition, but nowhere more than at four clubs who had had some initial trepidation at the prospect of another season of struggle. South London Storm, Kingston Warriors, Derby City and Crewe Wolves were well used to competitive games between each other, but receiving heavy defeats against their remaining divisional adversaries - 2002 was the beginning of a new dawn for them. They were not always victorious, but they were now a different proposition for sides that might just have been a touch complacent in the past. For the Storm, in particular, the season was a revelation. Another indication of an increase in intensity and playing standards was that Hemel Hempstead Stags and Rotherham Giants – two sides certainly not expected to struggle – didn't pick up any points until the third round of the competition.

The Giants featured in the match of the first month. Gary Tasker picked an absolute corker of a game to attend on 11 May, with Rotherham hosting Chester Wolves. The early signs were more than promising, a tit-for-tat opening half with the highlights being an interception length-of-the-field effort from Giants' centre Graham Batty and the leadership and all-round qualities of Wolves hooker Drew Povey. It was 12-12 at the break. What ensued was more of the same, but with time ticking on towards 80 minutes, every score could have been decisive. When Sam Moore made and finished a break from the half-way line to put the Yorkshiremen 22-20 ahead, it appeared that the Wolves had had their moment. But not a bit of it: in a dramatic finale, Danny Heaton crossed the line from close range with little more than five minutes remaining and Chester hung on for a 24-22 win.   Another fixture also stood out, but perhaps more for symbolic reasons. North London Skolars' defeat of Kingston Warriors was expected (though a lot closer than in previous seasons), but it was the venue that attracted attention. The game was held as a curtain-raiser to the London Broncos versus Leeds Rhinos Super League fixture at Griffin Park. It was yet another illustration, not only of the close relationship between the Broncos and local amateur rugby league, but of the lure of the RLC competition. Lionel Hurst's replacement as Broncos' chief executive, Nic Cartwright, commented in *Rugby League World:* "We certainly see these clubs as being an integral part of the bigger picture in terms of southern development."

June 2002 was the Queen's Golden Jubilee. In celebration of this, it became also the month of the York Golden Jubilee Rugby League Festival. Inspired by Lionel Hurst, among others, this international nines tournament had received official recognition, and was one of the first events under the auspices of 1895 International at which Hurst had spoken, in its previous guise as the 1895 Club, so convincingly and eloquently six years previously about an amateur summer rugby league competition that would eventually become the Southern Conference League. A crowd of 2,000 saw RLC sides Teesside Steelers and Cardiff Demons do battle with representatives from

Ireland, Scotland, France, North Wales, York itself, the services and most exotically, two amalgamated outfits, the South Asia Bulls, containing players from Hindu, Muslim and Sikh communities, and the London Koogas, a representative mixture of players from a variety of London teams all with RLC experience. Both Teesside and Cardiff reached the quarter-finals, but the London Koogas went on to make the final where a fantastic defensive display from Chris Thair and a momentous try from captain Jake Johnstone, gave them a 20-14 victory over the French side Lezignan.

Internationalism was the flavour of the times, as the amateur Four Nations tournament was also underway. With eligibility for selection confined to players from domestic competitions (in the case of Ireland, Scotland and Wales), the RLC or the student under-19 competition, this covered all desired sources for the four contenders. Notwithstanding this, it was obvious that the English team had an advantage with a far larger pool of players. However, the other three nations had experience of playing such games, and their desire to beat the English could not be ignored. The opening salvos went true to expectation – the Welsh, with 12 players from the RLC, beat the Scots 40-22 in West Glasgow, and the England Lionhearts inflicted a 32-10 defeat on the Irish in Waterford. Tournament director Graeme Thompson reflected in *Rugby League World* on progress in the RLC after taking in the Waterford clash: "I attended Ireland versus England in Waterford and the basic skills in the Totalrl.com Conference have improved no end over the past couple of years, in terms of ball retention, field position and understanding of defence."

The next round of fixtures in July also seemed to follow the pre-tournament forecasts. England travelled to Old Anniesland, Glasgow and destroyed the Scots 58-8. A hat-trick of tries from both Parminder Tutt, now back at Wolverhampton Wizards following his experience at the Warrington and Salford academies, and captain Richard Smith of the Hemel Hempstead Stags helped the Lionhearts to their total, but the Scots' performance was creditable. Their side also contained RLC representation through Paul Campbell of the Bridlington Bulls. Back on home soil, the Welsh matched the English in scoring 50-plus points, though the Irish Wolfhounds responded with 20. The Irish recovered some pride by administering the heaviest defeat of the tournament on the Scots on 18 August, and that just left England versus Wales as the tournament decider. With the business-end of the RLC competition dominating proceedings during the course of August, that winner-takes-all game was postponed until after the Grand Final, when it provided a memorable end to the trilogy of big games at the Prince of Wales Stadium in Cheltenham.

Back to domestic matters and with all clubs in competition for play-off places, every game carried great significance. Teesside Steelers and North London Skolars were running away with their respective divisions, remaining unbeaten throughout and playing enterprising rugby league football. The result of the second half of the regular season was arguably Crewe Wolves' astonishing 54-12 victory over the Rotherham Giants on 13 July. Admittedly, Rotherham were not the force they were in previous seasons, but to dwell on that would be an injustice to a rejuvenated Wolves side who produced arguably their finest performance in the competition to date. Two tries each from Chris Arnold and Mike Ward, plus others from John Pemberton, Rob Condry, Rob Hall, Andy McGrain and Paul Cooper served notice that Crewe would be one to look out for in the Shield play-offs.

But there was more. In terms of sheer drama, two games really stood out. A 79th minute field goal from full back Evan Powell on 8 June gave Cardiff a thrilling 29-28 victory against Gloucestershire Warriors who had fought back tenaciously from 22-8 in arrears to draw level.

The final round of fixtures in Phase One put Luton Vipers and St Albans Centurions together and the 80 minutes that followed lived up to the pre-match expectation. Not only local honour was at stake, but the Eastern Division title was up for grabs as well. The Saints needed a victory to overtake their rivals from up the M1, and with seven minutes to go looked well-placed to achieve that with a commanding 22-8 lead. Unbelievably those final minutes witnessed three tries for the Vipers. Evans Onyango started the ball rolling and almost immediately afterwards, Paul Harmon went over from 60 metres. Surely it was too late though as injury time drew near. Drawing on every ounce of energy, skill and bravery, Luton gained possession again, kept the ball alive on the final tackle and were rewarded when James Fee dived joyously over in the corner. They were still two points behind however, and all depended on Fee converting his own try from the touchline. With nerves of steel, he kicked the ball between the posts and Luton had pulled off the greatest of escapes! The first phase of 10 matches came to an end, with the positions and fixtures now determined for the play-off phase.

	North East Division	Pl	W	D	L	F	A	Diff	Pts
1	Teesside Steelers	10	10	0	0	563	85	478	20
2	Durham Phoenix	10	5	0	5	245	288	-43	10
3	Bridlington Bulls	10	4	0	6	182	264	-82	8
4	Newcastle	10	3	0	7	170	319	-149	6
5	Sunderland City	10	3	0	7	180	375	-195	6

	North Division	Pl	W	D	L	F	A	Diff	Pts
1	Manchester Knights	10	9	0	1	390	109	281	18
2	Chester Wolves	10	8	0	2	324	164	160	16
3	Rotherham Giants	10	3	0	7	259	245	14	6
4	Crewe Wolves	10	3	0	7	212	395	-183	6
5	Derby City	10	2	0	8	122	403	-281	4

	Midlands Division	Pl	W	D	L	F	A	Diff	Pts
1	Coventry Bears	10	9	0	1	486	125	361	18
2	Leicester Phoenix	10	6	0	4	362	237	125	12
3	Nottingham Outlaws	10	5	0	5	380	276	104	10
4	Birmingham Bulldogs	10	4	0	6	210	309	-99	8
5	Wolverhampton Wizards	10	0	0	10	104	616	-512	0

	East Division	Pl	W	D	L	F	A	Diff	Pts
1	Luton Vipers	10	8	1	1	380	185	195	17
2	St Albans Centurions	10	7	1	2	271	152	119	15
3	Ipswich Rhinos	10	5	0	5	283	214	69	10
4	Cambridge Eagles	10	4	0	6	166	342	-176	8
5	Bedford Swifts	10	1	0	9	185	371	-186	2

	South Division	Pl	W	D	L	F	A	Diff	Pts
1	North London Skolars	10	10	0	0	428	140	288	20
2	West London Sharks	10	7	0	3	300	220	80	14
3	Crawley Jets	10	6	0	4	329	235	94	12
4	Kingston Warriors	10	3	0	7	224	324	-100	6
5	South London Storm	10	1	0	9	208	452	-244	2

	Central South Division	Pl	W	D	L	F	A	Diff	Pts
1	Hemel Hempstead Stags	10	8	0	2	491	140	351	16
2	Cardiff Demons	10	6	0	4	332	284	48	12
3	Gloucestershire Warriors	10	5	0	5	344	343	1	10
4	Oxford Cavaliers	10	4	0	6	290	338	-48	8
5	Worcestershire Saints	10	0	0	10	120	590	-470	0

An underlying ethos of the competition has been to encourage, support and instil in clubs an understanding that from a solid and vibrant operation off the field can stem playing strength and success on it. One of the most endearing qualities of the competition and a vivid illustration of its success is that, for many clubs, it has taken very little persuasion or coercion from the organisers to recognise this. Clubs have, in many cases, simply got on with the job, taken opportunities that have arisen and pursued all possible roads to achieve stability and viability. Some have led to *cul-de-sacs*, but this has failed to stem the enthusiasm and determination to seek another route. Of course, centralised assistance has been forthcoming – otherwise there would have been only a marginal role for an administrator or organisational team.

A good example of this occurred on 23 June when RLC club delegates attended a seminar on central government funding initiatives held at Hopwood Hall College in Rochdale. However, a brief selection of good club practice from the early months of the 2002 season shows clubs' industry, and innovation. Cardiff Demons appeared on HTV television programme *Hot Pursuit*. Cambridge Eagles launched Swoop 'n Scoop, an in-house lottery. In recognition of their hard work in developing the sport in east Manchester, the Knights received a Community Cash Back Award from the Royal Bank of Scotland. They were also successful in gaining sponsorship from Asda Supermarkets. Lastly, a sevens tournament organised by Crewe Wolves but assisted by Ruskin College and the Super League Warrington Wolves, formed part of an event involving local schools and other sports to celebrate the Manchester Commonwealth Games.

The middle of the summer saw a greater clarity on the National Leagues situation. The BARLA league (the subject, as we have seen, of considerable work and debate) was beginning to take shape – at least in terms of what would be expected of applicants. Clubs from this sector could also play in the traditional winter leagues, and applications would be accepted on an open basis rather than just inviting the stronger National Conference League clubs.

A financial package had been devised, and clubs were also to be encouraged to adopt their town name as part of any formal title within the new competition. While all this had no direct impact on any RLC club operation, indirectly the ramifications were considerable because it was becoming increasingly clear that ties between the BARLA and RLC-orientated national divisions were going to be close - indeed they were ultimately a lot closer than initially envisaged. As it transpired, following a protracted and in some ways complex process of changing ideas and adapting to circumstances, the concept of two separate divisions was dropped. There were insufficient BARLA clubs committed to the project to make a separate league viable. Accordingly, National League Three was to comprise clubs from both areas of the game in a unified division. Some RLC clubs were already making their interest in National League selection clear, while taking stock of their strengths, weaknesses and aspirations. And finally, in July, National League Three application forms were sent out to RLC clubs.

For London Skolars, good news came on 31 July when the RFL officially approved the entire national league structure for the sport. The Skolars were accepted into National League Two for the 2003 season alongside York City Knights. Only two clubs – Workington and Hunslet – voted against the inclusion of a second professional club in the capital. Their fantastic journey from the London League to national and professional inclusion in eight short years was complete, and was a supreme achievement. Mark Croston, the club's head coach and chief operating officer, also paid tribute to the RLC in providing a setting for the Skolars to fulfil their dreams and in which others might indeed follow. In *Rugby League World* he said: "The RLC has given the game a truly nationwide aspect for the first time and this should be carefully nurtured – we have laid down our own solid foundations and the time is now right to start building on them."

With Phase One of the RLC over, the revamped play-off series began. However, there was a potential loop-hole in the structure. As a result of the way the fixtures were arranged it was possible that a team could go through the second phase, which was also a league structure, undefeated and still be eliminated. Though the formula had been devised by Julian Harrison, this anomaly had not been picked up by any of the strategy board members or any club representatives when the system was announced. In Harrison's defence, he had requested that the board and various individuals check the working arrangement for any problems, and none had been picked up. Unfortunately, one club, Manchester Knights, were the innocent victim of the loophole and, despite leaving the competition, Harrison felt responsible for this outcome. He could do nothing about it, but that did not appease his regrets. Nevertheless, leaving aside this major blemish, the play-off series was successful. The intention was to prolong interest in the competition for all clubs. Theoretically, though perhaps unrealistically, it was possible for a club to lose all fixtures in Phase One and then recover to perform victoriously in Phase Two and compete for a trophy.

For Bedford Swifts and South London Storm, this almost proved to be the scenario. Both sides had only one victory to their name in the first 10 weeks of the season. However, the transformation in both during the next four games was miraculous. On the last weekend of the scheduled four, both clubs travelled to opponents that on past form were strong favourites to win. But Bedford triumphed 22-10 at Birmingham and South London were 20-12 victors at Oxford. That Crewe and Newcastle also looked strong in the Shield was less of a surprise. The former had improved immensely on the field and the Geordies were always capable of putting together a run of form, which was just what was required in this mini-series of games.

The Harry Jepson Trophy play-offs also produced compelling rugby. Teesside looked impressive in inflicting heavy defeats on Rotherham and Durham, though Bridlington proved to be a much tougher proposition. Hemel too, were showing signs of impending glory, and they couldn't have picked a more appropriate season to strive for honours. The club was celebrating its 21st year of existence. In playing terms, they had experienced successes and reversals, but £250,000 raised during this time from their weekly cashline lottery to help support their development programmes was perhaps their most notable achievement. Hemel's games against Crawley Jets had been real highlights of previous campaigns, but the first game in the play-offs was notably different. The Jets were not the force of yesteryear and Hemel's 54-14 victory was emphatic. Crawley's demise continued throughout the series. They suffered a record home defeat, 0-88, against North London Skolars and it was clear from the outset against the Stags that they would not be in the running for honours in 2002.

Ipswich Rhinos had defeated Coventry Bears in East Anglia during the first phase. When the sides were scheduled to meet again during Phase Two, a close contest was expected, especially as Ipswich were difficult to beat on their own turf. The result was anything but close. Coventry's determination to avoid the disappointment of the previous year was obvious, and a 78-0 victory sent a significant message to the rest. However, with National League Two on the horizon, many people saw North London Skolars as the overwhelming favourites to repeat their 1997 success. Their form in the four-game play-off series did nothing to dissuade those opinions.

With Manchester unfortunately eliminated on points difference, despite playing success, the semi-final line up for the main trophy pitched Coventry against North London and Teesside versus Hemel (in a repeat of the previous year's semi-final). In the Shield, South London were to play Crewe Wolves, with Bedford taking on Newcastle Knights.

Two venues had been chosen (the Prince of Wales Stadium in Cheltenham, and Sheffield's Hillsborough Arena) for double-header games over the course of two days. First on the field were South London and Crewe. A close game was won by the Londoners 21-14 with a superb display from full back Corey Simms catching the eye. Simms had been introduced to rugby league at Coombe Hunter Prison near Oxford, where he was serving a sentence for armed robbery, by Andy Lindley of the local side, the Cavaliers, and the RLC Lionhearts. He found that Simms had a natural gift for rugby league, the game's requirements of strength, speed, stamina and athleticism suiting Simms's own talents that had previously, perhaps, lain dormant. He was a revelation and on semi-final day in Cheltenham he scored two tries as the Storm progressed to the Shield final. Though the two clubs concerned would, of course, not consider it such, many at the ground on that day considered that game to be an appetiser to the main fare: Coventry Bears versus North London Skolars.

Semi-finals seem to bring out the best in the RLC. The previous season's contests were still fresh in the memory, but this was a real test of strength and quality. For all but two minutes of the game, the Skolars led the way. Unfortunately for them, the two minutes in question began in the 78th minute, for it was then that James Cathcart slotted over two points to convert a Francis Slater try for the Midlanders. When Cathcart repeated the dose shortly afterwards with a penalty to seal a 21-18 victory, the Skolars were left distraught. Luck was not with them on the day - they had a try controversially disallowed - but the Bears' determination to reach the final had proved to be ample motivation. There was another reason for their success, as captain Alan Robinson admitted in *Rugby League World*: "We had faith in our own ability and continued to finish our sets of six. I must pay tribute to sides in our division like Leicester and Nottingham. Tough matches against them prepared us thoroughly for this battle. Reaching the final again was a personal goal after last season's disappointment, we are more determined; we have a winning attitude this time."

The following day saw two equally enthralling spectacles to thrill a large crowd at the Hillsborough Arena. Bedford Swifts narrowly defeated Newcastle Knights 22-20, player-coach Richie Bower's second drop-goal cementing their victory in the last minute. The Swifts, so long accustomed to the sole joys of participation, now experienced a new sensation, that of semi-final victory on a national scale. Though hard on Newcastle, it was just reward for a club that had won so many friends over the years. *Déjà vu* was also a sensation when Teesside and Hemel entered the fray. Twelve months before, the North Easterners had revelled in the underdog tag and inflicted heartbreak on the Hertfordshire outfit. Revenge might be too strong a word, but the opportunity to rectify matters is a powerful weapon. Phil Caplan's report referred to the opening half as: "The best 40 minutes the Conference has seen". The teams reciprocated each other's efforts and scores, producing a match of great fervour and quality. Richard Smith, captain of the Lionhearts as well as player-coach of his club, produced a man-of-the-match performance, scoring two tries to inflict Teesside's first ever defeat in the RLC - Hemel winning 24-16.

Referee Paul Gluck, who had already been appointed to officiate the final and had witnessed both semi-final matches, looked ahead with glee in *Rugby League World* to what he considered to be his biggest day in his rugby league career so far: "Having seen this competition develop, there is no question that the quality is getting demonstrably better each year and it is a real pleasure to be involved in its development. The Grand Final will be my biggest appointment and I am really looking forward to officiating two great sides on what promises to be a special occasion."

Prior to looking at Grand Final day in Cheltenham, it is worth reflecting on significant advances in rugby league development that would affect the RLC and the game in general in the South East. Five new full-time staff were appointed as a result of a £500,000 investment from Sport England. This enabled further work to build on the growing successes in ventures such as the champion schools programme. On a wider front, the move towards greater collaboration with other initiatives and sectors that had characterised the RLC over the past two years became more formalised through the new approach adopted by Gary Tasker for his development department. Tasker referred to a "new holistic approach to rugby league development" and, in addition to specific operational staff, the development and expansion group that comprised people with RLC connections such as Bev Risman and Ian Cooper, would have a noteworthy role to play. For the RLC, a leading player in the development field and the vehicle for much of the intended work, the opportunities were available for more concrete support.

As far as the immediate future was concerned, optimism for further growth in the competition was high. This was based on the progress of fledgling clubs. Greenwich Admirals, for example, had stamped an immediate authority on the London ARL, ending the North London Skolars' 'A' team's 29-match unbeaten run in June and then winning the trophy by beating another RLC stalwart's 'A' side, Crawley Jets, 38-22 in the final. Their connections with Service Area and student rugby were also significant and showed a forward-thinking operation.

In Blackpool, the Sea Eagles emerged as a prospective RLC member. Also catching the media eye was the prospect of Rugby Raiders entering the RLC in the future. Ever since the RFL had engaged with the local Borough Council, school and – initially through the RLC – the rugby union club, it had been clear that a club in the Warwickshire town was a realistic target. The Raiders had been formed by former Leicester Phoenix player Colin Wood, and made their baptism against local rivals' Coventry Bears 'A' team on 3 August. The game was featured on the Sky Television rugby league magazine programme. These examples had been largely independent of specific RLC action – though of course influenced by the prospect of participation in the competition. However, under the auspices of Gary Tasker and Niel Wood, there was now a proactive campaign around the country to nurture sides to enter the RLC. This would yield almost immediate dividends.

Sunday 8 September dawned and it proved to be another memorable Grand Final day in the RLC. Four eager sides were present, all intent on carving their respective name for the first time on an RLC trophy. However, Bedford's arrival in Cheltenham was delayed as a result of problems en route, and, with no room for manoeuvre in the scheduling, they had little preparation time prior to taking the field to face the South London Storm.

Bedford Swifts: Chris Haines, Gavin Twigden, Paul Fairhurst, Will Richardson, Chris Aubury, Joe Bickerdike, Jez Britton, Tommy McCollin, Tony Pullen, Marrick Murphy, Justin Line, Parwaz Khan, Richie Bower.
Subs: Mark Whybrow, Martin Fairhurst, Chris Baker, James Lane.
South London Storm: Corey Simms, Brendan Bruce, Carl Zacharov, Allan Prout, Gavin Calloo, Caro Wild, Terry Reader, Nick Byram, Mark Nesbitt, Nathan Price-Saleh, Daniel Poireaudeau, Simon Drury, Keri Ryan.
Subs: Aaron Russell, Matt Fuller, Alun Watkins, Andy Binns.

That this scenario affected Bedford's concentration and performance is arguable, but highly plausible. Their sole points came from the boot of prop forward Tommy McCollin. The Storm, on the other hand, were a revelation, scoring 10 tries. Though pride of place would go to hat-trick hero Caro Wild, the contribution of all the players was the real reason for a 54-2 victory.

There would be no such pre-match problems for Coventry and Hemel. They lined up as follows to compete for the Harry Jepson Trophy:

Coventry Bears: Richard Pepperell, Steve Campton, Rob Lowe, James Cathcart, Francis Slater, Alex van der Walt, Joe Smith, Rich Davies, Matt Allsopp, Carl Southwell, Ian McGregor, John Nicholls, Matt Wright.
Subs: Alan Robinson, Scott Carver, Andy Lewis, Tim Stevens.
Hemel Hempstead Stags: Matt Cannon, Barry Jon Swindells, Liam Doubler, Scott Roberts, Jon Mason, Chris Caws, Grant Hathaway, Alex Murphy, Richard Smith, Ben Kay, Jimmy Daines, Gareth Martin, Charlie Adie.
Subs: Damon Marii-Metuarii, Paul Joyce, Adie McKenna, Ross Willoughby.

In contrast to the previous year, this was a relatively high-scoring affair. Hemel scored first through Scott Roberts. However, that early score was the last time the Stags were ahead for, despite never being out of the equation until the end, the rampant Bears were tantalisingly always just out of reach.

Both sides scored four tries. Roberts with two, Gareth Martin and Richard Smith, from close-range, crossed for the Stags. Steve Campton, Scott Carver and James Cathcart touched down for the Bears before fittingly player-assistant coach Alan Robinson went over unopposed to score the final four-pointer with two minutes left. No-one who had heard his dignified response to defeat at Rugby in 2001, would begrudge the big Ulsterman his moment of glory, though it was his friend and playing colleague, also from Enniskillen, James Cathcart who won the new Bev Risman medal as man-of-the-match. His seven goals to the lone score from Hemel's Charlie Adie were the real difference on the scoresheet. An enthusiastic crowd, boosted by a significant local presence as well as supporters from all the teams and the usual RLC following, had a good day out in the sun. So too had the hosts, who reported the busiest day in their history. The venue even ran out of hamburgers.

Coventry's Grand Final victory also had ramifications for the club's off-season, because for the first time, the RLC competition winners were to enter the Challenge Cup in place of the Lionhearts representative side. London Skolars had participated in 1998 following their success in the 1997 Southern Conference League, but their representation was through membership of the BARLA National Conference League.

The season was not quite over, though. The Cheltenham Festival of Rugby League still had to run its course. A week after the climax of the club season came the deciding clash in the Four Nations tournament. Fittingly, the two opposing full backs from the previous week's Grand Final played major parts, though this time for the same team. Coventry's Richard Pepperell put the Welsh ahead for the first time on the hour, before his counterpart from Hemel, Matt Cannon, sealed a 28-18 victory over England towards the end of the game. Wales were the first winners of the Cheltenham Regency Cup.

The end-of-season awards and recognition of achievements ceremony was held on 19 October at The Willows, Salford prior to the Super League Grand Final at nearby Old Trafford. The 140 club delegates heard a presentation on the new structure for National League Three and had the customary de-briefing session. But Great Britain international Adrian Morley's presence to present the various trophies captured the most attention. Richard Smith was a deserving Player of the Year with Corey Simms equally meritorious in the Young Player category. While the Team of the Year was expected, Coventry Bears, the choice of South London Storm as Club of the Year was perhaps less so, but certainly justified. The club's long, hard work at junior and youth development was now paralleled at open-age level and the future looked bright for both club and game in the deprived areas of London south of the Thames where the Storm worked. A testament to their progress was their end-of-season trip to the South of France to play Realmont XIII. Coach of the Year went to Coventry Bears' Steve Harrison-Mirfield, another string to his sizable bow in the RLC, and the refereeing award went to youngster Ian Jefferson, a match official of immense potential who was already a relative veteran in RLC terms, as he controlled games up and down the country accompanied by his parents.

The Dream Team again epitomised the all-round strength of the competition, with no less than 14 clubs represented in the following 17 chosen players:

Tom Howden (West London Sharks), Phil Pitt (Newcastle Knights), Jake Johnstone (North London Skolars), Ian Bryson (Manchester Knights), Gavin Molloy (Bridlington Bulls), Keri Ryan (South London Storm), Danny Atherton (Manchester Knights), Obi Ijeoma (North London Skolars), Richard Smith (Hemel Hempstead Stags), Paul Dodsworth (Teesside Steelers), Adam Millward (Derby City), Gareth Martin (Hemel Hempstead Stags), Nigel Arismendez (Leicester Phoenix), Richard Whitehouse (Worcestershire Saints), Ian Sheppard (Bedford Swifts), Mick Walker (Oxford Cavaliers), Matt Wright (Coventry Bears).

The 2002 season had been a campaign of change, both actual and impending, and of new dawns for some, and demise for others. For a competition that had lost a key organiser on the eve of the season, the performance of the organisational teams as well as the participants on the field deserved many accolades. Experience is a notable attribute. The RLC now had that in its own ranks as well as being able to draw upon support of others in the game. The prospect of entering the new era for the game league on the back of such a season of progress was less daunting now than it had been at the beginning of May.

10. 2003: Further expansion

Sizable expressions of interest in both the Rugby League Conference and National League Three from clubs currently outside their parameters were expected. However, the level of interest was amazing. As became clear when the composition of the RLC for 2003 was announced, this was a fresh beginning and a whole new stage of development. The competition was still accountable financially and otherwise to the RFL, but was free from the restrictions of the pre-season period 12 months earlier. The application process revealed many new clubs, some resurrections of famous old names, and some virgin rugby league locations. RLC supremo Niel Wood had a problem, but a nice one. At the end of 2002, following the end of the application process, he declared: "We have been massively encouraged by the applications for the new National League and the phenomenal interest shown in the RLC from around England and Wales."

He said the demand for RLC places was "staggering" and also revealed an 'over-subscription' for the places available for RLC clubs in the new National League Three. For RLC 2003, possibly the most exciting prospect was of significant inroads in Wales. At a time of heightened interest in rugby league – the Challenge Cup Final in Cardiff, consideration of governing body status, possible future professional and Super League franchises and Welsh coach Neil Kelly's interest in developing greater connections between heartland clubs and the domestic Welsh game – there was a downturn in the fortunes of Welsh rugby union. There was an opportunity to fill a gap in a country that had never been averse to rugby league. Wales, of course, had yielded some legendary figures in the sport's history. One of these, Mike Nicholas, the current Wales manager, captured the feeling of opportunity, saying in *Rugby League World*: "The Rugby League Conference is a new tactic for us. It's a new approach, something which we can take advantage of while we try to get a professional team on the go. We see it very much as a forerunner of a semi-professional league."

The clubs' location reflected the traditional Welsh rugby strongholds in the south of the country. A Wales division would also produce in rugby league the intense local rivalries that occurred in rugby union and football. However, current RLC side Cardiff, while welcoming new Welsh neighbours, were concerned at losing the ties with their English counterparts that had begun to develop – very successfully in some cases – in 2002. The remedy was sensible. Cardiff would continue to participate in the English part of the RLC, while the new Welsh clubs had a league of their own. Any notion that Cardiff's separation from the other Welsh clubs was due to greater playing strength in England, was dispelled when news of the players joining the new clubs emerged. Bridgend Blue Bulls, for example, included Kevin Ellis, John Devereux and Allan Bateman, all Welsh internationals in both codes.

New activity was not confined to Wales, and exciting new initiatives were happening in very diverse locations. New clubs were formed in Bristol, Lancaster, Carlisle and Gateshead. The latter two included some familiar names. Bev Risman was spearheading the Carlisle Centurions, and former

Gateshead Thunder pair Steve Worsnop and Rob Jones were masterminds of the Gateshead Storm.

Among the current RLC contingent there were also positive developments. Hemel Hempstead Stags received a deserved 21st birthday present by winning three awards at their local authority sports awards ceremony. Dacorum Borough Council honoured Derek Millis for his Service to Sport, Richard Smith as Sports Person of the Year and the club itself in the team performance category. The RLC was also producing more promising players – the number that had gone to professional clubs was evidence of this – but London Broncos wanted to search further into nooks and crannies that could foster potential Super League stars. Following television's *Pop Idol*, the club launched *Prop Idol*, their own promotional search for that elusive star. RLC clubs were part of this process, but the more enterprising could also use the concept to their own advantage.

Paradoxically, even when two clubs lost their coaches there was a positive news slant as St Albans and Luton's losses were gains for Gateshead Thunder and Warrington Wolves. The RLC was now both a hotbed of playing talent and a veritable nursery for aspiring coaches.

There was, unfortunately, nothing constructive from the season's Challenge Cup campaign. Coventry Bears reached the second round, but only by default as Newcastle Knights (the North Eastern representative but also, a fellow RLC club) failed to raise a side to play the Bears at the end of November. The Bears then took on BARLA National Conference side East Hull, who won 48-8. The odds were always stacked against victory due to the competition being played in the RLC off-season, but Coventry gave a good account of themselves. Cardiff Demons fared little better at Shaw Cross in the first round, losing 56-12. Many Cardiff players had played union the day before – not the best preparation for a cup tie in Yorkshire.

The waiting was soon over on how the RLC and National League Three would run in 2003, and, more significantly, who would participate. On 9 January rugby league was again present in Parliament. As had been the case in 1998, there was significant news to announce. The first National League Three line-up was revealed. It contained six RLC 'graduates' - Coventry Bears, Hemel Hempstead Stags, Teesside Steelers, St Albans Centurions, Manchester Knights and Crawley Jets - to complement the four sides from the BARLA ranks with their town names: Bradford-Dudley Hill, Sheffield-Hillsborough Hawks, Warrington-Woolston Rovers and Huddersfield-Underbank Rangers. The club representatives were photographed in playing kit with snow on the Westminster grass. For the RLC, the unprecedented interest in the application process translated into reality. Of 52 clubs, 23 were existing members, four were 'A' teams from National League Three outfits, South Norfolk Saints returned after a season's absence, and sensationally, there were 24 new locations for RLC rugby. The divisional line up was:

North West: Blackpool Sea Eagles, Bolton le Moors, Carlisle Centurions, Chester Wolves, Lancaster, Liverpool Buccaneers.

North East: Bridlington Bulls, Durham Tigers, Gateshead Storm, Newcastle Knights, Leeds Akademiks, Scarborough (soon to be renamed the Yorkshire Coast Tigers), Sunderland City, Whitley Bay Barbarians.

London and the South: Crawley Jets 'A', Greenwich Admirals, Gosport Vikings (soon to become the Gosport & Fareham Vikings), Hemel Hempstead Stags 'A', Kingston Warriors, North London Skolars, South London Storm 'A', West London Sharks.

East: Cambridge Eagles, Essex Eels, Ipswich Rhinos, Luton Vipers, St Ives Roosters, South Norfolk Saints.

South Midlands: Bedford Swifts, Birmingham Bulldogs, Coventry Bears 'A', Leicester Phoenix, Telford Raiders, Wolverhampton Wizards.

North Midlands: Crewe Wolves, Derby City, Mansfield Storm, Nottingham Outlaws, Rotherham Giants, Worksop Sharks.

Wales: Aberavon Fighting Irish, Bridgend Blue Bulls, Cynon Valley Cougars, Rumney Rhinos, Swansea Bulls and one more to be confirmed.

West: Bristol Sonics, Cardiff Demons, Gloucestershire Warriors, Oxford Cavaliers, Somerset Vikings, Worcestershire Saints.

Though the sixth club in the Welsh Division was not yet known, the new membership revealed many successful outcomes to initial enquiries received during Julian Harrison's time as RLC administrator, such as Leeds Akademiks, Bolton le Moors, Greenwich Admirals and Worksop Sharks. Other operations were based on - or at least, heavily made up of - players from the services (Gosport & Fareham Vikings and Somerset Vikings). Nevertheless, Niel Wood's policy of active recruitment had produced instantaneous success, with widespread new rugby league centres. Though Wood revealed that three of the new clubs - Bristol Sonics, Liverpool Buccaneers and Essex Eels - had emerged from discussions on the Totalrl.com website, the more telling influence in translation into practice was Wood's own pursuit of new clubs, the support from the new development department at Red Hall, and the reality of a durable structure into which such novice clubs could slot.

With a new pre-season RLC Cup competition and news of greater links between RLC junior development and the game's Champion Schools and Active Sports programmes, there was much to gladden the hearts of rugby league expansionists, including the RFL executive chairman. Richard Lewis commented in *Rugby League World:* "The expansion of the Conference, together with the nationwide grassroots development activity taking place, shows that our sport is continuing to grow throughout the UK. This year in London alone the game will be played in 23 out of the 32 boroughs and our Active Sports programme will provide new participation opportunities."

A perfect day concluded with a feature on BBC Radio Five Live's evening sports show. RFL director of marketing, Chris Green (London-born and a past player in the London League) was joined by Hemel's Derek Millis to outline the RLC's work and development, and, in Millis' case in particular, to promote the virtues of the sport to a national audience many of whom may have been unaware that the game had a national appeal and national presence.

January also witnessed the baptism of the professional London Skolars. The club had strengthened their squad, but coach Mark Croston was determined to give opportunities to the players responsible for the club's elevation in their amateur days. Off the field, the club were realistic. Budgeting for gates of 250, they sold 110 season-tickets. Increased merchandising and sponsorship ventures were successfully pursued. The club's subsequent performance in National League Two would have wider ramifications, as rugby journalist Huw Richards outlined on the *Play the Ball* website: "...National Three must in time become a test bed for transition to the professional ranks. How the Skolars handle the leap will have a considerable influence on how soon the game's rulers are ready to contemplate that shift."

Meanwhile, pre-season preparations for the RLC were gathering pace. February saw the announcement of the sixth club in the Welsh Division, Torfaen Tigers (from the Pontypool area). The new Lancaster club made news by going 'back to the future'. The club were to play their home games at the Lancaster City FC's Giant Axe, the late nineteenth century habitat of the original Northern Union club in the city. The ground also hosted the Lancaster Charity Cup in the 1930s and 1940s, and the new Lancaster rugby league outfit were looking for the missing trophy.

Coaching appointments also received media attention, with Bristol and Derby revealing new names from the amateur game, Bob Lovell and Dave Lawson, and Carlisle, South London and Gloucestershire announcing sensational coups by capturing Gary Murdock (former Carlisle and Workington player), Darryl Pitt (former London Bronco) and Dave Ellis respectively. Ellis, now defensive coach at Gloucester rugby union club, had experience in the professional and development sectors in England and in France, with Paris St Germain and the French national team.

Greenwich Admirals were yet to play in the RLC, but their achievements were recognised by the local Borough Council who awarded them the prestigious title of Team of the Year. The Admirals aimed to attract players of all ages and become a real community club. The club were seeking to emulate Telford Raiders in establishing a firm junior and youth base from which future players would evolve. Raiders' driving force were Dave and Janet Berry, who had done so much in Shropshire but also for the RLC in previous seasons. That was rewarded as around 60 per cent of the club's current open-age side had come through the club's youth development.

Swansea also turned towards youth. Their under-15 side attracted the attention of Sky Television's *'Boots 'n' All'* programme by journeying to Yorkshire to play Ovenden of Halifax and then having a coaching session as part of the Bradford 'Bulls Connection'. Those responsible for the general game in Wales also had plans to extend development at all levels from juniors, through the schools and into the student and representative sectors, and also to produce more qualified coaches and match officials. There was also a longer-term aim to expand the number of clubs playing rugby league football in Wales in the RLC from six to 16. This would embrace North Wales in addition to spreading the game in the valleys.

March saw the beginning of the inaugural RLC Cup. Originally, the plans were for 19 sides to participate in six groups. Not surprisingly, though, not all those signing up for the competition were able to compete. This was still the rugby union season, and clubs which relied more on players from the other code were more likely to struggle in playing them in formalised 'pre-season friendlies' because of important cup or league games in rugby union. That a great number of matches took place was testament to the clubs and the lure of a new competition. North and South London made encouraging starts, as did Coventry Bears and Rotherham Giants. Other clubs, such as Worcestershire Saints, saw it as a chance to prepare for the season without having to arrange their own matches.

Launch events are a particularly beneficial method of promotion, advertising and club and team bonding. Carlisle Centurions attracted a former Carlisle player from the RFL days - Kiwi legend Dean Bell, who brought with him from Wigan the Challenge Cup trophy. At the beginning of April, Gloucestershire Warriors and Leeds Akademiks also held memorable events, the former an introduction evening and training session and the latter a prestigious occasion with guests Ray French and David Oxley (the chairman of the Student Rugby League). Club director of rugby Graeme Thompson outlined the new club's ambitions and they revealed "one of the most significant sponsorship deals in the competition's short history", according to the RLC website. The sponsors were Code Blue Marketing Services Ltd, their director being a former stand-off at Huddersfield University, demonstrating the benefits to the sport of graduates from the student game. The Akademiks were not alone in attracting new monies into rugby league via club operations. The following are just some examples: Crewe Wolves and Fiat through their Stoke on Trent dealers, B. S. Marson & Son; Derby City and Work it Out (a teambuilding management company with a specific relation to sports clubs); Gateshead Storm and catering company On the Go; and, though not new agreements, the retention by Coventry Bears and Ipswich Rhinos of deals with Workforce Direct and Bellway Homes respectively showed that the clubs were doing many things right and were attractive propositions for business support.

With the National League Divisions One and Two now operational, a further illustration of the benefits of a unified structure was given at the RLC clubs meeting on 5 April in Rochdale. It was now possible for any player from the RLC to qualify for representation at Great Britain level, providing that eligibility criteria were met. This was the case for the Emerging Nations World Cup in 2000, but what was now in place for the European Nations Cup in November was potentially a sustainable system for the future. The selection process and road to stardom was complex - beginning with regional trials for the England Lionhearts and culminating in an RLC squad participating in Great Britain trials – but there were now avenues for both clubs and players at RLC level to advance. As a means of attracting participation and providing incentives, this was the 'icing on the cake'.

April also witnessed the climax of the RLC Cup competition. South London continued to attract attention for their strong performances. Corey Simms established a new RLC record when he scored a try 10 seconds into their match against Greenwich Admirals on 6 April. But the Storm went out in the semi-final to the Skolars. The other semi-final saw Rotherham Giants defeat old rivals Coventry Bears 41-22 and the final would be a north versus south clash on the eve of the Challenge Cup Final in Cardiff. The Demons' base at Old Penarthians was the venue for a game that promised to be close, but failed to live up that expectation. The London side were dominant throughout and tries from Dave Petch, Nick Dodinski, Paul McCorkell, Cory Bennett and two from man-of-the-match Kirk King saw the Skolars capture the inaugural cup as they had done the inaugural league, winning by 30 points to a sole Dan Lynch try for the Giants.

London Skolars had more pressing priorities; being competitive in the professional game was the key aim. Despite some big defeats, their performances showed glimpses of promise and there was a determination and edge to their play. On some days, 'glimpses' were more enduring. They came close to upsetting Dewsbury at Ram Stadium and then secured their first ever professional league competition point at York. The coaching staff were introducing new players to rugby league at this level all the time. What immediately captivated any new visitors was the Skolars' go-ahead ambition and enthusiasm. Sponsorship packages were secured with the Portman Group (encouraging sensible drinking habits), Arriva buses (enabling the Skolars image to be shown as people were bussed around the local area), and a local hostelry became the Skolars pub. To complement this, the club recruited quality development and backroom staff to continue the excellent work of previous years. Successful off the pitch, they now strived to change their fortunes on it. Their patience and hard work were rewarded before the season was over.

While the Skolars' future prospects looked rosy, there was a contrasting fate for another of the RLC's traditional 'big guns'. Crawley Jets were the most successful team in the early years of the competition. Their place in National League Three was virtually 'par for the course'. There was shock throughout the RLC and National League 3 when the club announced that they were withdrawing from the latter before the season had commenced. Following consultation with the players, the club management decided to focus exclusively on the RLC. For chairman Mark Richardson, the realisation that not everyone shared his vision for the club was a bitter blow. His commitment to the Jets had never wavered and his input, both personal and financial, had been immense. Crawley's success had owed as much to Richardson's drive and dedication to the cause as it had to Steve O'Reilly and the players on the pitch. For Niel Wood, as competition organiser, it meant a replacement had to be found. That was South London Storm, their first team and second teams in effect moving up a division to National League Three and the RLC respectively. The selection of the Storm had some irony. Many people had compared South London with Crawley in the junior and youth development versus open-age success debate relating to long-term viability. Now the Storm were ahead in both areas - elevation to the National League while further strengthening their roots. One major result of their development work was shown when Storm youngster Adam Janowski was selected to play for the England under-18s against Wales in Aberavon.

The rapid rise of the South London Storm showed how far some clubs had come in a very short period. Their participation in the RLC was one significant factor among many. St Albans Centurions, also to embark on a new challenging voyage into the National Leagues, were another case in point. The club had moved to a fantastic state-of-the-art facility at Woollams, and were now attracting players who had played at lower grade in Australia's National

Rugby League (NRL). The club were intent on challenging for further advancement through the new pyramid structure.

Teesside's Lloyd Darby encapsulated the feelings of many on the eve of the season in *Rugby League World:* "We are very excited about this new venture and honoured to be a part of it. We've brought in some players with hardened Rugby League experience from Yorkshire and Cumbria, such is the competition's appeal, but we are nervous because we don't know what to expect in the coming months."

This was not confined to those in National League Three. The RLC too, had reached a new stage. Excitement now stretched to new locations and in Wales in particular there was an anticipation of a new dawn for the sport.

The 2003 season got underway on Saturday 3 May. It was like 'manna from heaven' for rugby league expansionists everywhere as the sport descended on previously virgin and more familiar territory. Such a significant growth in clubs increased the possibility of cancelled fixtures and there were fears amongst many observers concerning the viability of some operations. RLC organiser Niel Wood considers the first day of the 2003 season as his most memorable moment in the competition that stretched back to 1997. His reason is simple. All the games took place, months of preparation came to fruition, and to see the results of fixtures from Durham to Kingston, Blackpool to Bridlington, Bristol to Mansfield and Telford to Essex appearing on Teletext was thrilling. And, of course, it was not only the RLC that sprang into life. National League Three kicked off and did so with a sensation. Coventry Bears, fresh from the RLC and only four years old, defeated the seasoned campaigners from Warrington-Woolston Rovers. If that wasn't enough, South London Storm (recruited at the 11th hour), triumphed over Huddersfield-Underbank Rangers, and as an example of club progress, Teesside Steelers travelled to their away fixture at St Albans by plane! Martyn Sadler, in *Rugby Leaguer and League Express* captured the historical essence of the new competition's dawn: "It all points to a great future for Rugby League, and is a great tribute to the tremendous work done by so many people for Rugby League at the grassroots in the last ten years. When you see names like Coventry, St Albans, Teesside, Hemel and South London, you realise that Rugby League will surely never be the same again."

For the RLC, clubs getting to the starting line and launching themselves off at the pistol was one thing. Finishing the course without suffering major injury, setback and handicap was another. The pitfalls of any season were to be expected, but there was a sense of expectation and profile in 2003 that mirrored the first season in 1997, and long-standing RLC participants and observers remembered that there was a casualty (Kingston) six years previously in the pilot initiative. However, the season's early weeks delivered on the pre-season intentions. Games were largely competitive, and those teams that might be struggling on the pitch were compensated by the raw enthusiasm and thrill of taking part. Certain sides caught the eye. Leeds Akademiks and Carlisle Centurions had flying starts, as did established clubs Birmingham Bulldogs and Ipswich Rhinos. In Wales, however, there was something akin to 'rugby league heaven'. The Welsh Division kicked off 24 hours later than the most other fixtures, but when a crowd of more than

1,000 turned up at Bridgend to watch the Blue Bulls, including Ellis, Bateman, Devereux, take on and beat Aberavon Fighting Irish, the wait was most certainly worthwhile. What was more encouraging was that many of the sides had embryonic, if not thriving, junior and youth sections. The RLC provided a shop window for the ambitions of talented young rugby players across South Wales who previously had only played union. Rugby league seemed to realise the moment. There had been false dawns and missed opportunities in the past. There was now both promise and hope, but also definite action. The Cardiff Challenge Cup Final, the appearance of ex-Welsh legends promoting the new competition, the junior development work underpinning everything and the support of Super League clubs came together. Neil Kelly, then coach of Widnes as well as Wales, took his side down to the Valleys at the beginning of June, both to take on London Broncos in an on-the-road fixture in Aberavon, but also to witness the home RLC side defeat Cynon Valley Cougars 66-14. The standard in the Welsh Division was high and pointed a successful competition.

Another sign of competition maturity was the staging of the RLC's first Regional Championships on 24 May. This was a selection vehicle for the England Lionhearts squad. The concept was based on one used by Student Rugby League and 150 players took part representing six regions. Yorkshire beat the South West 18-0 in the final, but the day gave the opportunity to players like 17-year-old twin brothers, Phil and James Berry, the sons of Dave and Janet, from Telford, to display their skills on a national stage.

Another RLC protégé, Oxford Cavaliers' Darrell Griffin, had initially joined the London Broncos. But on 11 June, he made his Super League debut for Wakefield Trinity Wildcats, for whom he had signed an 18 month full-time contract, against Huddersfield Giants. He was the first player to come through the RLC to play in the game's elite competition (though not the first player from an RLC club prior to the advent of the Southern Conference League - Leicester's Lawrence Taylor for example played for Sheffield Eagles). This was both a personal achievement and a collective one for the RLC. It was now more than possible that a future Super League player or even international could emanate not only from Leeds or Wigan, but also from Leicester or Worcester. Griffin led the way, but others soon followed. Joe Mbu, initially with London Skolars, moved to the Broncos. Leeds Akademiks' Andy Rigby attracted the attention of Leeds Rhinos Academy, and Dene Miller of St Albans did likewise at St Helens, while Matt Cook, the former Bedford Swifts junior, moved to the Bradford Bulls, the local paper referring to the new recruit as "Rugby League's Wayne Rooney".

There were other indications of an increasing profile. Leeds Akademiks captain Dom McCormack appeared on Radio Leeds as the draw for the second York Nines tournament took place. Bristol Sonics were boosted by the public support of Wigan-born Bristol City football manager Danny Wilson. Birmingham Bulldogs included Commonwealth Games athlete James Hillier in their line-up for a friendly game against RAF Cosford, and the club also launched a pioneering text service of club updates. Luton Vipers pulled off a transfer sensation by attracting three influential players from Hemel Hempstead Stags, including England Lionhearts captain Richard Smith. On the development front, particularly noteworthy was the formation in London of new women's sides by three of the most enterprising RLC clubs, London Skolars, South London Storm and Kingston Warriors. A regional tournament was held on 11 May prior to the Skolars home National League Two game against Barrow. In a short space of time, a basic representative system was in place enabling the best players to participate in the National Women's Nines Tournament in Blackpool as part of the BARLA Cup Final activities. Also in May, another 'first' occurred in the RLC. The re-arranged fixture between Bolton le Moors and Lancaster was played mid-week. An increasing number of clubs with close geographical ties, though the distance in this case was not small, allowed for such an eventuality. Bolton made home advantage count, winning 14-6 having withstood a severe test from their visitors.

But in June, news came that Bedford Swifts would not be continuing in the competition, shocking people throughout the RLC. After struggling to field sides, and actually failing to do so, club manager Tracey Hirons made the heartbreaking decision to withdraw the club before draconian action was taken by the RLC management. Niel Wood paid tribute to the club's input into the development of the sport in the area, which was strong enough to ensure that a new Bedford club, the Tigers, would soon emerge from the ashes of disappointment. The realisation that the competition had lost its first club mid-season since Kingston's demise in 1997, was compounded by the fact that the Swifts had been a stable operation, and had won the RLC Club of the Year trophy in 2001. However, this showed that should unfavourable circumstances befall a club, there is a risk that however strong that operation may appear on the surface, cracks in the edifice may bring the whole thing down. Looking on from the outside, and with the benefit of this perspective plus past experience in dealing with non-fulfilled fixtures and potential club disasters, Julian Harrison commented: "Knowing how hard Tracey had worked in keeping the club going and how devoted she was to the cause of rugby league in Bedford, I knew just how hurt she would be feeling. No-one likes having to cancel games and no-one does this by choice. It is a last resort when all other eventualities have been pursued, but what some fail to recognise is the human emotions as well as the desperate work that go into such circumstances. It is very easy to castigate clubs when they pull out of fixtures - until those throwing the punches have to take them themselves."

Mid-summer meant the re-emergence of internationalism. The Four Nations tournament started and shared the limelight with the York Nines Festival, England defeating a Scotland side featuring eight players from RLC clubs in their squad by 28-20. The other opening fixture saw Ireland defeat reigning Champions Wales 32-28, showing the development of the Irish side.

Further recognition came when the York Nines and its younger sibling in Middlesex came under the auspices - for the first time - of the European Rugby League Federation. French club Lezignan captured the Fairfax Cup in York, but RLC clubs were far from disgraced. Reigning champions London Koogas went out in the quarter-finals and Lancaster, Worcestershire Saints and Carlisle Centurions all made the last 16. Leeds Akademiks reached the York City Knights Shield final, losing narrowly to Zuid Holland. The Royal Engineers were victorious in the Middlesex Nines, defeating hosts London

Skolars 20-14 in the final, but the event also served - as its sister in York continued to do - to introduce new sides and possibilities for international competition and the RLC. Embracing teams from many areas, the South East in particular, it included London Nigerians, a team of players of Nigerian descent that in time could provide the basis for a full national side. One year later, teams representing South Africa and the West Indies were taking part.

In the June edition of *Rugby League World*, Phil Caplan illustrated the growth and development of the RLC, by revealing a current total of 2,580 registered players, only 4 per cent of whom were also registered with BARLA. Potential new RLC clubs were organising friendly fixtures to demonstrate their suitability for future inclusion. These included North Wales Coasters, Peterlee Pumas, Rugby Raiders and Wetherby Bulldogs. The regular series of RLC fixtures, 10 in total, drew to a close at the end of July. It had been - the Bedford situation apart - a greatly encouraging start to the campaign. Only three clubs - Carlisle Centurions, Bridgend Blue Bulls and Birmingham Bulldogs – had 100 per cent records, though Leeds Akademiks would have joined them had they not slipped up against Yorkshire Coast Tigers on 19 July by drawing 6-6. As usual, the London and South division was extremely competitive, with Crawley finishing top. This was mirrored by the North East. Newcastle Knights, Bridlington Bulls and Gateshead Storm pushed Leeds Akademiks tremendously hard, and Sunderland City and the Scarborough-based Yorkshire Coast side were both competitive. Only points' difference separated Nottingham from Mansfield at the top of the North Midlands Division. Elsewhere, South Norfolk Saints and Cardiff Demons held off determined challenges to capture their respective divisional titles.

	North East Division	Pl	W	D	L	F	A	Diff	Pts
1	Leeds Akademiks	10	9	1	0	347	121	226	19
2	Newcastle Knights	10	8	0	2	402	198	204	16
3	Bridlington Bulls	10	7	0	3	508	110	398	14
4	Gateshead Storm	10	7	0	3	357	151	206	14
5	Sunderland City	10	4	0	6	253	429	-176	8
6	Yorkshire Coast Tigers	10	3	1	6	263	304	-41	7
7	Durham Tigers	10	1	0	9	172	465	-293	2
8	Whitley Bay Barbarians	10	0	0	10	126	650	-524	0

	North West Division	Pl	W	D	L	F	A	Diff	Pts
1	Carlisle Centurions	10	10	0	0	554	104	450	20
2	Chester Wolves	10	8	0	2	398	258	140	16
3	Bolton le Moors	10	6	0	4	335	267	68	12
4	Liverpool Buccaneers	10	3	0	7	210	371	-161	6
5	Blackpool Sea Eagles	10	2	0	8	200	476	-276	4
6	Lancaster	10	1	0	9	162	383	-221	2

	North Midlands Division	Pl	W	D	L	F	A	Diff	Pts
1	Nottingham Outlaws	10	8	0	2	402	143	259	16
2	Mansfield Storm	10	8	0	2	289	170	119	16
3	Crewe Wolves	10	7	0	3	307	190	117	14
4	Rotherham Giants	10	4	0	6	332	258	74	8
5	Derby City	10	3	0	7	214	297	-83	6
6	Worksop Sharks	10	0	0	10	77	563	-486	0

South Midlands Division	Pl	W	D	L	F	A	Diff	Pts
1 Birmingham Bulldogs	8	8	0	0	453	80	373	16
2 Leicester Phoenix	8	4	0	4	204	219	-15	8
3 Wolverhampton Wizards	8	3	0	5	135	239	-104	6
4 Telford Raiders	8	3	0	5	137	258	-121	6
5 Coventry Bears 'A'	8	2	0	6	196	329	-133	4

Bedford Swifts record expunged

South West Division	Pl	W	D	L	F	A	Diff	Pts
1 Cardiff Demons	10	9	0	1	510	123	387	18
2 Gloucestershire Warriors	10	7	0	3	468	178	290	14
3 Somerset Vikings	10	6	0	4	324	207	117	12
4 Oxford Cavaliers	10	3	0	7	247	393	-146	6
5 Worcestershire Saints	10	3	0	7	133	482	-349	6
6 Bristol Sonics	10	2	0	8	226	525	-299	4

Wales Division	Pl	W	D	L	F	A	Diff	Pts
1 Bridgend Blue Bulls	10	10	0	0	608	197	411	20
2 Aberavon Fighting Irish	10	7	0	3	500	285	215	14
3 Torfaen Tigers	10	6	0	4	363	357	6	12
4 Rumney Rhinos	10	3	0	7	344	411	-67	6
5 Cynon Valley Cougars	10	2	1	7	247	552	-305	5
6 Swansea Bulls	10	1	1	8	244	504	-260	3

East Division	Pl	W	D	L	F	A	Diff	Pts
1 South Norfolk Saints	10	9	0	1	495	181	314	18
2 Ipswich Rhinos	10	8	0	2	512	162	350	16
3 Essex Eels	10	6	0	4	532	258	274	12
4 Luton Vipers	10	5	0	5	452	330	122	10
5 St Ives Roosters	10	2	0	8	158	640	-482	4
6 Cambridge Eagles	10	0	0	10	72	650	-578	0

London & South Division	Pl	W	D	L	F	A	Diff	Pts
1 Crawley Jets	10	9	0	1	563	179	384	18
2 West London Sharks	10	8	0	2	438	185	253	16
3 Gosport & Fareham Vikings	10	8	0	2	403	233	170	16
4 North London Skolars 'A'	10	6	1	3	358	199	159	13
5 Kingston Warriors	10	4	0	6	239	342	-103	8
6 Greenwich Admirals	10	3	1	6	298	350	-52	7
7 South London Storm 'A'	10	1	0	9	100	596	-496	2
8 Hemel Hempstead Stags 'A'	10	0	0	10	157	472	-315	0

The play-off format had been changed to a system akin to the Australian NRL and Super League models. Despite the increase in tension and importance, both sides of the draw, Harry Jepson Trophy and Shield, produced some free-flowing rugby league and tight knock-out contests. Carlisle's 68-2 destruction of Leeds Akademiks side in front of 400 supporters at Gilford Park rekindled memories of past triumphs by the Border Raiders, the game's previous incarnation there. On 1 August, over 700 fans witnessed Bridgend's 38-16 triumph over Cardiff. The game was featured on Sky Television's *Boots n' All* programme, and the sense of occasion was captured on the Totalrl.com website in its reference to the fixture as "the biggest game in its (South Wales) post-war history between two Welsh clubs."

In the Shield, three new clubs dominated - Torfaen Tigers, Bolton le Moors and Somerset Vikings - though Rotherham Giants threatened to emulate past glories, reaching the semi-finals before falling to Bolton 38-16.

Notwithstanding the disappointment of defeat, it was encouraging to hear positive reflections that encapsulated the RLC ethos. Bristol captain Ben Morris declared on the Totalrl.com website: "At the start of the year many of our players had never seen a rugby league game on television, let alone played it. Now they love the sport and can't wait for the next season to start. There have been some disappointments this season, but also some great highs, like the York Nines and our recent win over Somerset. We've got to take those positives into the next campaign when it starts in the spring."

At the end of a gruelling, yet rewarding series of matches, the semi-final stage resulted in victories for Carlisle over Birmingham by a convincing 44-2 and Bridgend over Ipswich by a closer 44-24 in the Harry Jepson Trophy, with Torfaen joining Bolton le Moors in the Shield Final courtesy of a 36-26 victory over Gosport & Fareham Vikings. It was hard on Birmingham and Ipswich, ever-present members of the RLC, who had made massive strides over the previous 12 months. Both gained confidence from a season of success, and for the Rhinos players at Broadstreet, Coventry, there was some consolation in the knowledge that they had played against and pushed hard some prestigious names in the Bridgend ranks. The occasion featured the remarkable sight of Ipswich personnel asking for autographs and requesting photo opportunities with at least one of their opponents – dual code international Allan Bateman.

While the RLC had attracted clubs from virtually every area of England and a large part of South Wales, there was still interest in the possibility of extending the concept further. Scotland had their own summer Conference, with beginnings of efforts to nurture a closer relationship with England. There was also a domestic game in Ireland, predominantly centred on Dublin. However, there were indications that Rugby League Ireland were contemplating their own Rugby League Conference, based on the model over the water, with three regional leagues. Such was the spirit of the times that - despite some hurdles to overcome with rugby union in the Emerald Isle - this vision was rapidly to become reality. Links with the RLC were already in place, both through the Four Nations competition and individual player connections, largely from the student game. Coventry Bears' Alan Robinson and Gavin Gordon of London Skolars and West London Sharks fame both had footholds in Student Rugby League and the RLC. They began to form an Ireland Exiles team as part of strengthening the overall Irish international structure. A Scottish equivalent already existed.

Before bringing consideration of the 2003 RLC season to an end, a glance at the National Leagues would make interesting viewing to anyone with an affinity to the summer Conference. In a remarkable continuation of their success in the RLC, Teesside Steelers had reached the inaugural National League Three Final at Winnington Park rugby club, the home of the Crewe Wolves. They had confirmed the worthiness of development clubs when faced by heartland opposition, by going to Bradford-Dudley Hill in the qualifying semi-final and coming away with a 10-8 victory to secure their final berth.

They were not the only club with RLC connections to succeed, as South London Storm and St Albans Centurions in particular had carried the fight to more fancied outfits and gained new-found respect and accolades. The Steelers story was not to have a happy ending, however, as they found the enforced lay-off as a result of their early succession to the final difficult, and were no match for a classy and more deserving Warrington-Woolston Rovers side who played magnificently in the Final to win 42-6.

Nevertheless, the end of season recognition of achievement deservedly acknowledged the input of the Steelers and other development sides. Teesside's Tom Sibley won the Young Player of the Year award and Peter Tonkin of St Albans won the coaching award. The inaugural National League Three Dream Team featured one player from South London, two from Teesside and three from St Albans. Further up the national scale, 24 August was a momentous day for London Skolars as they won for the first time in their professional history, walloping Gateshead Thunder 48-14. Their season now included a positive result along with all the other developments that had transformed the club in an unprecedented fashion in a few short years. Further achievement came their way when South African Rubert Jonker was included in the National League Two representative side to face the New Zealand tourists in October. It all showed what a good grounding participation in the RLC had been.

The lead-up to the RLC Final had been dramatic off the pitch. On securing their respective places in the Grand and Shield Finals, both Bridgend Blue Bulls and Torfaen Tigers had contacted Niel Wood to point out that, due to players contracted to rugby union clubs, they would have severe player availability problems for the original date of Saturday 6 September. They both requested a postponement for 24 hours. Memories of 1998 and Crawley versus South Norfolk came flooding back, but there was also an additional dimension in the form of the venue. The possibility had arisen of playing a pre- and post-match game at Wilderspool around the Super League fixture between Warrington and Halifax. The lure of such a venue, especially considering Warrington's impending move away from the legendary ground, combined with the media-friendly and nostalgic return of ex-Warrington players Ellis and Bateman, ensured that this was a really attractive proposition. Nevertheless, a precedent had been set five years previously. Following extensive discussions and the co-operation of all the competing clubs, it was decided to take up the Wilderspool option and the game date was moved. Niel Wood paid tribute to the players and officials of the four clubs in question: "The fact that they worked together to come up with such an amicable agreement speaks volumes for the spirit, camaraderie and sense of togetherness engendered by the competition."

Nevertheless, there were dissenting voices. Paul Kelso in *The Guardian* commented: "The credibility of this summer's encouraging developments in Wales has suffered a blow" and that "the withdrawal [of Bridgend from the original scheduled Saturday] is a blow to any hopes of a Bridgend team entering National League Two next season". Only time will tell whether there will be any lasting damage to the promotion prospects of the two clubs in question. Of immediate concern once the switch had been confirmed was the fact that some players would play competitive games in two different sports on consecutive days. If there were aching limbs and tired minds, they weren't apparent when it came to the 'wire'. At half-time in the Shield Final, it looked like Torfaen were on the way to victory. Leading 20-12 with four tries in the process, things looked ominous for Bolton. However, hooker Craig Kay had other ideas. A fine hat-trick complemented by two tries from Dave Hindley, overturned the deficit and sealed a deserved victory, 28-21.

The Grand Final between Bridgend and Carlisle followed a similar pattern, though this time there was a decisive twist towards the end, to the benefit of the team from the Valleys. In a magnificent contest well officiated by local referee and RLC stalwart (despite his young age) Garath Illidge, the Blue Bulls were ahead 16-10 at half-time. However, 20 minutes further on and the Cumbrians were leading 26-22, delighting their many fans in the ground and listeners back home receiving the commentary live on BBC Radio Cumbria. Richard Campbell, Paul McGee and Chris Sawyers had scored tries in 10 minutes, and the onus was now on Kevin Ellis and his Welsh side to respond. Man-of-the-match Karl Hocking quickly levelled matters and there was no looking back. A further try from full back Mark Davies and three points from goals by John Williams secured a 33-26 win, and for the first-time the Harry Jepson Trophy was journeying outside England. The teams lined up as follows:

Torfaen Tigers: Nolan Nickolin, Damian Smith, Adrian Fowler, Luke Bingham, Mike Stephens, Richard Jenkins, Gareth Jenkins, Steff Jones, Jason Hill, Jammie Juene, Lee Taylor, Damian Hudd, Phil Marsh.
Subs: Kevin Jones, Nick Blake, Gareth Davies, Mike Davies.
Bolton le Moors: Ryan Kelly, Andy Bowling, Dave Hindley, Mark Bolton, Darryl Leach, Kevin Coward, Martin Fisher, Gary Dooney, Craig Kay, Mark Cain, Chris Brett, Rob Whittaker, Dave Peel.
Subs: Nick Cook, Mark Brindell, Marc Simon, Darren Wright, Paul Crook, Anthony Robinson, Carl Kelly.
Bridgend Blue Bulls: Mark Davies, John Williams, John Devereux, Geraint Lewis, Lenny Woodard, Allan Bateman, Kevin Ellis, Nathan Strong, Dan Williams, Karl Hocking, Paul Morgan, Phil Wheeler, Marcus Sainsbury.
Subs: Craig Fox, Gareth Bartlett, Griff Davies, Dan Shore.
Carlisle Centurions: Craig Stalker, Andrew Sawyers, Jamie Watson, Martin Sawyers, Dean Haney, Dale Semple, Mike Marsden, Richard Nicholson, Steven Brough, Paul McGee, Richard Campbell, Richard Massey, Eddie Robinson.
Subs: James Mackay, Russ Stewart, Chris Sawyers, Gary Murdock.

An indication of the impact the RLC's final was now making could be seen after the game. While Bridgend stand-off Allan Bateman called for further assistance for rugby league development in Wales, the Carlisle players enjoyed a civic reception. RLC media manager Phil Caplan revealed the massive surge of interest in the competition's big day, with congratulatory phone calls even being received from France due to media coverage in the international editions of a number of newspapers, including the *Daily Mail*. It had taken a good few years for equivalent development finals, such as the student Varsity match to really gain a foothold in the rugby league calendar. However, only six years had passed since the inaugural SCL final, and comparisons with that match, North London versus Leicester, were striking in terms of wider levels of interest and acclaim.

The growth in prominence of the Grand Final encapsulated the 2003 season overall. Many clubs reported successful media work. Leeds Akademiks featured on both Radio Leeds and Sky Television's *Boots n' All*, for example, and the August edition of *Rugby League World* covered further club successes in this area. Radio was a particularly beneficial medium. There were so many positive things to report in addition to the competition itself. Development positions at London Skolars and in Hertfordshire, links to Active Sports and Service Area programmes, a new breath of life for rugby league in Wales reflected in support from both within and outside the game, even venturing to rugby union with some extremely warm words from Aberavon RFC director of rugby Chris O'Callaghan, all illustrated the 'feel good' factor surrounding the RLC.

In Wales, Aberavon Fighting Irish were the first winners of the '*Rugby League World* Amateur Club of the Month', and national coach Neil Kelly's full squad for 2003 included five players who had played in the RLC that summer. To top it all, the Welsh amateur team regained the Cheltenham Regency Cup as winners of the Four Nations, again defeating England in the crunch fixture, this time 28-18 in Port Talbot. If there was a previous halcyon era for Welsh rugby league, the present period must be a strong rival to it, and it promises to get even better.

The clubs celebrated their achievements with end of season functions, choosing their own recipients of individual awards and attracting some notable guests. St Ives Roosters' Junior Night, for example, featured rising St Helens star Mike Bennett. This was quite a coup, though the fact that his brother Steve was the inspiration and driving force behind the Cambridgeshire club might have had some bearing.

As far as the league awards were concerned, an increase in the number of categories meant more trophies to be won. RLC clubs gathered in Widnes in early October when all was revealed. In addition to recognising the divisional champions, the following were successful:

Best Programme: Worksop Sharks; *Best Media & PR:* Bristol Sonics; *Best Administration:* Telford Raiders; *Best New Club:* Gateshead Storm; *Referee of the Year:* Garath Illidge; *Club of the Year:* Ipswich Rhinos; *Team of the Year:* Bridgend Blue Bulls; *Coach of the Year:* Kevin Weaver (Torfaen Tigers); *Young Player of the Year:* Sean O'Brien (Aberavon Fighting Irish); *Player of the Year:* Craig Stalker (Carlisle Centurions).

The chosen 'Dream Team' also reflected the great all-round strength of the competition, with 12 clubs represented in the final line-up:

Craig Stalker (Carlisle Centurions), Tom Brown (Gloucestershire Warriors), Paul Curphey (Chester Wolves), Jamie Watson (Carlisle Centurions), Lenny Woodard (Bridgend Blue Bulls), Peter LeMarquand (Ipswich Rhinos), Dan McCormack (Leeds Akademiks), Mark Baines (Birmingham Bulldogs), Rob Brown (Nottingham Outlaws), Scott Eccles (Bridlington Bulls), Darren Ryan (Aberavon Fighting Irish), Chris Storey (Mansfield Storm), Tony Emmins (Crawley Jets).

Despite setbacks, the 2003 season must be classified as a success. With such an increase in the number of clubs entering the RLC and a new competition in National League Three that put greater demands on its

141

constituent clubs and brought RLC and BARLA backgrounds together, there was always a chance of unrealised expectation. Would the moving train that was the RLC - varying in speed throughout its previous six years - significantly slow down and possibly even stop? Would the compromise that was the inaugural National League Three format and composition simply reveal a gulf between established operations in the north, and the ambitious newcomers from elsewhere? The answer to both questions was clearly 'no'. Moreover, there were already movements towards 2004. The RFL invited clubs to register their interest in both RLC and National League Three, and Essex Eels and Bramley were both keen to be considered for the latter.

While the powers that be contemplated adjustments to the current structures, some clubs in the Midlands and South simply got on with playing. A winter Merit League was organised by Midlands referee Nick Evans and had attracted interest from as far apart as Scarborough, Greenwich, St Ives and Telford. It all showed the enormous strides the competition and its clubs had taken, borne out of hard work, dedication, perseverance and no shortage of bravery. All these attributes could equally be applied to Ian Cooper, a man who had done much to assist the developments he now announced he was leaving. The BARLA chief executive was to take up a position outside of rugby league with the West Yorkshire Probation Board. It was undoubtedly a great loss to the game as a whole, not just the amateur sector that he served so well for many years. As people within the RLC and National Leagues contemplated with satisfaction the progress that had been made and looked forward to what 2004 would bring, a moment of reflection to consider the input of the affable and always dependable Cooper would also have been appropriate.

11. 2004: Into the heartlands

The clubs meeting in Widnes on Sunday 5 October revealed information on the 2003 season that showed massive achievements and encouraged all involved in the competition. For example, a fantastic 92 per cent of matches took place, involving over 3,000 registered players. Interestingly, only 20 per cent of respondents to the clubs survey said they were heavily reliant on rugby union players. The meeting's purpose was to analyse the 2003 season and use the information from the survey to assist in the competition's development. From that perspective, the overriding message appeared to be a call for organic growth and against significant change; though an increasing movement towards partnership working with Scotland and Ireland and also in the direction of National League Three, were also telling conclusions that didn't necessarily contract those general feelings.

However, the admission of so many new clubs in 2003 and the prospect of more for 2004 was a marked change in direction. Phil Caplan indicated in the *BARLA Bulletin:* "With credibility established, and more importantly in 2003, six clubs graduating to National League 3 – a sure fire indication of improving standards – the management philosophy deliberately changed to be one of encouraging participation wherever there was a demand."

The RLC in 2004 was to have a slogan that reflected both club and league administration aims. The RLC was to be 'bigger, better and stronger'.

The clubs were doing their bit to justify the slogan. London Skolars held a festival for years 7 and 8 pupils as a culmination of six weeks intensive coaching, introducing the game to a new local audience. None of those taking part had played the sport before. The Skolars were also nurturing further links with the London Broncos, with academy players moving between the clubs to enhance their development, though the first beneficiaries were Broncos under-18 players being given opportunities in North London. Across town, Greenwich Admirals were also busy. The club announced the appointment as joint head coach of former Sheffield Eagles and Batley Bulldogs player Steve Walker, and also had significant representation in the London and the South regional sides at under-14 to under-16 level. Despite being in existence for only a year, the impact made by the exuberant Essex Eels had been immense. This was recognised by their local BBC radio station as the Eels received the 'best club' title at their annual sports awards. And across the region, a tremendous 151 teams entered the Powergen Champion Schools competition.

The good news was not confined to the South East. Striving for entrance into the RLC for 2004 were the Peterlee Pumas, who had been encouraged by near neighbours Teesside. There was an RFL-appointed development officer in the North East, the benefits of which were evident as a new County Durham Service Area for the sport came into existence. The new body's inaugural chairman was Rob Laverick, the instrumental force behind the Peterlee club. A mini-league festival was held at the Pumas' home ground with teams from five local primary schools. A further illustration of the relationship between the student and RLC sectors was the launch of the Leeds Varsity Nines competition. The Akademiks were the graduate arm of the university game based in north Leeds, and the Nines strengthened links between all respective playing channels.

As usual, the RLC off-season was dominated by international competition. Places in the Great Britain amateur side were up for grabs and a selection festival at Leigh on 18 October included players from the RLC in the Four Nations Select side. The team's captain was an RLC stalwart, former Gloucestershire and now Somerset Viking, Chris Richards. This was a notable achievement, but was arguably bettered by the choice of five Conference players in the full Welsh side that beat the Russians in Aberavon eight days later. Amidst seasoned full international players such as Paul Atcheson, Adam Hughes and Hefin O'Hare were veterans Kevin Ellis and Allan Bateman and the less well-known Damian Hudd, Aled James and Lennie Woodard. The latter made quite an impression, scoring a hat-trick of tries. Wales coach Neil Kelly was delighted with the result and a new source of players of an appropriate standard. He commented in *Rugby Leaguer and League Express:* "...I've been impressed with the Conference players like Woodard and Hudd, we'll be looking closely at that league for more new recruits."

Though Woodard and Hudd were missing (Woodard returned for the fixture against England in the European Nations Cup), the other three players were included against Australia a week later. Also taking on an Australian team were South London Storm, boosted by recruits from other London amateur sides. This side from down under was slightly different. It included Craig Coleman, Andrew Farrar, Rod Wishart and Trevor 'the axe' Gillmeister in a legends team, and a crowd approaching 400 witnessed the novel encounter that had come about through the input of club sponsor *The Elusive Camel*, who also happened to be hosting the Australian visitors. Such was the camaraderie engendered by the occasion that a reciprocal visit was arranged for summer 2004. The other on-pitch adventure of the off-season was the Challenge Cup. Four RLC and National League Three sides were in the first round, though none were successful. All went out to BARLA clubs, hampered by the perennial problem of playing out of season.

Notwithstanding the start of rugby league's most famous competition, the sporting attention of the nation was focused on rugby union in Australia for their World Cup. England, inspired by former league man Jason Robinson, won the Webb Ellis Trophy, but it was not just the XV-a-side game that benefited. In early December, *Rugby Leaguer and League Express* reported greater interest in participation in rugby league, and mentioned some RLC clubs, such as Derby City, as examples. An interest in rugby of either code coupled with the playing opportunities now available in league throughout the country clearly had a significant effect.

The stream of club initiatives grew and grew. Of notable interest were new signings. Coventry Bears attracted former St George and Penrith loose forward Troy Perkins to Coundon Road as player-coach with the prospect of further Australians from the Sydney Metropolitan Cup. Manchester Knights also turned their attention to the southern hemisphere and Brisbane in particular, confirming the recruitment of three players from the Broncos Academy. Bristol Sonics appointed their first director of coaching in Ian Newman, and Liverpool Buccaneers pulled off a mammoth coup by securing the services of England students coach Lee Addison. This did not go unnoticed by the higher echelons of the Rugby League Conference.

One of the competition's leading officials, David Asquith, reached a personal milestone, refereeing his 1,000th game. In *Rugby Leaguer and League Express*, he recalled an amusing incident in the 2003 RLC season: "I was refereeing Blackpool and Chester in last summer's Conference and after the game a woman came up to me and said: 'I've been watching you for 20 years, Asquith, and you're still bloody crap'." Officiating at that many fixtures requires talent and appreciation. Asquith has both. His commitment to the RLC has been monumental, regularly taking games far from his York home.

Finally, sponsorships continued to be negotiated. One of the most eye-catching (literally!) was Newcastle Knights' deal with a local lap-dancing establishment. The RLC continued to set new parameters for the game.

Niel Wood had not waited too long into the off-season before revealing the format and schedule for the 2004 season application process. With another anticipated flood of new applications, it was important to establish clear procedures and a time framework. He also spent a week in November visiting applicants for the 2004 competition. Clearly if the competition was to expand, careful consideration had to be given to each formal enquiry. Not that existing clubs' continuation in the competition was guaranteed. Three of the 51 clubs in question were asked to resubmit their applications due to various concerns over performance.

Wood was equally concerned with entrants into National League Three. That certain clubs (Essex Eels, Carlisle Centurions and Bramley Buffaloes, for example) were putting themselves in the running was no secret. With decisions made, the customary embargo on public announcement was put in force, but did not go according to plan. In December, *Rugby Leaguer and League Express* revealed that National League Three was to increase to 14 clubs, including the three clubs mentioned above and Birmingham Bulldogs.

However, for the RLC, things were less settled. A consultation paper had been circulated detailing the possible inclusion of sides from traditional league strongholds such as Hull, Cumbria, Wakefield and Widnes. Though clubs were asked for their views, it appeared on the surface that the possibility was high (perhaps bordering on probable) that the change of policy specified two months previously would manifest itself in this significant geographical expansion. If there was a demand for RLC rugby in these areas of northern England, that demand could now be satisfied. Such an undertaking was never likely to be universally agreed upon, and questioning voices were quickly heard. It was a radical departure from the competition's original *raison d'être*, and flung open barriers that had been carefully (but not conclusively) erected in previous seasons with debates on the extension of the boundaries to include Chester, Manchester and Rotherham.

Early in the New Year the same newspaper that had broken the story regarding National League Three did likewise on the RLC. There was nothing surprising in the news that the heartland clubs' admission was to be rubber-stamped, though it was revealed that two existing clubs had requested - without success - that such clubs be ring-fenced to reduce the chances of one-sided contests. On 21 January, a press conference and launch at

Birmingham's Civic Hall revealed the admission of 18 new clubs, two new divisions in Cumbria and Yorkshire, an amended play-off format to reflect the uneven numbers per division and the inception of a Welsh Grand Finals Day. The new divisional composition was as follows:

Cumbria: West Cumbria, Copeland Athletic, Barrow Shipbuilders, Penrith Pumas, Carlisle Centurions 'A'.

North East: Gateshead Storm, Newcastle Knights, Whitley Bay Barbarians, Sunderland City, Durham Tigers, Yorkshire Coast Tigers, Peterlee Pumas, Jarrow Vikings.

Yorkshire: Bridlington Bulls, Leeds Akademiks, South Wakefield Sharks, Hull Phoenix, Wetherby Bulldogs, Sheffield-Hillsborough Hawks 'A' (moved to North Midlands), Huddersfield-Underbank 'A', Bradford-Dudley Hill 'A'.

North Midlands: Derby City, Nottingham Outlaws, Mansfield Storm, Worksop Sharks, Thorne Moor Marauders (moved to Yorkshire), Rotherham Giants.

East: Ipswich Rhinos, South Norfolk Saints, Cambridge Eagles, St Ives Roosters, North London Skolars, Middlesex Lions, Hemel Hempstead Stags 'A', Luton Vipers.

South: Gosport & Fareham Vikings, Greenwich Admirals, Crawley Jets, West London Sharks, South London Storm 'A', Kingston Warriors.

North West: Lancaster, Blackpool Sea Eagles, Liverpool Buccaneers, Bolton le Moors, Chester Wolves, North Wales Coasters, Widnes Saints, Crewe Wolves.

Wales: Swansea Valley Miners (new name), Aberavon Fighting Irish, Bridgend Blue Bulls, RCM Cougars (new name – then changed to Valley Cougars), Cardiff Demons, Newport Titans, Torfaen Tigers.

South West: Somerset Vikings, Bristol Sonics, Gloucestershire Warriors, Worcestershire Saints, Oxford Cavaliers, Telford Raiders.

Midlands: Leicester Phoenix, Rugby Raiders, Wolverhampton Wizards, Birmingham Bulldogs 'A', Coventry Bears 'A'. St Albans Centurions 'A' later admitted.

Not surprisingly, the focus was on the new clubs. Niel Wood revealed the openness in the debate concerning the admission of clubs in 'heartland' areas, with a desire to seek, though not necessarily incorporate, all views. He said that the majority of clubs had not "felt the need to comment". In addition to the much-publicised slogan, the rallying call and new era was "making the game open to everyone everywhere". Nevertheless, certain central tenets of the RLC would not change. A commitment to participation was one. A commitment to development was another, whether that be in Widnes or Whitley Bay. That development would differ depending on local circumstances. In Cumbria, for example, it meant an assurance that clubs would not field professional players. Arguments will always rage over what exactly constitutes 'development', but what was clear was a sense of process, not only for 2004, but also for the future of the competition which would almost certainly lead to further stratification, this time with respect to playing and other standards, not simply geography. The 2004 arrangements were a 'stepping stone' towards the premier league(s) concept much talked about in competition circles for a number of previous years.

The Birmingham occasion was shared between the RLC and National League Three, for the latter also had much to shout about. The rise of the

146

Essex Eels was astonishing. Their elevation to National League status owed much to the club philosophy of working in the community. For the local side in Birmingham, advancement - in contrast to the Eels - had taken longer to come to fruition, though again an emphasis on community development was at their core. A return to their old ground at Moor Lane was also on the cards, though it would be a very different facility to the one from their early years in the RLC and EMARLA. Part of the University of Central England, the venue was the subject of a £1.2 million facelift. It was a new beginning and a new challenge, but one both clubs - and Carlisle Centurions - were determined to face.

It had been another memorable day. In *Rugby Leaguer and League Express*, Tim Butcher alluded to the immediate impact: "Within hours of the joint launch of the National League Three and TotalRL.com Conference seasons at Birmingham Civic Hall, stories were springing up on local Ceefax news sites on television sets all around the country. Rugby League is reaching places it never reached until the Conference came along."

While the opening clashes in the RLC and National League Three were still some months away, the opening of National League Two was just around the corner. London Skolars had had a successful off-season. The joy of that inaugural win against Gateshead had translated into further optimism and re-energising for 2004. National recognition had come in a readers' poll conducted by *Rugby Leaguer and League Express*. The Skolars had come fourth in the Club of the Year category, behind Bradford Bulls, York City Knights and Warrington Wolves. The club progressed to the fourth round of the Challenge Cup. And in the Arriva Trains Cup, they beat Sheffield Eagles 16-14. The club also supported an Active Sports initiative that culminated in the creation of the Haringey Hornets playing at the New River Stadium.

In St Albans on 12 February, the London Broncos took on a Barbarians side composed of players from RLC clubs in and around Greater London. The Broncos Super League prowess shone through, but what was significant was that a Super League club in the south felt that they could find appropriate opposition in their own area to help their pre-season preparations.

That the day also witnessed an extensive regional programme of action in the Powergen Champion Schools competition only reinforced the progress made, as did the number of players emanating from RLC and National League Three clubs in the Broncos 2004 Academy squad. Among the represented clubs were London Skolars, Greenwich Admirals, West London Sharks, St Albans Centurions, South London Storm and Kingston Warriors.

More competitive than the contest at St Albans was the second season of the RLC Cup. Beginning at the end of February with 22 scheduled sides challenging to emulate London Skolars inaugural season success, it had a similar pattern to the previous season, with a host of non-fulfilled games and the same concentration of support. For some, there were other distractions. Moves to affiliate the Welsh RLC clubs to counterparts in Super League were in their early stages. Equally significant were changes in the England Lionhearts set-up. A new coach was needed to replace the outgoing Connor Gissaine, and the successful candidate was Liverpool Buccaneers' Lee Addison. Replacing Duncan Merrill (who had tendered his resignation) was

Nick Evans, who was familiar to the RLC as a referee. The same regional championship format was to operate, but supplemented by a series of regional advisors scouting playing talent throughout the RLC.

Also new was a club in Bedford. The Swifts' demise during the early stages of the 2003 season had been one of the most disappointing episodes in the RLC's entire history. The Bedford Tigers were initially to play in the London Amateur League.

It was ironic that this development agenda and the arrival of so many new sides coincided with the demise of two recipients of the Harry Jepson Trophy. Crawley's fall had begun 12 months earlier when they opted out of the inaugural National League Three. Nevertheless the news that they were now withdrawing from the RLC still came as a massive shock. The departure of key individuals was a major factor, but the failure to put down firm roots from which players could emerge hastened their end. It was not for the want of trying. The club had made moves in development, with both Rod Chinn and former Scotland development officer, Ian Johnstone involved at various stages. However, the effort had not been translated into practical results.

If the Jets' exit was a shock, the departure of Teesside Steelers from National League Three was greeted with disbelief. Only a few months previously the club had reached the inaugural NL3 final, despatching Bradford-Dudley Hill on the way. There were a number of premeditating circumstances. Criticism was levelled at the club for an absence of any youth development. While there were no teams at this level, the club had hardly benefited from significant assistance in this work, and attention - with restricted resources and manpower - had focused on the open-age set-up to ensure a competitive face in both the RLC and the National League. The demands of the 2003 season had been great, especially with Teesside's geographical position. The club had voiced concerns regarding away games in the south. In a desire to maintain the impetus of the previous two seasons, Teesside had also cast the net far and wide to bring in quality players. At the same time, they were, to an extent, victims of that success as players left, attracted by the lure of a higher standard of rugby, their talents brought to the attention of others through their displays for Teesside. It was heartbreaking for club founder Phil Gowing, but there was little alternative for him and his colleagues. The Steelers, like the Jets before them, had left an indelible mark on the RLC. Their contribution was immense and nothing would erase memories of their achievements, sportsmanship and work for rugby league expansion.

Niel Wood's immediate task was to find replacements. Reigate Crusaders were brought in to replace Crawley, but didn't play a competitive game. They also withdrew, leaving the South Division to continue with one less club. There couldn't be a similar outcome in National League Three. Gateshead Storm were approached as the most appropriate outfit to perpetuate a North East presence in the league, and accepted. Coached by Rob Jones who had previously held a similar position at Newcastle Knights, the Storm also received support from their professional counterparts in Gateshead. It was an unforeseen addition to Wood's workload, but it didn't significantly disrupt pre-season preparations. The clubs meeting was on the 18 April in Widnes. Nearly

200 delegates discussed a variety of issues, not all related to the 2004 campaign. It was a good opportunity to look once more at the potential for league re-organisation in 2005. Delegates were encouraged to discuss regional concerns as well. The principal announcement was the unveiling of Parkhouse Recruitment as a new associate sponsor. The deal embraced not just the RLC and its match officials, but the Four Nations tournament and Student Rugby League as well. New referee's kits were to be paraded and a weekly and monthly announcement on player, team and coach performances were to be features of the season. With new coaches and players coming into the competition all the time, it would be difficult to differentiate between performances and select specific individuals each week. On the coaching front alone, some talented individuals were recruited. Newcastle Knights confirmed the continuation of Gateshead Thunder captain Stephen Rutherford as their head coach for 2004. Across the country, Carlisle Centurions announced that former Workington Town player Colin Armstrong was to succeed Gary Murdock.

April was a month of frantic activity: New sponsorship deals, significant publicity and promotional initiatives, prestigious launches, heightened media interest, increasing numbers of young players knocking at the door of RLC clubs desperate to learn the game, and numerous fixtures. Some were friendlies; others were in the RLC Cup that reached its conclusion on 25 April. North London Skolars retained the trophy, narrowly defeating Gateshead Storm 38-34 at Derby.

The customary reference to the mouth-watering prospect of the 'best season ever' was made. It was certainly going to be the biggest ever season, but an eye was always going to be on the repercussions of success or failure in the 2004 campaign. With the possible advent of 'Premier Leagues' to come and potential National League places for those with lofty ambitions, all the competing teams had much to play for.

There was an additional dimension to interest in the new clubs with many from traditional rugby league areas and therefore expected to do well. Widnes Saints certainly fulfilled pre-season expectations in the competitive North West division, but elsewhere there were encouraging signs for those who had come through the more accustomed RLC route. Leeds Akademiks and Wetherby Bulldogs provided a new - and much welcomed - rivalry, based both on geography and equitability on the pitch. The honeymoon period for Welsh rugby league continued into the season. Of long-term significance were the formal links established between domestic clubs and counterparts in Super League. Only time will tell whether these prove to be valuable (memories of past 'false dawns' with respect to twinning relationships are still relatively fresh), but St Helens' encouraging start in Aberavon - supporting development programmes, for example - must bode well for the future.

A new development in Wales was the origin match between East and West on 9 June. Organised as an extra, but necessary, tier in the representative system, it provided a platform for new talent to state their case for higher recognition. Won by a West Wales side featuring players from Aberavon, Bridgend and Swansea, it illustrated the depth of playing ability in South Wales. Lancaster also had an origin match. A crowd of over 400 saw

Morecambe triumph over Lancaster by 24-15. Lancaster's 'Giant Axe' home was, of course, a blend of past achievements and future hopes. The same could be said of rugby's spiritual home, The Close at Rugby School. There was now a permanent rugby league presence in the Warwickshire town, and though the Raiders' normal home base was elsewhere, on 8 May they arranged for their first competitive home fixture to be played at the famous location. Amidst the backdrop of the school and the commemorative plaque, and the filming of a new production of *Tom Brown's Schooldays*, Rugby Raiders took on Wolverhampton Wizards in the RLC. It was a game to remember - the visitors victorious but only after a spirited fightback from the enthusiastic locals. The game had attracted the whistle of Super League's Russell Smith and a sizeable contingent of onlookers (including Les Cusworth, the former England union international), though the vision of rugby league preparations in the background while the book that contained references to the original 'rugby football' was being filmed was another abiding memory of the day.

The inclusion of second teams from National League Three outfits was another new feature of the 2004 RLC season. Though this was significant in itself, that only one of them was successful on the pitch, and that club was not from the heartlands, was most revealing. It illustrated the growing depth of talent in relatively new rugby league areas. The club in question was Coventry Bears and their battle with Leicester Phoenix for the title of South Midlands divisional champions was one of the most captivating aspects of the first phase of the competition.

The Challenge Cup Final weekend was increasingly being used to showcase new developments in the sport and 2004 was no exception. The Powergen Schools competition was coming to its conclusion with fittingly a side from Cardiff (Whitchurch) featuring prominently, though it was the Four Nations clash between Wales and Ireland that figured more significantly on the day of the big game itself. The outcome was a memorable Welsh victory. For England, the regional championships at the end of May provided the platform for representative cases to be made. In sweltering conditions at Nottingham Outlaws' home, the honours were shared between the East Midlands and Yorkshire, but the main purpose was to provide selection options for Lionhearts' coach Lee Addison. The day was a success. A fortnight later the chosen players battled to a 28-26 victory in Scotland, but the development of the Celtic nations was a prominent characteristic of the season. Wales' prowess was already known (they were, after all, the only winners of the tournament), but the Scots and Irish were catching up. One month later, Ireland beat England 28-24 in Dublin.

In reviewing progress one month into the new season, RLC media manager Phil Caplan announced a record match completion rate of 96 per cent. He also revealed that plans were developing for the 2005 season. A Premier League format, with as many as four leagues in operation, was being proposed with application forms distributed for a competition that would be longer and, unsurprisingly, have more stringent entry criteria, including junior development. The RLC would remain the same in format and scheduling, but its status in the grand scheme of things would possibly change - perhaps an unavoidable outcome of a differentiation process based now on standards and ability rather than solely on geography?

National League Three was also underway with mixed fortunes for the new boys. On the plus side, Birmingham followed up an impressive victory at Carlisle by defeating Huddersfield-Underbank Rangers and Hemel Hempstead Stags at home. Conversely, Essex Eels' baptism was traumatic. On the opening day, they visited reigning champions Warrington-Woolston Rovers and an 86-18 reversal rather set the pattern for the season for the men from the south. While only experiencing a season in the RLC, the club demonstrated much of the competition's ethos, that hard work and progress off the field would reap dividends. Fellow National League Three members South London Storm and St Albans Centurions had shown the way, and they were eager to follow.

Coventry Bears had probably underachieved in 2003, but 2004 was a different matter. A new sponsor (resulting in the incorporation of 'Aquatic' in between 'Coventry' and 'Bears') coupled with the forthcoming move to their impressive new home at the Butts Arena, provided an additional surge of energy to the Midlanders and with their second team also leading the way in the RLC, their prospects looked very promising. The same was true for South London Storm. Their season incorporated an unforgettable trip to Australia, as a legacy of hosting the 'legends' side the previous November, as well as more mundane journeys to St Albans, Gateshead and Huddersfield.

Regrettably, things were not so rosy in Manchester and northern Cumbria. Carlisle were the innocent victims of bureaucratic decisions made by their local BARLA league that severely affected the availability of players for summer rugby. As a consequence, the Centurions relinquished their position in the RLC to focus on the National League. Even that didn't prevent the embarrassment of having to cancel a game at Coventry. For Manchester Knights, a worse fate awaited. The problems of running a side can culminate in unavoidable decisions having to be made on future participation. The Knights were the latest operation to suffer from a series of major setbacks and the club reluctantly withdrew from the league in the latter stages of the season. A viable future for the club, potentially in the RLC, was still possible and this was welcome news. Niel Wood pointed to such a scenario in the official press release announcing the news of their withdrawal: "We believe that events such as this should be viewed as not unexpected during a period of rapid and successful expansion which Rugby League has recently undergone. This also does not detract from the overall success of the new League... The Knights decision to step down is a growing pain that is common to many new competitions and League structures and we will now work with the club to place them at a more appropriate level of competition".

For the league as a whole, there was an added incentive to do well, for the National League Three Final was added to those of the higher two divisions in a one-day feast of rugby to be held on 10 October at Widnes's Halton Stadium. For a lengthy period, London Skolars did not rule out hopes of making the National League Two play-offs. Their improvement was quite staggering. In 2003, the team had to be content with a win and a draw, 12 months on and they achieved some sensational results, beating Swinton Lions 28-26 at home, and winning 41-8 at Dewsbury.

The RLC was well represented at the third York Nines tournament. The two-day event had stepped up another notch on the ladder in size and status. Worcestershire Saints, Newcastle Knights, Cambridge Eagles, Carlisle Centurions, Lancaster and Bristol Sonics all took part, as did Essex Eels from National League Three. None shone in a tournament that reflected the varied sectors of rugby league participation in this country and an international dimension. The winners were the new West Indies side (including RLC players) who defeated the York Ironsides in the final in dramatic fashion.

There was further RLC and National League representation at the Middlesex equivalent event. Such was the interest in the southern-based Nines that a qualifying tournament, (won by the West Indies again) had to be held at St Albans to finalise the 16 competing teams. London Skolars, Greenwich Admirals, Ipswich Rhinos and South London Storm all did themselves proud, and RLC players again permeated some of the other teams that took part.

Ipswich reached the semi-final stage before bowing out, but the Skolars went two steps further and triumphantly lifted the trophy on home soil, defeating the gallant Royal Engineers 16-12 in the final. Such events were no longer novelties or isolated occurrences. They had a purpose and place in the annual rugby league calendar, providing a different form of rugby entertainment, comradeship and competition across league or national dividing lines. As a means of promoting rugby league, they were invaluable.

Nevertheless, there was no diminishing of the eminence in which the RLC trophies were held, and the battle to reach the respective finals had now reached the play-off stage. The first phase had seen some memorable moments and some keenly-contested games, and the final division tables were as follows:

	North West	Pl	W	D	L	F	A	Diff	Pts
1	Widnes Saints	10	9	0	1	524	152	372	18
2	Chester Wolves	10	9	0	1	475	186	289	18
3	Bolton Le Moors	10	8	0	2	280	177	103	16
4	Liverpool Buccaneers	10	6	0	4	289	204	85	12
5	Crewe Wolves	10	4	0	6	270	314	-44	8
6	Lancaster	10	3	0	7	208	294	-86	6
7	Blackpool Sea Eagles	10	0	1	9	104	445	-341	1
8	North Wales Coasters	10	0	1	9	160	538	-378	1

	Yorkshire	Pl	W	D	L	F	A	Diff	Pts
1	Leeds Akademiks	10	9	0	1	374	170	204	18
2	Wetherby Bulldogs	10	9	0	1	351	170	181	18
3	Hull Phoenix	10	5	1	4	368	217	151	11
4	Bridlington Bulls	10	5	1	4	335	276	59	11
5	South Wakefield Sharks	10	5	0	5	235	306	-71	10
6	Thorne Moor Marauders	10	3	1	6	213	297	-84	7
7	Bradford-Dudley Hill 'A'	10	1	1	8	206	435	-229	3
8	Huddersfield-Underbank 'A'	10	1	0	9	200	411	-211	2

South West	Pl	W	D	L	F	A	Diff	Pts
1 Somerset Vikings	10	9	0	1	526	154	372	18
2 Gloucestershire Warriors	10	8	0	2	434	200	234	16
3 Bristol Sonics	10	5	1	4	340	334	6	11
4 Oxford Cavaliers	10	4	1	5	254	416	-162	9
5 Telford Raiders	10	1	2	7	178	340	-162	4
6 Worcestershire Saints	10	1	0	9	202	490	-288	2

South	Pl	W	D	L	F	A	Diff	Pts
1 West London Sharks	8	7	0	1	424	116	308	14
2 Greenwich Admirals	8	7	0	1	274	180	94	14
3 Kingston Warriors	8	3	0	5	218	252	-34	6
4 Gosport & Fareham Vikings	8	3	0	5	182	248	-66	6
5 South London Storm 'A'	8	0	0	8	88	390	-302	0

Midlands	Pl	W	D	L	F	A	Diff	Pts
1 Coventry Bears 'A'	10	8	0	2	447	226	221	16
2 Leicester Phoenix*	10	8	0	2	569	144	425	14
3 Birmingham Bulldogs 'A'	10	6	0	4	276	248	28	12
4 St Albans Centurions 'A'	10	4	0	6	340	303	37	8
5 Wolverhampton Wizards	10	4	0	6	174	358	-184	8
6 Rugby Raiders	10	0	0	10	118	645	-527	0

*points deducted for not fulfilling fixture at Birmingham.

Cumbria	Pl	W	D	L	F	A	Diff	Pts
1 Barrow Shipbuilders	10	9	0	1	416	142	274	18
2 Penrith Pumas	10	5	2	3	391	222	169	12
3 West Cumbria	10	5	2	3	317	149	168	12
4 Copeland Athletic	10	5	2	3	240	223	17	12
5 Carlisle Centurions 'A'	10	0	0	10	72	512	-440	0

Wales	Pl	W	D	L	F	A	Diff	Pts
1 Bridgend Blue Bulls	12	12	0	0	544	197	347	24
2 Aberavon Fighting Irish	12	9	0	3	464	291	173	18
3 Torfaen Tigers	12	7	0	5	459	289	170	14
4 Newport Titans	12	6	1	5	426	315	111	13
5 Cardiff Demons	12	3	0	9	358	442	- 84	6
6 Swansea Valley Miners	12	2	1	9	235	647	- 412	5
7 Valley Cougars	12	2	0	10	266	571	- 305	4

North Midlands	Pl	W	D	L	F	A	Diff	Pts
1 Rotherham Giants	10	9	0	1	510	94	416	18
2 Nottingham Outlaws	10	8	0	2	318	197	121	16
3 Derby City	10	7	0	3	210	160	50	14
4 Mansfield Storm	10	4	0	6	230	288	-58	8
5 Sheffield-Hillsborough Hawks 'A'	10	2	0	8	142	394	-252	4
6 Worksop Sharks	10	0	0	10	138	415	-277	0

North East	Pl	W	D	L	F	A	Diff	Pts
1 Jarrow Vikings	10	9	0	1	382	128	254	18
2 Newcastle Knights	10	7	0	3	324	209	115	14
3 Sunderland City	10	7	0	3	270	213	57	14
4 Peterlee Pumas	10	4	0	6	287	166	121	8
5 Yorkshire Coast Tigers	10	4	0	6	231	318	-87	8
6 Durham Tigers	10	1	0	9	172	418	-246	2
7 Whitley Bay Barbarians	10	1	0	9	94	496	-402	2

	East	Pl	W	D	L	F	A	Diff	Pts
1	Ipswich Rhinos	10	10	0	0	531	116	415	20
2	North London Skolars	10	8	0	2	576	108	468	16
3	South Norfolk Saints	10	7	0	3	474	229	245	14
4	Luton Vipers	10	7	0	3	392	217	175	14
5	St Ives Roosters	10	4	0	6	200	424	-224	8
6	Hemel Hempstead Stags 'A'	10	2	0	8	212	440	-228	4
7	Cambridge Eagles	10	2	0	8	156	446	-290	4
8	Middlesex Lions	10	0	0	10	107	668	-561	0

The play-offs were no less impressive as clubs jockeyed for positions and the advantages of a home draw. With different numbers in certain divisions, some preliminary stages (elimination contests) had to take place which meant the end of the road for North Wales Coasters, Middlesex Lions, Bridlington Bulls and, perhaps surprisingly, the previous season's Shield finalists Bolton le Moors, who went down to Liverpool Buccaneers. With the number of teams still left in the bag decreasing weekly, it was time for big defence and that bit of inspiration that could make all the difference. Some much fancied teams joined Bolton through the exit door. Coventry Bears 'A' team lost at home to Leicester. Rotherham did likewise at home to Nottingham. Gloucestershire's fine season came dramatically unstuck at Somerset Vikings and Lancaster were surprised by Blackpool Sea Eagles. The first big domestic trophy occasion occurred on 7 August. The inaugural Welsh Grand Finals day attracted a crowd of around 600 to Aberavon Greenstars RFC. Cardiff were successful in the Shield Final, defeating Newport Titans 38-35 to recover some positives from a season that had been disappointing up to that point. In the main game, Bridgend's unbeaten record in the RLC came under serious threat from the home side, the Fighting Irish. In a pivotal day for Welsh rugby league the Blue Bulls moved to within two of Wigan's World Record number of consecutive unbeaten games. Their 26-21 victory was number 27. The teams on this historic day were as follows:

Aberavon Fighting Irish: Richard Price, Paul Morgan, Dean Scully, Dai Hawkins, Richard Lewis, Liam Gadd, Dan Hawkins, Mark Jones, Mark Burke, Roger Howard, Darren Ryan, Ceri Thomas, Nathan Davies.
Subs: Jason Massey, Rhodri Morris, Richard Thomas, Andrew Suter.
Bridgend Blue Bulls: Jon Williams, Grant Epton, Dai Owen, Carle Ellis, Gareth David, Allan Bateman, Kevin Ellis, Nathan Strong, Craig Fox, Jon Purnell, Karl Hocking, John Devereux, Marcus Sainsbury.
Subs: Matthew Wareham, Paul Morgan, Gareth Bartlett, Geraint Lewis.

The Bridgend side had two more hurdles to overcome to achieve parity with Wigan. They came sensationally unstuck at the first. West London Sharks travelled to Wales to take on Kevin Ellis and his team of invincibles, and achieved what no-one else had yet managed to do - victory over Bridgend. The Londoners' 30-18 win was a wonderful achievement and just reward for captain and loyal servant Alex Sanerive. Though much of the media prominence went to Trevor Leota (the Samoan rugby union international who had been given permission by his union club, London Wasps to play league in their off-season to keep him fit), Sanerive's inspirational leadership was still predominant.

Of all the quarter-finals, one stood out as only a single point separated Thorne Moor Marauders and Durham Tigers at the end of 80 minutes frantic rugby. The victory delighted many in the Doncaster area, and also perhaps former world heavyweight boxing champion, Mike Tyson. He was friendly with Marauders supporter Andy Booker who had photographed Iron Mike in a Thorne Moor shirt. They progressed to the Shield semi-finals with St Albans, Cardiff and Crewe. Widnes Saints, Ipswich Rhinos and Wetherby Bulldogs joined West London in the last four of the Harry Jepson Trophy.

Amidst the thrills and spills of RLC play-off rugby, the spotlight was unexpectedly shone on rugby league in development areas and, indirectly, on the Conference and associated competitions, when the subject came up in BBC Radio Five Live's *Any Sporting Questions*. The bone of contention for those working tirelessly for the cause of grassroots rugby league were disparaging comments made about the game in London and the South by presenter John Inverdale. That the remarks appeared to be supported by prominent league personality Bobbie Goulding only added fire to the indignation of most listeners who were followers of the game. Inverdale even alluded to Bedford as 'simply 13 players running around the field' and questioned whether this was indeed rugby league. There was a strong case for a response because of the tone of their remarks. It produced heated responses on the Fans Forum on the Totalrl.com website, with emails and letters flowing from clubs and supporters to Mr Inverdale, some inviting him to games. To his credit, he responded, but there was little sign of a retraction. The Bedford Tigers had 40 members at the time, and statistics from the RLC and RFL have further discredited the comments made.

The 2004 RLC season had seen over 95 per cent of the games played (a new record) and over 4,000 registered players. The RLC was singled out by the RFL as one of the four main areas of growth for the sport; growth that had seen a rise in participation of 94 per cent since 2002. The other three areas also had a significant development element: the Powergen Champions Schools programme, National League Three and Girls rugby league.

Another indication of development success was that Matt Cook, one of the England Academy stars (and the scorer of two tries) in their historic victory over Australia in Sydney on 21 August had, of course, received a rugby league education in Bedford. He was now with the Bradford Bulls.

On 9 August an announcement by the Rugby Football League may well culminate in a further illustration of the game's depth outside the heartland areas. Red Hall revealed that a 34th professional place was up for grabs, possibly as early as 2006, because of the need to balance the number of clubs in the current divisions. With London Skolars having already shown the way, heads turned in the direction of National League Three outfits. Two had already demonstrated considerable credentials through participation in the RLC: Coventry Bears and Hemel Hempstead Stags. The latter were believed to be showing an interest in entering a side in the RFL's Junior Academy and they had been there before when it came to professional potential. Coventry's joint rugby club status and new stadium would undoubtedly be massive advantages should an interest be transferred into active application. All will be revealed in due course.

Meanwhile, the RLC semi-final weekend dawned at two venues, Bradford-Dudley Hill and Hemel Hempstead Stags. In the Shield, Cardiff Demons marked their 50th competitive appearance by producing one of their greatest ever displays. Playing almost faultless rugby at times, they swept away St Albans in a 66-14 victory. The other semi-final was much closer and provided a memorable finish with Thorne Moor hanging on grimly to a two point lead, overcoming Crewe Wolves 30-28.

In the Harry Jepson half of the semi-final weekend, Widnes Saints fought off dogged resistance from Wetherby Bulldogs to earn their place in the final - winning 29-6. The other game promised one of the clashes of the season, unbeaten Ipswich Rhinos taking on West London Sharks. It didn't fail to live up to expectations. Though a 40-8 margin for the Londoners suggested a one-sided contest, it was anything but that. Sharks' greater forward power combined with the deft skills of Gavin Gordon, who opened the scoring, the pace of Clae Morgan and Andre Wilson and terrific combination play set the platform for an impressive victory. It was only in the last quarter that West London piled on the points.

That only left the principal day in the calendar to come. Who would triumph on 5 September at Woollams, St Albans, to join the other victorious champions of development area rugby league? Fife Lions had won Scotland's Grand Final, defeating Edinburgh Eagles 36-24, and Clontarf Bulls were the Irish Conference Champions with a close win against Dublin Blues. Bridgend Blue Bulls, as we have seen, were the inaugural Welsh Grand Final winners. In the London League, Haringey Hornets beat Bedford Tigers 28-22 in the final to lift the Gordon Anderton Trophy. In all areas of the British Isles, amateur rugby league was flourishing in development competitions. The statistics didn't lie. There were new players, coaches, sponsors and supporters enjoying rugby league. For the 2004 season, the jigsaw needed to be completed.

Sweltering conditions greeted the four competing teams, dignitaries and around 500 supporters at St Albans on Sunday 5 September. The players could be forgiven for treading cautiously given the intense heat, but this was finals rugby in the RLC. There was much to live up to from previous years and two fantastic contests provided sufficient evidence that all four sets of players were up to the test. The teams took to the field as follows:

Cardiff Demons: Jamie Iles, Idris Evans, Rhodri Thomas, Neil Thomas, Andrew Bradshaw, Gareth Jones, Peter Moore, Graham Hughes, Mark Bow, Anthony Loxton, Mark Dando, Dave Roberson.
Subs: John Byers, Pat Howell, Tom Young, Kyle Blake,

Thorne Moor Marauders: Craig Hookway, Kevin Lake, Shaun Carvell, David Knott, Craig Linsdell, Mark Roach, Ryan Noble, Andy Evans, Martin Rowlands, Wayne Rafferty, Brett Stavely, Gareth Monroe, Steve Allen.
Subs: Ernie Lake, Shane Lake, Nathan Hazelwood, Chris Allen.

West London Sharks: Andre Wilson, Phil Astbury, Pat Wadwell, Clae Morgan, Dan Coffey, Mark Barnes, Dan Wright, Lawrence Ross, Gavin Gordon, Dan Oliver, Nathan Bennett, Ben Hinze, Alex Sanerive,
Subs: Will Armor, Paul Richards, Graham Robbins, Stephen Lamb.

Widnes Saints: Greg Lawrenson, Danny Liguri-Badham, Danny Yates, Andy Benson, Mike Lamb, Lee Campbell, Mark Birmingham, Anthony Kirwan, Anthony Hollins, Waitangi Halatuna, Paul Borg, Carl Leach, Neil Bourke.
Subs: Keiron Walker, Stuart Martin, Paea Liku, Mark Keenan.

Cardiff Demons produced another scintillating display during the first half of the Shield Final. The Welshmen scored four tries and prevented Thorne Moor Marauders from notching a single point. When Graham Hughes extended the lead after 51 minutes, the writing was on the wall for the South Yorkshiremen. In true RLC finals tradition, the fightback began, and such was the extent of their recovery that the Demons were grateful to the boots of Pete Moore and Gareth Jones to preserve a wide-enough margin to prevent nerves from setting in. Star of the show, however, was Marauders' Shaun Carvell. The talented centre went over for four tries, and was unlucky not to bag a fifth when he was deemed to have dropped the ball in the tackle when over the line. He didn't deserve to be a runner-up, but then neither did a Cardiff side that ensured consecutive successes for Welsh sides in RLC finals - the final score being 29-20.

The battle for the Harry Jepson Trophy also had a nerve-wracking final quarter. West London Sharks were without the talismanic Trevor Leota, who was in New Zealand, but it seemed to make no difference during an opening 24 minutes in which they scored four tries (two each to Clae Morgan and Dan Coffey) and opened up a 16 point lead. Their pace stifled the Widnes Saints, but the Cheshire outfit didn't panic and stuck to their game plan that saw the tide begin to turn in their favour. By half-time the West London lead was only four points and within minutes of the restart the Saints went ahead for the first time when centre Danny Yates gleefully touched down following enterprising play from hooker Anthony Hollins, Stuart Martin and Bev Risman Medal winner Neil Bourke. Widnes' Liguri-Badham and West London's Will Armor then exchanged converted tries before Waitangi Halatuna sealed victory for the favourites from the heartlands by scoring a four-pointer in the corner with Neil Bourke superbly converting. A magnificent match ended with Widnes victorious 36-28. For them, it was success in their inaugural season. For West London, it was one game too far in a season that had seen them lay the ghosts of previous last-ditch disappointments in the regular rounds. It had been a long journey since their initial incarnation in the 1997 season, and 2004 had been the summer when potential translated into achievement on the field. Only time will tell if they will be able to follow in the successful footsteps of North London Skolars, Crawley, Chester, Teesside, Coventry and Bridgend in claiming the ultimate prize in RLC rugby league, the Harry Jepson Trophy.

As the trophy was paraded, celebrations and commiserations begun, and the sun finally went down on another momentous day in the history of the competition, thoughts might have drifted back to that first Saturday at Saffron Lane, Leicester in 1997 as the home side took on Birmingham to begin an adventure that no-one would realistically have predicted would have reached such an advanced stage in such a short period of time. It was but seven years ago, a totally different era and context, and it seemed a lifetime away.

The victorious Morecambe team from the Origin match against Lancaster
at the historic Giant Axe ground in Lancaster in 2004 (Photo: Kristen Madden)

12: Into the future

The story of the Rugby League Conference to date has been one of continuous growth. As thoughts turn towards further amendments to formats, structures and the impending Premier Leagues, it is an appropriate time for reflection. Following my resignation from the post of administrator in the spring of 2002, I initially deliberately distanced myself not only from the RLC but from rugby league as well. However, the game as we all know acts like a magnet, attracting attention from devotees, both new and old. I have subsequently spent many a long hour since the onset of researching and writing this book, pondering the changes taking place and the future direction of a competition in which I am proud to have played some part.

Like everyone else, I have been thrilled by the success of the RLC concept. There is no doubt that, generally speaking, the RLC and its associated developments (particularly the incorporation of RLC clubs into the National Leagues) have been nothing short of sensational and quite staggering to behold. Certainly beyond the expectations, I would think, of those like myself that sat in cafés and leisure centre rooms putting the ideas into practice back in 1996 and 1997. Pride in achievement also comes into the equation, but so too does concern. Like any parent contemplating the development of his or her child into adolescence and adulthood, it's a process that brings with it a whole mixture of emotions, some conflicting. In hearing the views of many people involved in the RLC today, it is clear that my concerns are shared by others.

The RLC has grown in size and profile. Of that there is no doubt. But is this naturally all movement in a progressive direction? In 2004, there was an acknowledgement from within the RLC hierarchy that a significant change of policy or ethos had occurred. This principally centred around the incorporation of 'heartland' clubs and therefore the opening up of the competition to anyone interested in participation, wherever they might be located (in England and Wales at least). I always believed that there needed to be an assimilation of competition between new and traditional rugby league operations; that the RLC could not always act in isolation, protecting relatively new clubs from the extra rigours of facing more experienced clubs. What I did believe was also appropriate was that assimilation should be gradual and not forced upon those who were not at the relevant stage of development. This was borne out of the recognition that there is nothing more off-putting and disheartening to newcomers in whatever field (sport or otherwise) than being confronted by too great an inequality in standard too soon. Bev Risman in his Foreword to this book, mentions Hector McNeil's vision and plan for the future. Hector, a man of remarkable energy and innovation, recognised the importance of assimilation - of clubs testing themselves against quality BARLA opposition - in this pioneering document. Many people have also asserted the benefits to their own club and player development of playing against opponents of a higher standard. Clearly, this is the way forward and is widely acknowledged. But there has to be a balance and a careful consideration of timing. The question I would pose is 'has the RLC got that balance and timing right?'

The RLC was established to represent and cater for the development of clubs outside the traditional heartland areas of rugby league. I would accept that this should never prevent the incorporation of clubs from the heartlands. Nevertheless, the central tenet of 'development' that I would argue should remain as a core of RLC philosophy is a preservation of that focus on strengthening clubs from development areas so that, given time, they are in a position to compete with those from Yorkshire, Lancashire and Cumbria. In practical terms, that does mean the eventual formation of Premier Leagues for those who are in a position to challenge on a weekly basis the stronger clubs from the North. It may also mean looking a little more strategically at the RLC Cup as a vehicle for seeing how other RLC outfits handle the prospect of a draw against the likes of Widnes Saints, Hull Phoenix and some of the Cumbrian clubs, without having to inflict regular contests (and potential mismatches) on them.   I would also argue that the pinnacle of the RLC season, Grand Finals Day, should continue at a venue within a development area. In my view, to have a final in Warrington (as was the case in 2003) was detrimental at this stage of the RLC's development. The day should focus on showcasing the very best of RLC talent to an audience that can more readily be influenced into getting involved in our great sport.

Near the end of the 2004 season, the following words were issued by an RLC spokesperson in *Rugby League World:* "Totalrl.com RLC VII could turn out to be a seminal year for a number of clubs who have traditionally relied predominantly on rugby union players to make up the bulk of their squad. For the integrity of the RLC to be maintained and enhanced, they may need to give an undertaking and commitment as to which is their priority sport in the overlapping stages of the season, especially around the play-offs, if their future applications are to be endorsed by the governing body."

This is all very laudable, and of course, there should be an aim by all concerned to increase the number of *bona fide* rugby league players, of people who make the sport their first choice whether they play rugby union or any other sport as well. However, circumstances and contexts are different depending on the club and the area in which they play. In areas of current union dominance, the more talented players are perhaps more likely to focus primarily on that sport and many of them will be contracted to union clubs. If the statement is taken as being an indirect edict to clubs to ensure prioritisation of rugby league, unless RLC clubs can offer something extraordinary and in many cases financial incentives, they may have to resign themselves to targeting players of lesser ability and those not so contractually obliged or important to union clubs. As a consequence, their playing performance may suffer and any chance of competing on the park against stronger, more experienced rugby league players will go as well. Surely a 'Catch 22' situation? More fundamentally, the RLC was formed to give those interested an opportunity and incentive to play rugby league, perhaps for the first time. From where does the RLC expect clubs to gain new recruits? Rugby union remains a key potential source and the sport is, in many areas, a mutually beneficial ally to our clubs. Can we really afford to put any obstacles in the way of this?

For the future, in my view the RLC should strive to ensure the following:

• Maintenance of quality minimum standards, both on and off the pitch. Appearances, first impressions and an attention to detail are vitally important, not insignificant inconveniences. Clubs have performed wonders in this regard, not always because they have been asked or told to do things by the RLC administration, but because they have felt the necessity and recognised the importance of such matters.

• A focus on development that reflects strengthening of roots and those aspects of the competition which are fundamental to the sustainability of clubs in development areas. This means looking at junior and youth development and at the opportunities for expanding the girls' and women's game. It means more qualified coaches and match officials. It also means looking at closer links with Scotland and Ireland. This is not to say that there shouldn't be a continuation of the heartland incorporation that we have witnessed in recent seasons. Rather, that greater focus should be given to collaboration and co-operation across national boundaries.

• Strengthening of the connection with the National Leagues so that the pyramid system operates in a productive and seamless fashion. This may involve the eventual creation of a National League Four as well as RLC Premier Leagues. It will mean more strategic thought being given to the inclusion into the pyramid structure of leading BARLA clubs who wish to try summer rugby. I believe there will be many who will want to do so.

• There should also be a greater consideration of assistance being given to development 'underneath' the RLC. I use the term 'underneath' not in a disparaging sense, but as a reflection of the structural edifice that exists at present. This will mean greater support for the London ARL and also the formation of similar leagues in other regions represented by RLC clubs.

• Most fundamentally of all, however, should be the preservation of the RLC's status. The role of the competition may change to reflect its place within the pyramid system as a lynchpin between regionalised leagues on the London ARL model and the National Leagues above it. However, the central tenets upon which the competition is based - development, participation and standards - should not be compromised in any way. Participation also involves the direct input of clubs in the decision-making processes affecting their development and that of the league as a whole.

I have no doubt that an exciting future exists for the competition. There are too many talented and committed people involved for this not to be the case. Where there is a will, there is a way. That was certainly true in 1996 and it is just as true today, in 2004. No doubt there will be people who disagree with my assertions, my values and principles with regard to the RLC and my ideas for the future. I accept that, and recognise and respect other opinions. I urge debate and thorough scrutiny of the consequences of actions and developments. Some consequences will be unintended and others may be undesirable. Too much work and devotion have been given to the development of the RLC for such a process not to be given the due reverence and careful analysis that the competition deserves.

161

Appendix 1: Matches, memories and people

This appendix is devoted to those who have contributed in a variety of ways to the development of the RLC. Many people outline their favourite memories from their involvement in the competition.

However, to begin, the author has picked out 10 memorable matches from the many hundreds that have taken place since 1997. This was not an easy task. Fixtures and occasions are memorable for a variety of reasons, their quality, their novelty and some for personal reasons. Readers will have their own views. The 10 chosen are here in chronological order:

Matches

Leicester Phoenix 36 Birmingham 23
17 May 1997

This was the first ever fixture in the summer Conference era. A small crowd gathered at Saffron Lane Stadium, Leicester, alongside distinguished rugby league journalists Ray French and Martyn Sadler and award-winning photographer Gerald Webster, to watch the historic occasion. Traditional rivals from EMARLA, the result was a win for the home side, the key being a magnificent try from Leicester centre Ben Harbottle which tipped the balance in favour of Phoenix.

Cambridge Eagles 18 Hemel Hempstead Stags 12
1 July 2000

The surprise result of this and many a season. Cambridge Eagles underlined their undoubted potential by toppling previously unbeaten Hemel Hempstead Stags on a memorable Saturday afternoon at a novel venue. The unavailability of their usual home at Grantchester Road meant club secretary Barry Butterfield had to find an alternative. He came up with RAF Waterbeach, and the fixture took place amid the festivities of an Air Force open day. Some new spectators were captivated by a thrilling display from an Eagles side including Japanese World Cup star Masohiro Komori.

Wolverhampton Wizards 32 Leicester Phoenix 20
8 July 2000

Despite the visitors arriving late with a depleted side, nothing could be taken away from a red-letter day in the history of Wolverhampton Wizards. This victory over Leicester Phoenix was their first in the RLC. It was fully deserved and stands out for Julian Harrison for the phone call he received from Wolverhampton club secretary Duncan Merrill, when the genuine pride and emotion of the victory and occasion came through forcefully.

West London Sharks 18 Crawley Jets 20
22 July 2000

If there was an award for the unluckiest side in the history of the competition, West London Sharks would be leading contenders. Time after time the club seem to be on the verge of end-of-term success before being denied at the eleventh hour. In 2000, a draw would have sent them to the play-offs at the expense of the Crawley Jets, and with two minutes left, the scores were locked at 18-18. Then the referee awarded a penalty to the Jets, and Steve O'Reilly delivered the goods to leave the home side devastated. Crawley had needed to win seven consecutive games to achieve a play-off position. That they managed this by beating West London, who had the best defensive record in the league format stage of the competition was testament to their fighting qualities.

Ipswich Rhinos 24 South Norfolk Saints 24
2 June 2001
Trips to Ipswich are always enjoyable not only for the quality of the entertainment on the pitch, but also the warmth of the hospitality. East Anglian derbies have become some of the most-looked-forward-to fixtures in the RLC calendar and when the Rhinos faced the Saints in June 2001, a drama ensued that would have rivalled any encounter between their Super League namesakes, Leeds and St Helens. 24-10 down with only 10 minutes left, the Rhinos, inspired by hooker and man-of-the-match Paul Roberts, drew on all their reserves of strength to force a draw with virtually the last play of the game.

Hemel Hempstead Stags 16 North London Skolars 10
11 August 2001. Play-off quarter-final
This was a clash between two of the giants of the amateur game in the south of England and a quarter-final play-off. This was compounded in August 2001 by the first – and (at the time of writing) only – extra-time period in the RLC's history. With so much to play for, points were at a premium and the scores were locked at 10-10 after 80 minutes pulsating rugby. A try from Andy Curtain and a goal from stalwart Chris Caws eventually saw the Hertfordshire club through to the semi-finals, where they were beaten by eventual winners, Teesside Steelers.

Edinburgh Eagles 20 Teesside Steelers 30
26 April 2002. Champion of Champions
Although not strictly an RLC fixture, this was nevertheless symptomatic of the success of the summer conference concept with the first fixture between the Scottish Conference and RLC champions. Played on the eve of the Murrayfield Challenge Cup Final between St Helens and Wigan, the occasion also marked the final working day of the RLC administrator, Julian Harrison. A large crowd gathered at Broughton RUFC, and Sky Television was also there to witness a terrific clash. Both sides were superb ambassadors for their respective countries, but it was Teesside who came out on top, winning 30-20. The presentation of the trophy to Steelers' skipper and club stalwart Lloyd Darby marked a memorable end to Harrison's tenure as administrator of the competition.

Coventry Bears 21 North London Skolars 18
24 August 2002. Play-off semi-final
For sheer drama, this semi-final at Cheltenham would be hard to beat. Phil Caplan reported that "inner belief, the weight of history and the boot of James Cathcart combined to give the Bears a sensational victory over the NFP-bound Skolars". Coventry, defeated so narrowly by Teesside in the 2001 final, found themselves 14 points behind late in the game to the talented London side and their dreams of going one step further than they had 12 months previously seemed to be edging away. Until the 78th minute, the Skolars were in front, but dramatically, winger Francis Slater dived over in the corner to bring the scores to 17-18. There have been few better kickers in the entire history of the competition than the Irish international James Cathcart. His conversion from the touchline put the Bears ahead 19-18 and a further penalty in the 80th minute capped a superb individual performance and a memorable team fightback.

Bridgend Blue Bulls 38 Cardiff Demons 16
1 August 2003. Harry Jepson Trophy qualifying play-off
The re-emergence of the Welsh game has been one of the highlights of the RLC in recent years. The Blue Bulls, inspired by legendary Welsh league (and union)

players Kevin Ellis, Allan Bateman and John Devereux would eventually win the Harry Jepson Trophy in 2003, but their earlier victory over previous sole Welsh flagship club, the Cardiff Demons, announced the quality of the domestic game in Wales to the wider rugby league audience. A crowd of more than 700, including another Welsh rugby hero, Jonathan Davies, saw the home side withstand a furious Demons onslaught to run out comfortable winners in the end. The new era for league was epitomised by the speed of Lennie Woodward in scoring the decisive try in the 70th minute.

London Skolars 48 Gateshead Thunder 14
24 August 2003. National League Two
Another slight deviance from the RLC, but nevertheless connected. This 2003 National League Two fixture is selected because the Skolars were the inaugural winners of the summer conference and almost six years on from that triumph over Leicester Phoenix, took to the field against fellow expansion club Gateshead Thunder in this semi-professional RFL competition in an attempt to record their first win at this level. That they did so is worthy of many accolades. Neil Fissler, in *League Express* drew attention to its significance: "The result is [a] milestone for Rugby League in the capital that ranks alongside Fulham beating Wigan [Fulham's first match] and the Broncos' wins over Canberra [1997 World Club Challenge] and Castleford [1999 Challenge Cup semi-final]." It showed what could be achieved by a club emerging from the RLC or amateur rugby league in development areas.

Memories and people

Mark Austin (Wolverhampton Wizards): "I will always remember the first game of the 2003 season, my second season, against Coventry Bears 'A' at home. After a winless year in 2002, it was great to start the new season with my first ever league victory for Wolverhampton Wizards. Yes, we weren't playing Coventry's first team but it was nevertheless a memorable victory. This immediately boosted confidence in the club after a miserable season in 2002."

Originally from Widnes, Mark Austin moved to Stafford in September 2001 to take up a new teaching post. He soon joined the Wolverhampton Wizards and after a season as a player, became club secretary when Duncan Merrill stepped down at the end of the 2003 season.

Alan Bacon (Greenwich Admirals): "For me it has to be the match in 2003, where against the odds Greenwich beat North London Skolars 'A' in the second round of the RLC Plate. It was my first game as manager of the team. Everyone thought Skolars would win easily, especially because it was at their ground. But Greenwich won that day, and had beaten the in-form Essex Eels the week before. The club was on a high."

Alan Bacon has achieved a lot in rugby league at the still-young age of 22. After playing rugby union, Alan spotted an advertisement in a local paper in which Graeme Thompson was appealing for local people to form a new club with the professional club about to move from nearby Charlton to Brentford. Responding to the advert led Alan to both playing and coaching. In addition to his role as youth development officer at the Admirals, he has also been involved in Service Area rugby, having a coaching role and managing the London and the South under-13 team.

Ron Banks (Coventry Bears): "Playing at Wilderspool in the semi-finals in 2000 is the event that stands out for me. We were given a £40 match ball. Ours impaled itself on the end of a scaffold tube. The odds against that happening must be astronomical.

In 2002, the Bears were crowned champions defeating Hemel Stags in the Grand Final at Cheltenham. As a result of this the Bears were invited to enter the Challenge Cup. I cannot explain how much that meant to me. As a youngster in Barrow I remember my father going off every year to Wembley for the Challenge Cup Final. I always got a toy from these trips, usually a pop gun.

In 1955 Barrow reached the Final and at the age of seven I went on my first trip to London and Wembley. My heroes, Willie Horne the Barrow skipper and Barrow's flying winger Jimmy Lewthwaite were both playing. Jimmy lived next door-but-one to me and his daughter was one of my best pals. Also playing that day was Frank Castle. Frank was a rugby union player who had turned pro and 'gone north' from Coventry of all places. Barrow beat local rivals Workington.

But, unfortunately the Bears' cup run was short-lived, East Hull gave the Bears a hefty defeat and brought us down with a bump. The guys at East Hull were great and we had a fine time with them after the game.

We have made some good friends playing rugby league, not only in the Midlands but also up and down the country too. There are a lot of hard-working people trying to raise the profile of rugby league and they are making a good fist of it.

One anecdote that made me smile happened before our fixture against Wolverhampton Wizards in 2002. I overheard some Wizards players talking in the car park. "Have you seen the size of those Bears forwards, they are massive". "Yes they are", someone replied: "Where are they now?" said another. "They have gone into the changing rooms". "How? We haven't got the key yet" came the question. "One of them ate the door," was the reply.

One of rugby league's true gentlemen, Ron Banks' dignity and professionalism in both Grand Final defeat and victory has left a lasting impression on many. Ron, originally from Barrow, has – alongside Bears' founder Alan Robinson – been instrumental in one of the great success stories of the competition, and is currently chairman of the club, a position he has held with great distinction for a number of years.

Paul Brookes (Gloucestershire Warriors): "The game that made the biggest impression on me since 1998 was our first game in 2000, at Leicester. It just stands out in my mind as a game in which we fought hard and well, and pulled back from being down to winning. As I recall, the day was very warm and we built up a good early lead, but then Leicester came back at us and by half-time we were behind by a point, I think. After the break we got back ahead and spent about 15 minutes defending the lead to win. It was a tough game to play in but we handled it pretty well even though I think we were all shattered by the end."

Paul Brookes was captain of the then Cheltenham Warriors during the club's inaugural season in 1998.

Tim Carter (Newcastle Knights): "In 2003, we played local rivals Gateshead Storm who prior to the game had predicted the outcome. Also, they had recruited one of our players from the previous season. This was the second derby game of the season, the first we won convincingly. The second game we won with the last play of the match scoring a try to level the scores and our 16-year-old full back converted the try from the touchline in front of their supporters. This win meant we went through to the Harry Jepson Trophy."

Student Rugby League paved the way for Tim Carter's involvement in the game. A player with the previous Gateshead Panthers and Benfield Lions clubs and then Newcastle Knights, Tim has 'almost' retired from playing to focus on the off-field running of the Tyneside outfit.

Gina Coldrick (Leicester Phoenix): "I can't exactly remember the game – but it was an away match because only 13 players had shown up. Teams travelled away in their own cars and if it was Birmingham or Gloucester you normally lost a car load along the way. I also cannot remember the names of the two players involved in the incident, but it still makes me chuckle when I think of it. During the game one of the Leicester props dropped the ball and one of our other players shouted 'Stupid'. The prop turned round and shouted back: 'Don't call me stupid' and then chinned the other player, knocking him out. The referee sent the prop off – for a blood-bin and the knocked out player off for being concussed. So we ended up with 11 men on the field and still won."

Gina Coldrick has a well-deserved reputation as one of the best media managers in the game. Currently employed by Warrington Wolves, her rugby league pedigree is impressive. She was first taken to watch Leigh by her father when aged four, but her interest and involvement in the game really took off when studying – both at undergraduate level in Salford and then while undertaking an MA in the Sociology of Sport at Leicester University. While in the Midlands city, she got involved at Leicester Phoenix and, after keeping in touch with the late Peter Deakin, whom she had approached for advice with regard to her studies, moved from the RLC to Super League.

Phil Cole (Bristol Sonics): "Bristol Sonics beating Somerset Vikings at home 48-44 in the 2003 season really stands out. The Sonics had suffered a long run of defeats and came up against a Somerset side looking to put up a cricket score to qualify for the Harry Jepson Trophy. Having played well, the Sonics found themselves behind with four minutes to go, but still managed to score two tries. The second won the game for us."

The driving force behind the Bristol Sonics club, Phil Cole is a recent convert to the game having first watched live rugby league at Odsal Stadium, Bradford in 1997 and then frequenting occasional Gloucestershire Warriors fixtures. Having posted a message on the Totalrl.com message board, Phil was encouraged by Niel Wood to form a club in Bristol. The rest is history.

Chris Collis (Crawley Jets): "Well, appearing in three Grand Finals and winning two is obviously very significant for Crawley. We played Oxford Cavaliers in the semi-final in 1999 at The Stoop as a curtain-raiser to a London Broncos match. Also, seeing Steve O'Reilly score two consecutive penalties in two minutes from his own half at Rotherham Giants to break that game open stands out as does Steve landing a last-kick-of-the-match penalty at West London in 2000 to win 20-18 and get into the play-offs. He had been concussed earlier, but came back to aim from the touchline at what he hoped were the middle set of sticks. If the ref had realised his state, he'd never have got back on."

Chris Collis was a spectator at Crawley Jets' first ever game, a friendly against Kingston Warriors in 1997. Having been spotted by chairman Mark Richardson at three games in a row, Chris became more involved in the club, eventually becoming secretary as well as press officer and club statistician. His partner and now wife, Lydia, were constant features of a club that, despite its recent demise, was the most successful in the RLC.

166

Ken Edwards (St Albans Centurions): "Our first ever game in 1998 against Oxford must be up there with any choice I make. We snatched a win in the last few minutes with a drop goal. I won man-of-the-match, it was a scorching hot day and Oxford had a really good side to boot. They had prepared a good event at home with a barbecue, good weather and a good media presence with radio and local newspaper reporters at the ground. It was an eye-opener in some ways; it showed the very real potential of summer rugby at our level and showed a small glimpse of what could be achieved by proactive clubs with initiative. It was a precursor of what was to come, which would eventually lead to NL3 and all the great developments I'm sure will arise in the future too.

Another game that springs to mind was the game at West London in 1999 when we played at Marble Hill Park in Twickenham. It was where the RFL had their development teams based and some junior rep rugby was played there too. It was a real nail-biter, where we won again at the death from a field goal after Wests went ahead early. It was a fierce, physical match watched by Ray French who wrote the game up as Match of the Round in his *Rugby Leaguer* column.

Yet another might be the rep match when the RLC side played the Royal Navy at HMS Collingwood (I think) in 1998 (I think, again!). I was playing/assistant coach with Brian Chambers and Dave Doran. With such a young and inexperienced side, more or less thrown together, we nearly won but lost at the death in a really close, physical and exciting game. The camaraderie of the squad and the fact that all the guys present felt they were doing something worthwhile and something historical was almost tangible."

One of the most influential people in the history of the competition, Ken Edwards grew up with rugby league in Australia, playing as a junior in Darwin. Eventually, he came to the UK and played for London Skolars in their foundation year. However, his lasting RLC legacy will be his contribution to the success of the St Albans Centurions, a club he helped found with Gary Tetlow. Ken has played, coached and latterly been involved in administrative matters as the club has moved on to National League Three. It is testament to their staying power, and the lure of the Saints, that both of them are still there eight years later.

Andy Fairhurst (Blackpool Sea Eagles): "The 2003 derby between Blackpool and Lancaster at Blackpool is my key memory. The loser finished bottom of the league and Blackpool held on to win in a heated match which was one of the best I'd played in for a while."

Andy's family are from rugby league stronghold St Helens. A student at Leeds University, his first contact with the RLC was during his summer vacation when he joined Blackpool Sea Eagles. However, with the close links between all three University sides in Leeds and the Leeds Akademiks club, Andy sees his future in his adopted city, where he is currently the Leeds University club captain.

Phil Gowing (Teesside Steelers): "Winning the 2001 Grand Final with half our first choice team unavailable is the moment I'd select. We had numerous contracted rugby union players who could not play in the Grand Final because their winter season had started so we had a very much weakened team. It was a fantastic day and a very proud moment. It was a great reward for a lot of hard work. But it was particularly pleasing to have some of the people involved who'd been with the club since the outset."

In Julian Harrison's view, Phil Gowing is one of the most dedicated individuals in the sport. After being introduced to rugby league while a student at Hull University, Phil founded the Teesside Steelers club in 1995. His double-act with player-chairman Lloyd Darby was a significant reason for the club's success in the competition.

John Harding (Gloucestershire Warriors): "I have an abiding memory of the game in 2000 at Chosen Hill when Birmingham Bulls visited us. The previous games that season had been mismatches of varying degrees and we'd heard that Birmingham were of a higher standard. It was a bright sunny day, and the Warriors kicked off facing the clubhouse. A bald or shaven-headed forward took the ball on about the Bulls 20 metre line, put his head down and went full tilt into the advancing Warriors defence. The hit was bone-splintering and Peter Chadwick and I turned to each other and said as one: 'We've got a game on today!' Indeed we had and although I don't remember the details the Bulls built up a biggish lead and the Warriors reeled them in to take the lead midway through the second half, but then lost it at the end. Birmingham ran out winners 40-32. It was a rumbustuous affair and perhaps overly competitive at times, but great entertainment. The return match up at Birmingham was also close and hard fought with the Bulls again triumphant 18-12. But that first hit-up at Chosen Hill will stay with me for many a long year."

John Harding is webmaster for the Gloucestershire Warriors.

Steve Harrison-Mirfield (Birmingham Bulldogs): "As a Birmingham player in the first season, I played in the first ever match at Leicester. Niel Wood was refereeing and I thought he made some terrible calls. I'll always remember it as I'd been out clubbing the night before and was violently sick before the match after only having about two hours' sleep after a stack load of beer. We lost as I remember, but the game was a good end-to-end match. Birmingham had a lot of great players at the time such as Tony Williams, who for me was the best player Birmingham ever had and such a gentleman to boot.

As a coach, I was involved with Coventry Bears for the 2002 and 2003 seasons and what a couple of seasons they were. 2002 saw us take the championship and I got the accolade of Coach of the Year. The funniest thing that happened all season was when I was sent from the touchline against Ipswich Rhinos. Paul Gluck was the ref and he ordered me onto the pitch to be sent off. We laugh about it with him now as I apologised at the very next match when he refereed us against Birmingham. Indeed I have a laugh with him all the time now because he visits our matches. He even comes out on the 'pop' with us now and again."

Steve Harrison-Mirfield's involvement spans the entire length of the competition. Currently coach at the Rugby Raiders club, Steve held a similar position at Coventry Bears, leading the Midlands side to a Grand Final triumph over Hemel Hempstead Stags in 2002. He has also refereed in the competition and offered administrative support to RLC administrator Julian Harrison. There are few people who have made a more all-round contribution to the RLC.

Martyn Hilton (Nottingham Outlaws): "I think winning the Club of the Year award in 2001 was a brilliant achievement for the club and as I was heavily involved in running the team then, it was a personal triumph as well. On the playing side some fantastic games against Coventry, even though we lost all of them, stand out as being really exciting events that have always been roared on by a great crowd."

Although coming from Oldham, playing rugby league at school and watching the Roughyeds from an early age, it was rugby union that Martyn Hilton gravitated to first, both at home and when he moved to Nottingham. The rise of the Nottingham Outlaws whetted his league appetite once more, and Martyn became immersed in playing and latterly administering. His input was a major factor in the Outlaws winning the RLC Club of the Year award in 2001.

Lionel Hurst: "I think a very significant game was the 1998 Grand Final. I thought the way the Cheltenham club organised it was outstanding. It was standards-driven to perfection. All the little detail – a beautifully mown and marked pitch and such-like – was spot-on. But also, it was the 'Wedding Final'. I think we stood tall there. People accused us of being this, that and the other.

South Norfolk wanted to have the final postponed because of a wedding that many of their players were attending. And we said: 'You know, we simply can't have that. We have a structure here'. And all credit to South Norfolk. They went away and came back with almost a new team. Although they lost heavily, the game was the winner, because the management stood tall, stood strong and said: 'I'm sorry, you know, we can't have the tail wagging the dog'. So those sorts of things, I think, sent the right message of credibility to people so that they could show respect for what we were all trying to do. That certainly stands out in the memory."

One of the key proponents of the competition and a leading light in the field of rugby league expansion over the last 20 years or so, Lionel Hurst's first serious memory of the game was of lifting the Lancashire Cup in the Warrington team dressing room, his father being one of the club doctors, after their triumph over St Helens in 1959. His list of achievements and locations in which he has made an impact is impressive – from Woolston and Formby, to Cheltenham, MASWARLA, the York Nines, London Broncos and the 1895 International club – and Lionel is perhaps the name most associated with the RLC.

Harry Jepson OBE: "The overriding memory for me was when in my capacity as President, we launched the Conference season at Coventry's Coundon Road rugby union ground in 2000. I had once been escorted from Coundon Road 50 years earlier as an undesirable person - that is a rugby league man."

The word 'legendary' is used widely, sometimes too widely. Julian Harrison's view is that Harry Jepson, along with Bev Risman, fits the term perfectly. His achievements are immense. Rooted in rugby league, his love affair with Hunslet began at the age of seven. In joining the staff of Bewerley Street County Primary School, in Hunslet, in 1949, his love of the game was encouraged by the headmaster, Edgar Meeks who was Hunslet's chairman. Harry's involvement in the club, including as secretary, ended in 1969-70, though his passion and support remains undiminished. He continued his illustrious career at Leeds and also as a director of the RFL. His enthusiasm for expanding the game's horizons led to a position on the London Rugby League development board and then an invitation to become president of the RLC, a position he currently holds and cherishes. His personal achievements are more than matched by his presence and the work and involvement he inspires in others. In Harrison's view, never has a trophy had a more fitting nomenclature than that competed for in the RLC.

Steve Kiely (Greenwich Admirals): "I will always recall when we played away in the first round of the Plate competition in 2003 and beat Essex Eels on a scorching hot day in Basildon. It was a brilliant performance by the lads against a highly fancied side which was lapped up by our local papers and radio."

Another man lured by the appeal to form a new club in the area, Steve is currently the press officer at Greenwich Admirals, though he has extended his involvement in the running of the club.

Derek Millis (Hemel Hempstead Stags): "My high point was receiving the RLC trophy as Personality of the Year in 2000 from Ray French prior to the RLC Grand Final. My best game memory is having been beaten by Teesside Steelers – the eventual winners - in the semi-finals in 2001 and meeting them again in the semi-finals in 2002 when we beat them in a most exciting game at Sheffield Hillsborough Stadium. This was their first defeat in two seasons in the RLC."

Derek Millis is one of rugby league's 'nice guys'. Dedicated to the Hemel cause, his contribution to the club, since being won over to rugby league in 1992, has been staggering. A director of Hemel Stags Ltd since 1998, he has latterly taken over team management responsibilities. His professionalism was recognised in 2000 when he won the RLC Club Personality of the Year Award. Always modest, he has an infectious appetite for the game.

Trevor Nunn (Derby City): "Going to Rotherham, 5 July 2003, and only losing by four points was the performance I remember best."

Derby City owe a large debt of gratitude to Trevor's son Richard, for it was he who – as a player for Ilkeston Toyota Tigers in EMARLA and then for Derby City – encouraged his father to get involved in the game. Trevor is both matchday manager and chairman of the club.

David Peachey (Ipswich Rhinos): "My memorable event would be Ipswich Rhinos losing with credit to Bridgend in the 2003 semi-final."

Although a longstanding follower of Widnes, David Peachey's move to Suffolk in 1993, (where he became director of education for Suffolk County Council) culminated in a more hands-on role when, after seeing publicity for the Rhinos game against touring Strela side from Kazan in 1998, he met club stalwart Dave Flaherty and volunteered his services. David forms a talented double-act with wife Barbara, the former as chairman, the latter as secretary, and with the rest of the committee have presided over a successful period in the club's history.

Daryn Reeds (Oxford Cavaliers): "My favourite memory would be a 1998 game at Crawley Jets. Crawley and Oxford were arguably the two outstanding teams of the season, but possibly the Jets were stronger. A good-sized crowd was in place at their very nice stadium, but it was the Cavaliers who won, with an outstanding length-of-the-field try from Steve Lacey, Oxford's full back as the moment which summed up the game. There were several great performances that day, from Lacey, also from centres Jonny Flatman and Steve Berry and from prop Adam Skordi that really led the Cavaliers to victory."

South African Daryn Reeds' initial sporting involvement was in rugby union and cricket, where he played for Worcestershire. The advent of Super League captured his imagination and Daryn contacted his local club, Oxford Cavaliers, and offered his services, initially as a player. His enthusiasm led to his taking over responsibility for the media and through Daryn, the club became widely known through local radio. He also made inroads into the development side of the club before leaving at the end of the 1998 season.

Bev Risman: "The most memorable thing for me has been the development of the game in Wales at long last through the RLC."

Bev Risman needs little introduction. A dual-code international and son of the legendary Gus, Bev was one of the founders of the competition and also had club involvement as chairman of West London Sharks. He is now involved at Carlisle Centurions.

Ruth Sigley (Gloucestershire Warriors): "It is difficult to choose just one match, but I eventually narrowed it down to three. The first is our first ever match, against Chester Wolves at the Prince of Wales Stadium on 16 May 1998.

We had an inexperienced team, with almost three-quarters of the players new to rugby league. We lost one of our most experienced players and captain, Paul Brookes, after only 10 minutes. Another experienced player, Ronnie Haines, followed him a few minutes later. Chester, because of their twinning with Warrington Wolves, had three players with Super League experience, and the rest were experienced amateurs. Despite this potential mismatch, the Warriors matched them tackle-for-tackle, kept playing for the full 80 minutes, and restricted them to one of their lowest scores all season. As a debut performance it showed the rugby league potential in Gloucestershire.

The second memorable match was almost exactly 12 months later – Chester once again at the Prince of Wales. Our side was more experienced, but Chester were still one of the clubs to beat. And we did beat them – which was perhaps unexpected by the rest of the Conference – and went on to reach the semi-finals that year. The jubilation of the players and fans when we started the season so convincingly carried us all the way to 11 victories in 1999.

Finally, I'd choose a match where the Warriors were the underdogs, but gained a famous victory. The 2000 season opened at Leicester, and there were only 13 players available, including coach Shane Crellin, who had to come out of retirement, strapped together by Mala. Andy Haughton volunteered to take the number 14 shirt 'just to get in Leicester's way.' Despite the numerical disadvantage, we took an early 18-point lead, before tiredness allowed Leicester back into the game, with a one-point lead at half-time. We regrouped in the second half, and stunned Leicester with two tries to regain the lead. The Leicester pressure was immense, but we stood firm, playing on through injuries, and came away victorious."

Ruth Sigley was chair of the Warriors from 1997 to 2002. Alongside partner Steve Rigby, they have made a magnificent contribution to the competition, both with their local club, for the RLC Lionhearts and their help in rugby league in the area, including the 2000 World Cup match at Gloucester RFC.

Steve Sudlow (Ipswich Rhinos): "Torn cruciate ligament, right knee, 25 minutes into the first SCL game in May 1997, Ipswich versus Cambridge Eagles, is my defining moment. It turned me from player into a coach."

Originally from Warrington and a player at Woolston Rovers, Steve Sudlow is one of East Anglia's rugby league pioneers. After playing for Cambridge Eagles, Steve switched his allegiance to the Rhinos when he moved to Colchester in 1996. Present as an Ipswich delegate at the inaugural Southern Conference League meeting in Oxford, Steve played, captained and coached the club before moving to St Ives Roosters where he is head coach.

Alan Tucker (Carlisle Centurions): "Without a shadow of doubt the abiding memory is of getting to the 2003 final of the Harry Jepson Trophy and narrowly losing to Bridgend. This, apart from losing of course, was in line with our planning and player recruitment and to see all that come to successful fruition was an unbelievably emotional occasion."

A man with considerable experience of the professional game in Cumbria, having been a board member and chairman at both Carlisle Border Raiders and Barrow, his enthusiasm for rugby league took a new direction at the end of 2002.

Enthused by Ray French about the RLC, Alan teamed up with Bev Risman and other former Border Raiders personnel to form Carlisle Centurions.

Nigel Wachs (Gloucestershire Warriors): "My most memorable game was when we won the Central Southern Division in our second season, 1999, against Crewe. They arrived and complained that the pitch was rock hard and had not been watered. It was a boiling hot day but, just after half-time, the heavens opened. There was a huge storm, which lasted until just before the end of the game. As the players were coming off the field, I asked the Crewe side whether the pitch was watered enough for them now. That was the first time we had nilled a side and dealt out a big thrashing at home."

Nigel Wachs is the club's matchday manager. He has also been involved behind the scenes with the RLC Lionhearts representative set-up alongside fellow Warriors Steve Rigby, Ruth Sigley and Shane Crellin.

Caro Wild (South London Storm): "My greatest memory is scoring a hat-trick in the 2002 RLC Shield final."

Currently the RFL's regional development manager for London and the South, Caro Wild is another successful rugby league graduate from the student sector. He founded and coached the Luton University club, before becoming a RFL development officer in Oxford. His current position led to a greater strategic involvement in the RLC, but he still found time to play for South London Storm.

Geoff Williams (Chester Wolves): "Though I'm tempted to say that Chester's 1999 defeat of Crawley Jets in the Final at Tottenham was the most memorable event during my involvement with the club, after we came from behind to snatch victory in the final minutes, our 2003 home victory over Bolton stands out. This was a ding-dong battle between the second and third-placed teams, which we managed to win in injury time, after Bolton had scored what seemed likely to be the winning try with seconds left."

Originally from Liverpool, Geoff Williams developed an interest in rugby. A spectator at Liverpool City, his move to Cheshire culminated in firstly a heavy involvement in developing the Chester Sevens tournament, alongside Phil Roberts and SRL co-founder Andrew Cudbertson and then, following a season's watching from the touchline, a position in administrating the Chester Wolves.

Tim Williams (North London Skolars): "In 1997, our home pitch at Clapton was council-owned. If I recall correctly, we turned up for our first home game and the pitch was unmarked. I mean completely unmarked, not even the vestige of the previous markings. Clearly this was a problem. And the embarrassment was enhanced when a journalist from *League Express* turned up to cover the game. But Hector McNeil nipped over to Netto and bought 12 bags of flour which we used to mark the pitch. Needless to say the ref and the opposition were bemused to arrive and find us pouring lines of flour as we walked backwards across the pitch. I think we won and there were no disputed 'line' calls because of the distinct puff of flour produced when someone crossed or touched the line. And the headline in *League Express*? London Homepride..."

For a stalwart of the London Skolars club, it is no surprise to find out that Tim Williams's involvement in rugby league stemmed from his student days at York University. Tim has played for the club since its days in the London ARL.

Chris Wilson (Gloucestershire Warriors): "There are a couple of games that stand out for me. The first is from the 2001 season when the Warriors played Cardiff at Chosen Hill. The game was close with the Warriors hanging on to a 10-6 lead and Cardiff pressing the try-line. They must have had three or four consecutive sets of tackles, but could not get through such was the Warriors' determination. We scored two late tries to take the game 22-6.

The second game took place a month later when Hemel Hempstead were the visitors. The Warriors struggled against a good side who were unbeaten at the time and trailed 30-17 going into the last few minutes. Two tries by Sean Howe and a John Mulraney goal brought us to within three points and the referee's whistle blew just after the conversion of the second try with very little injury time having been played. The reactions of the Hemel players at the whistle showed that they knew they'd been in a tough match, but the Warriors' spirit in chasing a seemingly lost cause still runs right through this club today."

Chris Wilson epitomises the lure of the RLC and indeed of the game in general. Having been born in Beckenham, a move to Wigan converted the ex-patriot southerner to the XIII-a-side code. Chris was a regular contributor to Wigan's match day programme and fanzines such as *The Greatest Game* and *London Calling!* Keen to continue his participation after moving to Gloucester, Chris became the press officer for the Warriors and is now club chairman.

Peter Wilson (Manchester Knights): "I recall very clearly our first day in the RLC in 1999 shown on Sky TV. Knights were playing Wolverhampton – I actually got a rollicking from Lionel (Hurst) for getting television coverage."

A journalist and writer on rugby league in Manchester from 1974 when he joined the *Daily Express*, Peter Wilson helped to metamorphose the old Tameside Borough club, which folded in 1997, into the Manchester Knights. Another RLC person from the Cumbrian town of Barrow, Peter had also 'done his bit' for rugby league expansion prior to the advent of the summer conference, when he helped to form the now defunct Corby Pioneers in 1969.

Niel Wood: "The best moment for me was the opening day of the 2003 season when after all the teams played the results began to come in from around the country. To see them all on Teletext was a great sensation."

Niel Wood's involvement in the RLC has come full circle. From an initial input into the idea and then more practically through the appointment of referees in the SCL pilot season, Niel's appointment as rugby league national development manager in 2002 led to him overseeing the competition and all open-age development. A talented all-rounder, Niel is one of the most significant figures in development. He is principally renowned for his astute and influential directorship of the Student Rugby League.

Appendix 2: Club profiles

Aberavon Fighting Irish: RLC debut in the Welsh Division in 2003, finished second and made the minor semi-finals of the Harry Jepson Trophy (HJT). Close links with Aberavon RFC. Continuing a long tradition of amateur rugby league in the town.

Barrow Shipbuilders: RLC debut season in 2004. Based in strong traditional rugby league area.

Bedford Swifts: Founder SCL members in 1997 (Central Division), competed in the East Division 1998-2002 making the Shield Final in 2002. Withdrew early in 2003 season. New club, Bedford Tigers now playing in London ARL.

Birmingham Bulldogs: Founded in 1989, and competed in MASWARLA and EMARLA. Founder SCL members. Entered NL3 in 2004, 'A' team continuing in RLC. Play at Moor Lane Sports Club.

Blackpool Sea Eagles: Founded in 2002, played first game in June against Lancashire Police. Entered RLC in 2003. Play at Mossom Lane in Blackpool. Rugby league journalist Dave Hadfield is club chairman.

Bolton Le Moors: Entered RLC in 2003 in North West Division. Shield winner in their first season. Based at Bolton RFC.

Bradford Dudley Hill: Longstanding BARLA club. Entered 'A' team in RLC in 2004, summer first team in NL3.

Bridgend Blue Bulls: Following in history of amateur league club in 1950s and the Bridgend professional club in 1984. Joined inaugural Wales Division in 2003, winning title and the Harry Jepson Trophy at Wilderspool against Carlisle. High profile due to recruiting dual-code internationals Kevin Ellis, Allan Bateman and John Devereux.

Bridlington Bulls: Founded in 1983, playing in both BARLA York and Humberside leagues. Were the first British club to play in Germany. In 1989 through BARLA played Bochalt Eagles. Joined RLC in 2003.

Bristol Sonics: Set up in September 2002, and joined the RLC in 2003 in South West Division. Based at St Brendan's Old Boys RFC. Hosted successful Nines tournament in 2004.

Cambridge Eagles: Founded in 1990, played in LARL. Founder SCL members in 1997. Home base is Cantabs RUFC.

Cardiff Demons: Long history of amateur league in Welsh capital and professional club Cardiff Blue Dragons between 1981 and 1983. Present club developed from an Academy side founded in 1998. First open age game in 1999. Had strong links with student game (UWIC). Played in Challenge Cup in 2000. Entered the RLC Central Division in 2001, won South West Division in 2003. Transferred to Welsh RLC in 2004 and winners of the Shield in that season. Based at Taffs Well RFC.

Carlisle Centurions: Long history of league in city since the 1930s, entered RLC in 2003 with immediate effect, making final at Wilderspool. Joined NL3 in 2004, 'A' team continuing in RLC. Play at Gilford Park, former home of professional club. Bev Risman amongst club founders.

Chester Wolves: Joined RLC in 1998 winning North Division in their debut season and the HJT in 1999, defeating Crawley in the final at New River Stadium.

Copeland Athletic: Based in West Cumbrian League amateur heartlands. First season in RLC 2004.

Coventry Bears: Joined RLC in 1998 and made final in 2001, won HJT in 2002, entered NL3 in 2004 and returned to spiritual home (new Butts Arena) in September. 'A' team continued in RLC.

Crawley Jets: Joined RLC in 1998 with immediate effect winning HJT. Finalists in 1999 and winners again in 2000. Pulled out of NL3 in 2003 to continue in RLC for a further season, but withdrew for 2004.

Crewe Wolves: RLC debut in 1999. Based at Winnington Park RUFC. Strong links with Warrington Wolves and Manchester Metropolitan University.

Derby City: Founded in 1990, played in EMARLA. RLC debut in 1999. Based at Asterdale Sports Centre.

Durham Tigers: RLC debut in 2001 in North East Division. Joined (as Durham Phoenix) after Gateshead Panthers withdrew from their proposed RLC membership for the 2001 season.

Essex Eels: Joined RLC in 2003. Won BBC Essex 'Best Club of the Year' in 2003. Entered NL3 in 2004.

Gateshead Storm: Entered RLC in 2003. Moved up to NL3 in 2004, following the withdrawal of Teesside Steelers.

Gloucestershire Warriors: Founded in June 1997. Joined RLC in 1998 as Cheltenham Warriors, won Club of the Year award. Top of Western Division in 1999. Changed name at end of 1999 to Gloucestershire Warriors. Based at Chosen Hill Former Pupils RFC.

Gosport and Fareham Vikings: Joined RLC in 2003, basing heavily on services personnel in Portsmouth area. Part of Gosport & Fareham RFC.

Greenwich Admirals: Founded in 2001 with the help of the London Broncos. First competitive season in LARL in 2002, and won the title, beating Crawley Jets 'A' in the final. Joined RLC in 2003. Based at Royal Artillery Barracks in Woolwich.

Hemel Hempstead Stags: Founded in 1981, playing in LARL and then MASWARLA. Premier southern-based amateur club in South in the 1990s playing in Rugby League Alliance, then BARLA National Conference League Premier Division and John Player Trophy. Entered RLC in 1999 and reached the HJT Final in 2002. Joined NL3 in 2003, 'A' team continuing in RLC.

Huddersfield-Underbank Rangers: Longstanding BARLA club. 'A' team entered RLC in 2004, summer first team in NL3.

Hull Phoenix: Based in the strong Humberside amateur area. Set up by Hull RUFC, and have close links with the RU club. Joined RLC in 2004.

Ipswich Rhinos: Founded in 1992 based on civil service south east team, as Felixstowe Eastern. Played in Eastern Counties League. Move to Ipswich in 1995 and joined LARL. Founder members of SCL in 1997. Semi-finalists for HJT in both 2003 and 2004. Based at Ipswich RUFC.

Jarrow Vikings: Joined RLC in 2004. New club based in South Tyneside. Based at Old Jarrovians RUFC.

Kingston Warriors: London based side entered SCL in 1997, but only played one game. Re-entered in 2000. Have successful youth set up.

Lancaster: Home of original Northern Union club. Founded in 2002, and entered RLC in 2003.

Leeds Akademiks: Based on London Skolars model. Entered RLC in 2003 and finished top in North East Division. Based at West Park Bramhope RFC.

Leicester Phoenix: Founded in 1986. Formerly in EMARLA. Founder SCL members and runners up to North London Skolars in 1997.

Liverpool Buccaneers: Joined RLC in 2003. Based at Sefton RFC.

Luton Vipers: Attempts were made to develop a club in the early 1990s, but did not last. Reformed in 2000, with base at Stockwood Park RUFC. Joined LARL in 2001, and reached final, losing to North London Skolars. Joined RLC in 2002 and finished top of East Division.

Manchester Knights: Joined RLC in 1999. Entered NL3 in 2004, but pulled out just before the end of the season. May rejoin RLC in 2005.

Mansfield Storm: Former base of professional club Mansfield Marksmen in the 1980s. Joined RLC in 2003. Based at Forest Town Welfare Club.

Middlesex Lions: Linked to Wealdstone RFC, the Lions joined the RLC in 2004.

Newcastle Knights: Trace their roots back to 1979, when amateur rugby league started in the North East. Initially played friendlies, then in York & District League. Played as Gateshead, joined Yorkshire League. Moved into the NE league in 1994, and merged with Newcastle Benfield Lions ARLFC in 1999. Joined RLC in 2001. Based at Old Novocastrians RUFC.

Newport Titans: Joined RLC Wales Division in 2004.

North London Skolars: Founded in 1995 as Student Rugby League Old Boys to keep people from the student game within the sport. Played in LARL, founder members of the SCL. Won East Division and SCL in 1997. In 2002 joined NL2 as London Skolars. 'A' team stayed in RLC. Cup winners 2003 and 2004. Also started Haringey Hornets in LARL in 2004. Strong youth set up.

North Wales Coasters: Originally played in North West Counties Amateur RL. Joined RLC in 2003.

Nottingham Outlaws: Founded in 1998 by former Nottingham Trent University players. Joined RLC in 1999. Finished top of North Midlands Division in 2003. Professional club Nottingham City played in the city in the late 1980s and early 1990s. Based at Nottingham Moderns RUFC.

Oxford Cavaliers: Founded in 1996, and were founder SCL members in 1997, made regional final in 1999.

Peterlee Pumas: Based in former East Durham coalfield area. Joined RLC in 2004. Formed by the Durham RL Service Area. Based at Peterlee Cricket Club.

Penrith Pumas: Formed in 1985 with one senior side. Formed junior section in 2003. Based in East Cumbria and joined RLC in 2004.

Rotherham Giants: Joined RLC in 2000 and made final in first season. Made play-offs in 2001 and Cup final in 2002. Shield semi-final in 2003.

Rugby Raiders: Based in Warwickshire town in which rugby football is claimed to originate. Joined RLC in 2004, playing first home game at famous Rugby School. Usual home venue is Old Laurentians RFC.

Rumney Rhinos: Joined the RLC for one season in 2003.

Sheffield-Hillsborough Hawks: Long established BARLA club. 'A' team entered the RLC in 2004, with first team in NL3.

Somerset Vikings: Services based, joined RLC in 2003.

South London Storm: Latest incarnation of longstanding amateur league presence in South London. Based at Streatham & Croydon RFC, outstanding youth development work has given them a secure base. Joined NL3 in 2003 when Crawley pulled out, 'A' team continuing in the RLC.

South Norfolk Saints: Joined RLC in 1998, reaching the Grand Final. Withdrew after 2001 for a one year break before resuming RLC membership in 2003. Based in Thetford.

South Wakefield Sharks: Entered RLC in 2004. Close links with Crigglestone All Blacks BARLA club.

St Albans Centurions: Joined RLC in 1998. Moved into NL3 in 2003, with 'A' team continuing to play in the RLC. Venue for 2004 RLC Grand Finals day.

St Ives Roosters: Joined in 2003. Based at St Ives RFC.

Sunderland City: Joined the RLC in 2001, as part of the North East summer incorporation into the RLC. The original Sunderland ARLFC was formed in 1979. Based at Nissan Sports Ground.

Swansea Valley Miners: Founded in February 2002 as Swansea Bulls. Based in an area from which many great rugby league players have originated. Based at Ystalyfera RFC.

Teesside Steelers: Joined in 2001 with other North East clubs. Won Grand Final in first season, and reached semi-final of HJT in second season. Winners of challenge fixture against Edinburgh Eagles in 2002. Joined NL3 in 2003 reaching the final, but withdrew before 2004 season.

Telford Raiders: Telford All Blacks played in the BARLA North West Counties League for some years as well as EMARLA. The present club was set up by Dave and Janet Berry in the early 1990s as Randlay Raiders youth team. This led to the development of a Shropshire youth league. Joined the RLC in 2003. Based at Oakengates Leisure Centre.

Thorne Moor Marauders: New entrants from Yorkshire to the RLC in 2004, runners up in Shield in first season. Based near Doncaster.

Torfaen Tigers: Joined the RLC in 2003 in the Wales Division. Runners-up to Bolton le Moors in 2003 Shield. Based at New Panteg RFC.

Valley Cougars: Founded in June 2001 as junior club in Abercynon. Joined RLC in 2003 as an open age club. Still has successful junior structure. Based at Pontypridd RFC.

West Cumbria: New entrants to the RLC in 2004. Based in Maryport.

West London Sharks: Founder members of the SCL in 1997. Formed from merger of Brent-Ealing, London Warriors and London Colonials, and became the 'Sharks' in 1998. Clubs from West London had competed in the LARL in various guises in the 1980s and 1990s. Have strong youth set up. Reached the HJT final in 2004. Based at Grasshoppers RFC.

Wetherby Bulldogs: New entrants to the RLC in 2004. Reached HJT semi-final in inaugural season.

Whitley Bay Barbarians: Joined the RLC in 2003. Based at Rockcliffe RUFC. The town has staged an annual rugby league junior festival for some years.

Widnes Saints: Joined the RLC in 2004. Based at long established Widnes St Marie's BARLA club, but draw players from various Widnes teams, including the local union side. Winners of HJT in first season.

Wolverhampton Wizards: Joined RLC in 1999. New club built from Wolverhampton Borough club which had competed in MASWARLA. Based at the Four Ashes pub.

Worcestershire Saints: Founder members (as Worcester Royals) of the SCL in 1997.

Worksop Sharks: Joined the RLC in 2003, continuing a tradition of rugby league in this East Midlands area. Based near Worksop Cricket Club.

Yorkshire Coast Tigers: Joined the RLC in 2003. Based in Scarborough, which was home to a professional club (the Pirates) for one season in 1991-92.

Appendix 3: Club performances

This table gives the position of each club in their Division, and progress in the post season.

Key: HJT: Harry Jepson Trophy (from 1998); GFW: Grand Final winners; GFR: Grand Final runners-up; SF: semi-final; ShFW: Shield Final winners; ShFR: Shield Final runners-up; PO: Play-offs; RF: Regional Final; RSF: Regional semi-final; MSF: Minor semi-final; WSh: Welsh Shield; wd: withdrawn.

The Shield was introduced in 2002.

The figure in brackets after the club name is the number of seasons in the SCL, RLC or NL3. Clubs in bold have competed in every season.

Club	1997	1998	1999	2000	2001	2002	2003	2004
Aberavon Fighting Irish (2)							2 HJT MSF	2 HJT 3 Wsh FR
Barrow Shipbuilders (1)								1
Bedford Swifts (6)	5	4	5	6	3	5 Sh FR	Wd	
Birmingham Bulldogs (8)	2 SF	3	3	1 PO	4	4	1 HJT SF	3* NL3
Blackpool Sea Eagles (2)							5	7 Sh 3
Bolton le Moors (2)							3 Sh FW	3
Bradford-Dudley Hill (1)								7* Sh 2
Bridgend Blue Bulls (2)							1 HJT GFW	1 HJT QF
Bridlington Bulls (4)					3	3	3 Sh QF	4
Bristol Sonics (2)							6	3
Cambridge Eagles (8)	4	3	4	5	5	4	6	7 Sh 3
Cardiff Demons (4)					3	2	1 HJT QF	5 WSh FW Sh FW
Carlisle Centurions (2)							1 HJT GFR	5* NL3
Chester Wolves (7)		1 HJT SF	1 HJT GFW	3	2	2	2 HJT QF	2 HJT 3
Copeland Athletic (1)								4
Coventry Bears (5)				2 HJT SF	1 HJT GFR	1 HJT GFW	5* 8 NL3	1* HJT 2
Crawley Jets (6)		1 HJT GFW	1 HJT GFR	2 HJT GF	1 HJT SF	3	1 HJT MSF	
Crewe Wolves (6)			5	6	4	4 Sh SF	3 Sh QF	5 Sh SF
Derby City (6)			4	5	5	5	5 Sh 2	3
Durham Tigers (4)					5	2	7 Sh QPO	6
Essex Eels (2)							3	NL3
Gateshead Storm (2)							4 Sh 2	NL3
Gloucestershire Warriors (7)		5	1 RF	3	2	3	2 HJT Elm PO	2 HJT 2
Gosport & Fareham Vikings (2)							3 Sh SF	4

179

Greenwich Admirals (2)							6 Sh QF	2 HJT 2
Hemel Hempstead Stags (6)			2 RSF	1 PO	1 HJT SF	1 HJT GFR	8*Sh QPO* 10 NL3	6* NL3
Huddersfield -Underbank Rangers (1)								8*
Hull Phoenix (1)								3 HJT 2
Ipswich Rhinos (8)	3	2	1 RSF	4	1 PO	3	2 HJT SF	1 HJT SF
Jarrow Vikings (1)								1
Kingston Warriors (6)	5 wd			5	5	4	5 Sh 2	3
Lancaster (2)							6	6
Leeds Akademiks (2)							1 HJT MSF	1 HJT 3
Leicester Phoenix (8)	1 GFR	2	2 RSF	4	3	2	2 HJT Elm PO	2 HJT QF
Liverpool Buccaneers (2)							4 Sh 2	4 HJT 2
Luton Vipers (3)						1	4	4
Manchester Knights (6)			2 RSF	1 PO	3	1	9 NL3	NL3
Mansfield Storm (2)							2 HJT MSF	4 Sh 2
Middlesex Lions (1)								8
Newcastle Knights (4)					2 PO	4 Sh SF	2 HJT Elm PO	2 HJT QF
Newport Titans (1)								4 Sh 3
North London Skolars (8)	1 GFW	5	4	1 PO	2 PO	1 HJT SF	4*Cup W* Sh 2* 10 NL2	2* HJT 3 NL2
North Wales Coasters (1)								8
Nottingham Outlaws (6)			3	4	2	3	1 HJT QF	2 HJT 3
Oxford Cavaliers (8)	4	4	2 RF	4	4	4	4 Sh 2	4 Sh 2
Peterlee Pumas (1)								4 HJT 3
Penrith Pumas (1)								2 HJT QF
Rotherham Giants (5)				2 HJT GFR	1 PO	3 HJT	4 Cup R Sh SF	1 HJT 2
Rugby Raiders (1)								6
Rumney Rhinos (1)							4 Sh 2	
Sheffield- Hillsborough Hawks (1)								5*
Somerset Vikings (2)							3 Sh QF	1 HJT 3
South London Storm (5)				6	4	5 Sh FW	7*Sh QPO* 7 NL3	5* Sh 3 NL3
South Norfolk Saints (6)		1 HJT GFR	3	2 HJT SF	2		1 HJT QF	3 HJT 2
South Wakefield Sharks (1)								5 Sh 3

Team	1	2	3	4	5	6	7	8
St Albans Centurions (7)		2 HJT SF	5	3	4	2 HJT	4 NL3 NL3 Elm SF	4* Sh SF* NL3
St Ives Roosters (2)							5	5 Sh QF
Sunderland City (4)					4	5	5	3
Swansea Valley Miners (2)							6	6 Sh 2
Teesside Steelers (3)					1 HJT GFW	1 HJT SF	2 NL3 NL3 Final	
Telford Raiders (2)							4	5 Sh QF
Thorne Moor Marauders (1)							6	6 Sh F
Torfaen Tigers (2)							3 Sh FR	3 HJT 2
Valley Cougars (2)							5	7 Sh 2
West Cumbria (1)								3
West London Sharks (8)	2 HJT SF	3	3	3	3	2	2 HJT Elm PO	1 HJT GFR
Wetherby Bulldogs (1)								2 HJT SF
Whitley Bay Barbarians (2)							8 Sh QPO	7
Widnes Saints (1)								1 HJT GFW
Wolverhampton Wizards (6)			5	6	5	5	3 Sh 2	5 Sh 2
Worcestershire Saints (8)	3	4	4	5	5	5	5	6
Worksop Sharks (2)							6	6 Sh 3
Yorkshire Coast Tigers (2)							6	5

* Denotes 'A' sides.

Appendix 4: Grand Finals

Southern Conference League

1997: North London 32 Leicester 16 at Staines

Rugby League Conference: Harry Jepson Trophy

1998: Crawley Jets 40 South Norfolk Saints 12 at Cheltenham
1999: Chester Wolves 26 Crawley Jets 24 at North London
2000: Crawley Jets 38 Rotherham Giants 22 at Coventry
2001: Teesside Steelers 12 Coventry Bears 10 at Rugby
2002: Coventry Bears 21 Hemel Hempstead Stags 14 at Cheltenham
2003: Bridgend Blue Bulls 33 Carlisle Centurions 26 at Warrington
2004: Widnes Saints 36 West London Sharks 28 at St Albans

Rugby League Conference Shield:

2002: South London Storm 54 Bedford Swifts 2 at Cheltenham
2003: Bolton le Moors 28 Torfaen Tigers 21 at Warrington
2004: Cardiff Demons 29 Thorne Moor Marauders 20 at St Albans

Sources & References

British Amateur Rugby League Association (BARLA), magazine *The Bulletin*

Cambridge Eagles RLFC, match programmes v Birmingham (31/05/97) and West London (26/07/97)

Farrar, D. and Lush, P. (ed.), *From Fulham to Wembley: 20 Years of Rugby League in London* (London League Publications Ltd, 2000)

Gloucestershire Warriors/Cheltenham Warriors RLFC, collection of match programmes and other information (courtesy of Chris Wilson)

Harrison, J.N., Rugby League Notes

International Festival of Rugby League programme, International Women's Challenge (Scottish Select v English Select), and Scottish Development vs. Ipswich Rhinos (08/02/98)

Ipswich Rhinos RLFC, match programmes vs. Cambridge University (05/03/97), Ipswich Rhinos University Students (21/12/97) and Club Captain's Invitation XIII (03/01/99)

Jackson, P., *Leicester Phoenix Rugby League Club History*

League Express, various copies

League Express Rugby League 1999-2000

League Leader (publication of the Student Rugby League Alumni), September and December 1999

Leicester Mercury 31/07/97 (Woman's View), 05/08/97, 12/08/97

London Amateur Rugby League programme for First and Second Division Trophies, 1997

London Amateur Rugby League programme for Gordon Anderton Invitation Trophy and Southern Counties Cup, 1998.

Moorhouse, G., *The Official History of Rugby League 1895-1995* (Hodder & Stoughton, 1995)

Open Rugby, various issues

RLC Lionhearts match programmes

Rugby Football League, various press releases

Rugby League Conference Grand Final programmes, 1998-2004

Rugby Leaguer, various issues, and James Lowes Column (09/06/97 & 16/06/97)

Rugby Leaguer & League Express, various issues

Rugby League World, various issues

Southern Conference League Final programme, 1997

The Guardian

The Inaugural 'Champion of Champions' Challenge Match: Edinburgh Eagles vs. Teesside Steelers programme, 26/04/02

Willacy, G., *Rugby League Bravehearts: The History of Scottish Rugby League* (London League Publications Ltd, 2002)

Wolverhampton Wizards RLFC, collection of match programmes (courtesy of Richard Lord)

Worcester Royals Rugby League Football Club newsletter, 1997

Websites: Birmingham Bulldogs, Ipswich Rhinos, Cambridge Eagles, Crawley Jets, Gloucestershire Warriors, Hemel Hempstead Stags, Oxford RFC, playtheball.com, Rugby Football League, Rugby League Conference, Totalrl.com, SRL Alumni, Wigan Warriors.

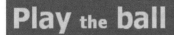

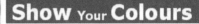

More Rugby League books from London League Publications:

Newlove
At the Centre of Rugby League
By Paul Newlove With Andrew Quirke
Published in November 2004 at £14.95 (hardback)
The autobiography of one the game's great stars of the past 15 years.

From Great Britain to Great Broughton
Peter Gorley – Rugby League forward
By Peter Cropper
Published in May 2004 at £9.95
Biography of a St Helens and Workington Town star

A Dream Come True
A Rugby League Life
By Doug Laughton with Andrew Quirke
Published in November 2003 at £14.95 (hardback)
The autobiography of a great player and coach

The Great Bev
The rugby league career of Brian Bevan
By Robert Gate
Published in August 2002 at £14.95
Biography of the game's record try scorer

Give it to Kelly!
A Rugby League Saga
By John D. Vose
Published in October 2003 at £8.95
Humorous account of mythical 1930s team Bramfield Rovers

All post free from: London League Publications Ltd, PO Box 10441, London E14 8WR (cheques payable to London League Publications Ltd). Credit card orders via our website: www.llpshop.co.uk